THE ARAB CENTER

MARWAN MUASHER

The Arab Center

THE PROMISE OF MODERATION

YALE UNIVERSITY PRESS   NEW HAVEN & LONDON

The map of the Israeli separation wall on p. 218 is redrawn with permission from B'Tselem

Set in Scala by Binghamton Valley Composition.
Printed in the United States of America.

Library of Congress Cataloging-in-Publication Data

Muasher, Marwan.
  The Arab center : the promise of moderation / Marwan Muasher.
      p.   cm.
  Includes bibliographical references and index.
  ISBN 978-0-300-12300-5 (clothbound : alk. paper) 1. Arab-Israeli conflict—1993—Peace. 2. Jordan—Politics and government—1952–1999. 3. Jordan—Politics and government—1999– 4. Arab countries—Politics and government—1945– I. Title.
  DS119.76.M825 2008
  956.05'4—dc22   2007043586

A catalogue record for this book is available from the British Library

The paper in this book meets the guidelines for permanence and durability of the Committee on Production Guidelines for Book Longevity of the Council on Library Resources

10 9 8 7 6 5 4 3 2 1

To Lynne
and to our children, Omar and Hana,
that they may have life,
and have it more abundantly

CONTENTS

ACKNOWLEDGMENTS

Immediately after the Madrid Peace Conference of 1991, I started the habit of keeping daily notes of events and meetings I participated in. I had no idea then that I would be involved in so many events affecting our region, but these notes, organized and filed during the past fifteen years, proved extremely helpful in writing this book. Someone told me that writing is a very lonely affair. Were it not for these notes, it would have been even lonelier.

I had one major incentive, however, in writing this book, which kept my adrenaline flowing. It is my deep commitment to the people of Jordan and of this region, who are so often dismissed by the West as a bunch of fanatics and who yearn for a peaceful and prosperous future for their children. This work is an attempt to create a better understanding by the West of the Arab world as much as it is also an internal appraisal of Arab society.

I am indebted to many people who contributed to this manuscript. Most of them have not been only professional colleagues but also friends and fellow believers in the need for reform in our region. First among them is Abdel Karim Kabariti, the first Jordanian prime minister I served with, who believed in the project and encouraged me to make it a reality. Our many discussions and his comments on the manuscript have enriched it tremendously.

Dr. Mustafa Hamarneh, the able director of the Center for Strategic Studies at the University of Jordan, gave me a home to write, brainstorm, and feel at ease. I am indebted to the many discussions we had, as well as to the help and contributions I got from the center's staff, including Dr. Muhammad Masri, Dr. Hassan Barrari, Dr. Faris Breizat, Dr. Nawaf Tall, and Dr. Ibrahim Saif. Salim Haddad served as my research assistant at the center and helped with the research.

Special gratitude goes to Dr. Rima Khalaf Huneidi, until recently assistant UN secretary general and head of the Arab section of the UN Development Programme, who meticulously reviewed the manuscript and offered many valuable comments. Gratitude also goes to the many people who read and commented on different parts of the manuscript. In particular, I would like to mention Taher Masri, Kamal Shair, Samir Khleif, Ted Baramki, Suheil Muasher, and Rania Atalla.

Jenny Hamarneh graciously made the archives of the English Jordanian daily *The Jordan Times* available for my use, as did Hamdan Al-Haj with the Arabic Jordanian daily *Al-Dustour*. I am grateful to both of them.

I want particularly to thank several individuals from the ministry of foreign affairs who worked with me both on the issues covered in the book as well as on reviewing parts of the manuscript. Ali Al-Ayed, Manar Dabbas, Ashraf Zaitoon, Bisher Khasawneh, Samer Naber, Haron Hassan, and Ali Al-Bsoul all helped me a great deal in carrying out my duties. Special gratitude goes to my able assistant at the foreign and prime ministry, Seta Issian. Toni Verstandig and Sam Gejdenson provided me with invaluable help through the different stages of production.

No one worked on the document more than Amy Henderson, my able "Jordanian" editor. She took an ordinary document and enriched it beyond recognition, offering not only amendments in style but, more important, suggesting matters that needed to be added or covered in more detail, as well as invaluable suggestions to chapters' structure and content.

I am indebted to my literary agent, Deborah Grosvenor, for guiding me through uncharted waters. I am also deeply grateful to Yale University Press, for believing in this project, and to my able "American" editor, Jonathan Brent, whose challenging comments, questions, and suggestions helped tighten up the document a great deal. Sarah Miller and Annelise Finegan, former and current assistant editors at Yale, were of great assistance to me. Laura Jones Dooley did a wonderful job of copy-editing and further refining the manuscript.

My greatest debt is to my wife, Lynne, and our two children, Omar and Hana, to whom I dedicate this book. They put up with me not only during the writing of this project but also during the countless days I was away from them in the past fifteen years. I am blessed to have them as my anchor and my support.

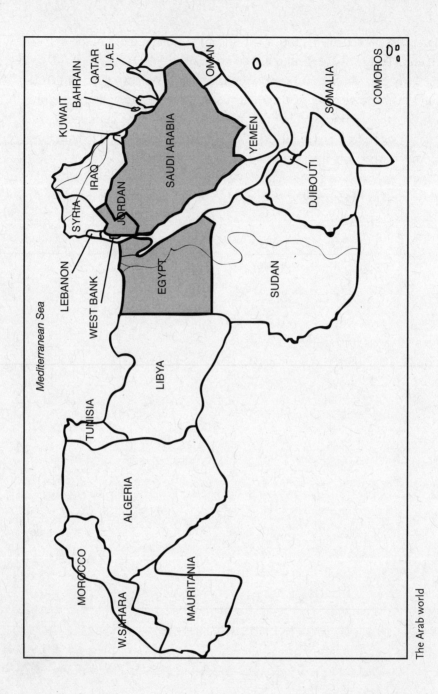

The Arab world

Introduction

ELEVEN-NINE WOULD GO DOWN IN HISTORY as Jordan's horrific
but eye-opening 9/11. On that day, November 9, 2005, three Iraqi terrorists belonging to Abu Musab Zarqawi's Al-Qaeda in Iraq entered Jordan
and carried out suicide bombing attacks against three Jordanian hotels
in the capital, Amman, killing sixty people and injuring scores more. A
fourth terrorist, an Iraqi woman and wife of one of the suicide bombers,
failed to detonate and was captured a few days later.

The night the bombers struck, I was attending a working dinner at
the home of a member of Jordan's parliament. I had been invited there
to talk to about thirty Jordanian activists on the outcome of the National
Agenda, a ten-year vision of political, economic, and social reform in the
country. I was making the case that political reform was no longer a luxury. For Jordan, it was key to advancing our wider ambitions for social
and economic development and our inclusion in the global economy.
Our future national security also required a more competitive environment for ideas, so that the radical discourse on the rise in the region
could be offset by voices of moderation in the public sphere.

I was explaining the details of the agenda's recommendations to the
government when the host interrupted to say that Al-Jazeerah television
had just reported that suicide bombers had hit three hotels in Amman,
killing an unknown number of people.

By November 2005, Jordan—along with several other Arab states—had already spent several years on the hit list of some of the world's most notorious terrorists. Their enmity toward Jordan stems from their radical ideology, which runs counter to the moderate discourse that Jordan has followed since its creation. The nature of Jordan's leadership and the country's geographical position have made the country an obvious target for extremists. The Hashemites of Jordan, descendants of the Prophet Muhammad who have ruled the country since King Abdullah I established modern Jordan after arriving from the Hijaz (today western Saudi Arabia) in 1921, have led the country with pragmatism and moderation and have eschewed religious extremism. The leadership's disposition has been reflected in Jordan's constitution. Jordan is today one of the most open and tolerant societies in the Middle East. The state has privileged cooperation over conflict as an efficient problem-solving mechanism, a disposition that has led it to pursue friendly relations with the Western world and regional peace and culminated in a peace treaty with Israel in 1994. Its policies have placed it at the heart of the Arab Center. Jordan's geopolitical position as a regional buffer state has also made it an attractive target for extremists, for, as it is often said, as goes the stability of Jordan, so goes the stability of the region. The kingdom has used its stability to help neighbors realize their own security. Jordan has, for example, made a major contribution to the training of Iraqi police and military personnel and has helped train Palestinian police and civil service personnel.

It is no surprise therefore, that Abu Musab Zarqawi, the head of Al-Qaeda in Iraq, who quickly claimed responsibility for the devastating Amman attacks, had Jordan in his sights. Zarqawi had thrived with Al-Qaeda in Afghanistan, and, although Jordanian, he harbored a special hatred for the Hashemites and the country. He, along with the rest of the Al-Qaeda leadership, regularly threatened Jordan, albeit from outside the region.

The fall of Baghdad in 2003 brought the group much closer geographically to its targets, since the chaos of Iraq provided an ideal arena for terrorist activity. From its haunts in Iraq, not only did Al-Qaeda in Iraq visit death and bloodshed on Iraqis, but the mother organization also exported terror to almost every country in the Middle East: Egypt, Saudi Arabia, Morocco, and Turkey. Jordan for a time had been spared, though not for a lack of trying on Al-Qaeda's part. Jordan's superior and highly professional security services, aided by an enlightened population, had in fact aborted many planned attacks.

Jordanians were acutely aware of these circumstances and events. For many Jordanians, a terrorist attack on the country had become a question of "when" rather than "if." Finally, in September 2005, Al-Qaeda managed a shot across the bow. From within a warehouse in the port city of Aqaba, the attackers fired three rockets at the *USS Ashland*, docked at port; all three missed the naval vessel, but one hit the dock, killing one Jordanian soldier and injuring another. Few in Jordan did not understand the significance of that event: the Iraq war had placed Al-Qaeda at Jordan's doorstep, and with the Aqaba attack, the group had announced its arrival.

In spite of the tremendous confidence Jordanians tend to have in the country's security services, from that day forward, few doubted that there would be more terrorism—more ambitious in terms of target, more spectacular in terms of execution, and certainly deadlier—in our country. But when the terrible day arrived, Jordanians were no less taken aback by the brutality unleashed on their country on 11/9 than Americans were on 9/11. That is the sinister "magic" of terror; it never fails to terrorize. Everyone in the room was shocked. People expected an attack, but not three simultaneous ones. As details were slowly being revealed on television, particularly regarding the suicide bombings at a wedding party, people in the room were sick to their stomach. Once the news started to sink in, everyone reached for their phones, frantically trying to call their loved ones. By now, the overloaded network was already down.

I had to leave immediately: as the official government spokesman and deputy prime minister, I would be responsible for keeping Jordanians informed about this horrific event and the investigation into it. I felt outraged, personally violated by a group who took it upon themselves to decide life and death for others. Amman, despite being a city of nearly two million people, is a relatively small place; any of my family or friends could have been at one of those hotels. I panicked about my wife and our children. As I sped, I frantically tried to reach my wife over my mobile phone, but the network was still down. I decided to take a short detour home before I headed to my office at the Prime Ministry.

As I drove home, flashbacks of September 11 kept coming to my head. I was then Jordan's ambassador to the United States and had left Dulles Airport at 8:40 a.m. on that fateful Tuesday, around the same time the terrorists did, for Houston, where I was to meet King Abdullah II, who was beginning an official visit to the United States. As we were about to land in Jacksonville, Mississippi, for a layover, the pilot announced that one of the World Trade Center towers in New York had been hit, as had the Pentagon, and that all US airspace had been closed. I felt the same outrage then that I felt now in Amman, with the same disbelief that any human being could do this to other human beings. I had also then tried to reach my wife to make sure she was okay, for a while without luck, since the mobile network was down.

After five long minutes, I reached home. Fortunately, both my wife and my two kids were there, safe. She was in shock, looking for answers to this madness, just as everyone was.

When I arrived at the Prime Ministry, the cabinet was preparing for an emergency meeting. The mood was somber. The cabinet discussed measures that needed to be taken both to calm citizens and to guard against future attacks. Suddenly, in the middle of the meeting, I felt that I needed to be on the scene. Jordanians expected and needed the government to talk to them directly. I promptly excused myself and went to the hotel where the largest blast had taken place, killing thirty-three people who had been attending a wedding there. The wedding hall, where one of the suicide bombers had blown himself up, was soaked in blood. I held an impromptu press conference there, facing the many reporters and cameras present, to give Jordanians the first official reaction to what had transpired.

From there, the prime minister, the minister of health, and I began visiting the wounded in the hospitals. At each, we were briefed on the emergency measures being taken. At one hospital, I found out that a close friend, Musab Khurma, a young and vibrant entrepreneur, was among those who had been killed. He was meeting his fiancé at one of the hotels when a suicide bomber detonated himself. His family was at the hospital, in total shock, wondering why his life had been cut short like this, without any reason. Another Arab-American, Mustafa Akkad, a Hollywood movie producer and his daughter, Reema, were fighting for their lives; both died a few hours later. Ironically, in the mid-1970s

Akkad had produced a Hollywood movie about Islam, *The Message,* starring Anthony Quinn and Irene Pappas, to portray Islam's true and tolerant message to the West. Now he had been killed by those claiming to speak and act in the name of Islam. At every hospital we visited, the same scene played out: family members wailing, overcome with grief at the loss of a loved one; others in tears, waiting to see if their loved ones would survive.

I could not help but feel proud, however, that all the medical teams we talked to were calm and efficient. Working under impossible conditions, they handled the situation with amazing professionalism. I saw many doctors, some of them friends, who just reported to the many hospitals we visited to offer their services. Jordan was united that night in a way I had not seen before.

As I drove home at 3:00 a.m., exhausted and still suffering from the shock of the past few hours, many questions came to my mind: Where was the Middle East headed? Why was it that the loudest voice in Islam today is that of Al-Qaeda rather than that of mainstream Islam, which advocates tolerance? Why was it that efforts to achieve progress on the central issues facing the Middle East—peace, reform, and the fight against terrorism—were all stalling? Was this predicament inevitable? Could the peace process have taken a different, more successful route? Has the slow pace of political reform in the region any connection with either worldwide terrorism or the peace process? Are the issues of terrorism and the peace process themselves linked in some manner? And why has the Arab region lagged behind in political reform when nearly all the other areas of the world have made significant progress toward democracy and good governance? Could the region, or indeed the world, afford a continuation of the status quo on all these issues?

Many of the problems of the Middle East are no longer localized. They are spilling over to the rest of the world. Terrorism, the emergence of Al-Qaeda and its transformation from a marginal movement into a key player in international affairs, the slow pace of political reform in the Arab world as well as the lack of progress on the Middle East peace process have undoubtedly affected the world at large.

Had there been voices in the Arab world that advocated alternative policies to those that had been practiced? Where did they succeed, and more importantly, why did they fail? Does the West really understand

the Arab world? Or vice versa? How did this lack of understanding contribute to many of the policy failures in all these areas? What lessons can
we draw from all this, if we are to chart a different course for the future?

Until late 2003, I was known in Jordan mainly as a "peace process" man.
It started when I was appointed as the spokesman of the Jordanian delegation to the Middle East peace talks in Madrid in October 1991. After
the talks concluded successfully in a peace treaty between Jordan and Israel in October 1994, King Hussein appointed me as the first Jordanian
ambassador to Israel, where I served until early 1996. Later, as Jordan's
ambassador to the United States from 1997 until early 2002, I followed
the peace process closely as one of my principal activities in Washington.

In early 2002, I was recalled from Washington to become Jordan's
foreign minister. In that year Arab states made a major effort to move
forward a peace process that had been going in reverse at high speed for
more than a year. I played a central role both in developing the Arab
Peace Initiative—an Arab plan that offered Israel a collective peace treaty
and security guarantees by all Arab states in return for an Israeli withdrawal from all occupied Arab territories and the establishment of a
Palestinian state—and then in developing what came to be known as the
Road Map—a plan of action to achieve the objective of a Palestinian state
in three years.

For three years, 2002–2004, I worked closely with Arab colleagues
and the international community to push forward both initiatives, until
the process was stalled again in 2004 by the continuation of violence
from both Palestinian and Israeli sides and by Israel's construction of a
separation wall that severely damaged the prospects of a two-state solution and continues to stymie negotiations today.

Because of my deep involvement in the peace process, I was somewhat surprised when King Hussein's successor, King Abdullah II, asked
me in October 2004 to leave the foreign ministry and become deputy
prime minister in charge of reform. Although I was known as a liberal
politician and a believer in political reform both in Jordan and in the
Arab world, my previous experience on the issue had been limited to my
role in convincing Arab foreign ministers to create a homegrown blueprint for political and economic reform in the Arab world, lest the
United States try to impose its version of reform outlined in the "Greater

Middle East Initiative." The initiative was an American scheme that was hatched not long after the tragedy of September 11. It was hastily assembled with little sensitivity to the wishes of the region, and certainly without much consultation with it. Although I shared with King Abdullah II my reluctance to leave what was by now my area of expertise and to wade into domestic politics that promised to be extremely problematic, King Abdullah II told me he thought I was best suited to head the effort and wanted me to do it.

At this new post, I headed an inclusive national committee, formed and instructed by the king to devise a holistic vision for political, economic, and social reform for the next ten years. This vision was to be arrived at through a consensus among Jordan's diverse political, economic, and social forces, including political parties, civil society, media, and the private sector, as well as the legislature, the government, and the judiciary. Our initiative was to differ from previous reform initiatives in that it would incorporate not only general recommendations on the types of reform needed but also specific initiatives in the political, economic, and social spheres, an agreed-on timetable for implementation, and benchmarks for performance to ensure that implementation could be measured against set targets.

The national committee met under my chairmanship throughout 2005. Arriving at a consensus on issues like political reform or women's empowerment was not easy. But the committee, after much deliberation, produced the National Agenda—the document that embodied this vision. The effort came immediately under attack from several quarters, particularly the status-quo political elite, forces in the country that saw in change a threat to the privileges they enjoyed. Within weeks those associated with the agenda were castigated as "neoliberals" doing America's bidding in the region.

Despite this heavy attack, much of it directed against my person (in part because of my reputation as a liberal politician who believed that the status quo needed to evolve), the committee succeeded, after months of serious, heated debates, in producing a forward-looking, measurable vision that promised, for the first time in the Arab world, a plan that moved beyond rhetoric to specific action with performance indicators. The drafting of the National Agenda was concluded in October 2005, and a meeting was planned to present the effort to King Abdullah II and launch a process of institutional and long-term change in Jordan. I was explaining the outcome of our months of hard work to the activists gathered that night when the terrible news hit us.

This book is about the story of the alternative, proactive moderate camp in the Middle East. It attempts to explain, through firsthand knowledge, the successes, failures, and frustrations of efforts to push through policies of moderation in the Arab World on issues of peace, reform and the fight against terrorism.

There have been many attempts to trace the roots of these problems and thus explain them; yet, few of these analyses are generated by those within the region. There may be many reasons—or, in some cases, excuses—for why this has been so. One key reason is that some Arab politicians are simply intimidated by the repressive atmosphere that prevails in some areas, and their stories have been simply denied the telling under the pretext of guarding state secrets. Whatever the reason, they rarely record their experiences, and of those who do, few are inclined to do so in English, leaving it for others to document the region's history from the periphery.

The book not only addresses developments on these issues through the eyes of a practitioner but also discusses the linkages among them and suggests courses of action. It details efforts by Jordan and other Arab states to push the peace process forward and counter claims in the West that the Arabs never wanted peace with Israel. It also forecasts the possible consequences of failing to realize a two-state solution to the Palestinian-Israeli conflict. Last, I hope it will help Western readers better understand Arab politics, address public attitudes in the region toward terrorism, and contribute to addressing extremist ideologies in the region.

In the Arab region, many—in fact most—politicians live by the credo "kiss, but don't tell." This book is an attempt at an honest account of events I witnessed or took part in. It is therefore part historical record and part autobiography. It provides many inside and as-yet unexplored stories about several important developments in the Middle East, including my time as Jordan's first ambassador to Israel; the succession in Jordan, which I witnessed from a unique perspective as Jordan's ambassador to Washington during King Hussein's last six months in the United States; and the development of both the Arab Initiative and the

Middle East Road Map. Beyond that, it is intended to be a statement on the current affairs of the Arab world. Partly through revealing some of the dynamics of Arab politics, I attempt to address how the Arab world is dealing with the triangular set of issues it faces today: peace, reform, and the fight against terrorism. I also discuss the process of opening up the political systems in the Arab world and the struggle to push for policies of inclusion as an alternative to the current stalemate that has trapped Arab citizens between the status quo, dominated by the ruling elites who have often failed to deliver development, freedom, and good governance to their people, and the more radical forms of political Islam, which many believe threaten to curtail political, personal, and social freedoms.

Given such a broad undertaking, this book is bound to be opposed by some who might disagree with many of its findings. But few will be able to disagree with its account of events. In any event, I hope it will be a positive contribution to the growing debate about the state of affairs in the region and how to overcome the seemingly insurmountable obstacles blocking the development of a stable and prosperous Middle East.

CHAPTER ONE

Jordan's Changing Role and the Evolution of the Two-State Solution Concept

During the negotiations that led to the signing of a free trade agreement between Jordan and the United States in 2000—America's first such accord with an Arab nation and only its fourth in the world—an Arab head of state was meeting with President Bill Clinton at the White House. His nation, too, had sought this coveted agreement with the United States but had not completed the changes in its trading practices to begin discussions. I was the Hashemite Kingdom of Jordan's ambassador to Washington, and I had been involved in a two-year effort to achieve this agreement. Jordan had met the requirements in record time, and our delegation had lobbied Congress, the administration, labor and environmental groups, and others before the Clinton administration agreed to negotiate and sign the accord, the first since the signing of the North American Free Trade Agreement with Mexico and Canada in 1993.

Administration officials who attended the meeting relate the story of the Arab head of state's repeated appeals to President Clinton for a similar deal. "Why are you giving it to Jordan, a small country in our region, as opposed to my country, which is bigger and more important?" he argued. When Clinton's attempts to explain that there were requirements met by Jordan but not by his country, the head of state protested, "If you are not willing to give it to my country, then you should not give it to Jordan." "Mr. President," Clinton said. "I honestly fail to see the logic."

THE U.S.-JORDAN FREE TRADE AGREEMENT is symbolic of the success that Jordan has made in reforming its economy and of the international prestige the country enjoys—a reputation that is disproportionate to its size and relative regional and international power. How is it that one of

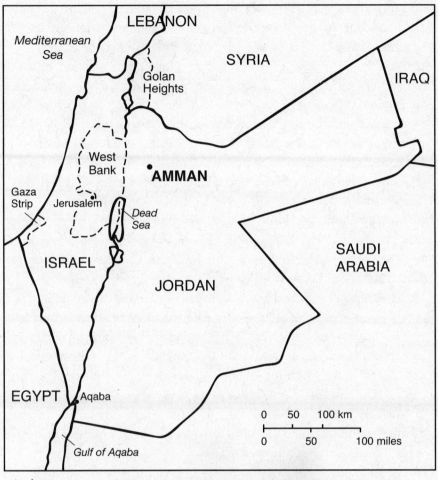

Jordan

the smallest countries in the Middle East—a nation of fewer than six million people that has no oil and limited natural resources—has come to enjoy such international stature? Jordan has managed to assert itself not only as a principal player in Arab-Israeli conflict resolution but as an originator of ideas and a bridge between the West and the Arab world— sometimes going against the grain of the Arab consensus (usually led by the country's larger and more powerful neighbors) but never far enough to violate that consensus.

Jordan, through enlightened leadership, has always pushed the envelope, adopting policies that advance Arab positions without abandoning

Arab principles and that accommodate international positions without compromising national interests. Since its founding in 1921, the kingdom has enjoyed a history of tolerance, and the Jordanian constitution explicitly forbids discrimination based on religion, ethnic origin, or language. Jordan's signing of a peace treaty with Israel in 1994 shifted its international standing in the West from being seen as a buffer state between Israel and the Gulf states and a bridge between East and West to offering a model of tolerance in the region that had long been lacking. The Jordan-Israel peace treaty presented a model of peace aimed at developing a new concept of cooperation and interdependence with all the states of the region, including Israel, as the only model that would ensure a sustainable development track for the region. Jordan was thus committed not only to the full implementation of the peace treaty but also to a proactive approach in seeking future areas of cooperation once the territorial conflict between Israel and Arabs was addressed.

The events of September 11 brought yet another qualitative shift in the international perception of Jordan. The Jordanian leadership, alarmed by the rise of Al-Qaeda and its distorted interpretation and practice of Islam, advocated a model of a tolerant Islam and sought to rally the silent moderate majority in the Muslim world into a clear stand against radical teachings and the murders that such teachings justify or even praise. The form of Islam advocated by Al-Qaeda is outside the teachings of any mainstream Muslim sect, for it sanctions the murder not only of non-Muslims but also of any Muslim who does not subscribe to its extreme ideology.

The brief history of Jordan that follows explains the evolution of conditions that have shaped Jordanian policy and its role in the Middle East today. It outlines the development of the Arab political center for which a two-state solution to the Israeli-Palestinian conflict has emerged as the foundation of its policy for lasting regional peace. The Arab center is a moderate force struggling to recapture the lead in a race against radical ideologies. That peace between Arabs and Israelis has eluded the region is due neither to the absence of Arab moderation nor to a lack of trying on behalf of moderate forces. But perhaps we need to shed light on Middle Eastern history to understand how such a center evolved.

A combination of factors—the disposition of its leadership, its geopolitical position, and its demographic composition—has kept Jordan at the heart of the peace process. Jordan's unique situation has been a source of opportunity as well as challenge, giving it a role in regional and international affairs that it might not otherwise have enjoyed. Jordan's activism has at times won the country a prime seat in the international community and at others brought it to the verge of war. Its moderation vis-à-vis the Arab-Israeli conflict and the burden resulting from the influx of hundreds of thousands of Palestinians as a result of the 1948 Arab-Israeli War brought it significant political and economic assistance from the West, particularly the United States, and the Arab world. This political and economic support has been crucial for Jordan's security, helping it to withstand the many conflicting pressures it has faced both from Israel and from other Arab regimes.

A BUFFER STATE

The contemporary Middle East was born of the 1916 Sykes-Picot Agreement, a convention secretly negotiated by Britain and France that defined their international spheres of influence in the post–World War I era. The agreement left Britain in control of the territories that today comprise Jordan, Iraq, and a small area around Haifa in what is now Israel. France secured control over what today are southeastern Turkey, northern Iraq, Syria, and Lebanon. The colonial powers were left free to decide on state boundaries within these areas. The area that came to be called Palestine was to be governed under an international administration pending consultations with Russia and other powers but was administered by the British in the interim.

Sykes-Picot contravened European promises to support Arab independence in exchange for Arab cooperation in felling the Ottoman Empire in World War I. Colonialism in the Middle East did not curtail Arabs' desire for independence, but the long history of colonial dependency meant that newly independent states were fragile, inducing a moment of intense regional competitiveness to ensure the nascent states' survival in the postcolonial era. These struggles for survival were intensified by the Balfour Declaration of 1917, which promised European Jews a national homeland in Palestine, introducing to the region a new competitor for power and influence.

Throughout the mandate period, the ascendance of Zionism among European Jews encouraged Jewish immigration to Palestine to establish a Jewish homeland there. Immigration to Palestine was also undoubtedly encouraged by the rise of Nazism and persecution of Jews throughout much of Europe. The Jewish longing for a homeland in Palestine was directly at odds with Arab aspirations for Arab independence in the same territory, which Arabs—of every religion—felt was theirs, if not by right as the inhabitants of the land, then at least by the promises made to them by the colonial powers. Jewish immigration proceeded apace with the help of the British, provoking the mobilization of a Palestinian resistance movement, which culminated in the 1936–1939 Arab revolt. The rebellion found ready support from the population of Transjordan, which supplied volunteers and arms to the Palestinian nationalist movement. It must be mentioned here that racial anti-Semitism was a European phenomenon that had no roots in Middle Eastern culture at the time. The conflict was strictly one over land, not religion or ethnic background.

That support was a natural outcome of a unique relation that had been established over centuries among the peoples of the territories straddling the Jordan River. Under Ottoman rule these were a complex articulation of economic, social, and cultural relations, along with political and administrative rules, that prevented the inhabitants from considering themselves as part of two fully separate entities. When Jordan became a state in 1921, the Jordan River became the western border of what was then known as Transjordan, but the mere drawing of a border did not sever the peoples of the two territories.[1] On the contrary, after the emergence of two entities, relations between Transjordan and Palestine remained intimate socially, economically, and even politically. Administered by the same colonial power, the two mandate administrations cooperated extensively, with many Palestinian mandate government officials taking up official posts in Transjordan.

The outcome of the 1948 Arab-Israeli War, which started after Israel declared statehood in May 1948 and several Arab armies came to the aid of the Palestinian population, transformed both Jordan's strategic milieu and its internal structure. After hostilities ceased, Jordan remained in a state of war with the newly declared state of Israel with all of the grave consequences of that status and in 1950 entered into a union with the West Bank. Jordan's role in the West Bank has been a matter of controversy for historians. One theory posits that King Abdullah I's decision was taken to prevent Israel's further encroachment on what remained of Palestine and its expansion beyond into Jordan itself. Some believe that

King Abdullah I, motivated by his own Arabist thinking, annexed the West Bank as part of broader territorial ambitions. Others contend that Jordan's inherent weaknesses in terms of material and human resources made territorial expansion imperative for its survival as a state. Still others believe it was a combination of all these factors.

The combination of the kingdom's state of war with Israel and its unity with the West Bank transformed Jordan's demographic composition. The country's population rose from an estimated 375,000 before the 1948 War to more than 1,270,000 after it, including almost half a million refugees.[2]

Refugees who had entered Jordan proper as well as those living in the West Bank became Jordanian citizens through a law passed in 1954. This new reality and Jordan's geographic proximity with Israel posed a fundamental challenge. Jordan now found that it had simultaneously to placate domestic public opinion—particularly, although not exclusively, among the aggrieved Palestinian population—which was very anti-Israeli, and to keep Israel at bay, particularly since neither Arabs nor Israelis were ready to accept the new borders and since Israel had its eye on the historic walled city of Jerusalem.

Even with the enlargement of its territory, Jordan remained a small country surrounded by three larger, stronger, and richer Arab states that often competed for regional hegemony and preeminence: Syria to the north, Iraq to the east, and Saudi Arabia to the east and south. And to its west was an enemy state, Israel. Jordan's geographical position made it a buffer among these states while also exposing it to conflicting pressures from all directions. Jordan was subject to pressure from revolutionaries who sought to overturn the status quo and reclaim lost Arab territory through military means and from conservatives who sought to preserve it, believing that Arab states could not match Israeli military capability and stood to compromise Arab interests and territory further if they tried to do so. Although one famous Egyptian commentator went so far as to call for wiping Israel (as a state, not as Israelis) off the map, the Palestinians at the time advocated establishing one democratic state in Palestine, with equal rights for Muslims, Christians, and Jews. Israel sought an exclusive Jewish state and considered this an unacceptable solution that would be the demographic equivalent of total military defeat.

Throughout the 1950s and 1960s, the revolutionary trend was ascendant, embodied in various Arab nationalist ideologies, especially Nasserism, an inspiration of Egyptian president Gamal Abdul Nasser. Nasserism was a revolutionary, Arab nationalist ideology that adopted some aspects of secular socialism and was vehemently opposed to colonialism. It was robustly opposed to Zionism and viewed Israel as a new Western colonizer that had come to replace the old. These ideas appealed to large segments of Jordan's population. They were most frequently promoted by Jordan's revolutionary and far more powerful neighbors, Egypt and Syria, each of which looked to boost its regional power and influence at Jordan's expense. The Jordanian state was in many ways hostage to these radical forms of Arab nationalism. In 1955, for example, domestic and regional pressure, particularly from the forces of Nasserism and pan-Arabism, prevented Jordan from joining the Baghdad Pact, even though the state agreed with its general principles. The pact, an initiative of Britain, Turkey, and Iraq (which the Hashemites also then ruled), was designed to confront Soviet expansion southward and would have bolstered Jordan's resources against the more immediate threats posed by Egypt and Syria.

Western fears of Soviet expansion were heightened after the Suez War in 1956 and Britain's withdrawal from Egypt. This episode signaled the end of colonial power in the region and opened the playing field to competition between the United States and the Soviet Union. American fears that the Soviets would rush to fill the vacuum were shared by Jordan: the atheism inherent in communism was incompatible with the ideals of the Jordanian leadership. In 1957, the United States announced the Eisenhower Doctrine, and President Dwight D. Eisenhower appealed to Congress to authorize increased economic and military aid and even direct U.S. protection of any Middle Eastern nation willing to acknowledge the threat posed by communism. The Jordanian state's ideological opposition to communism, together with a leadership that was considered open and pro-Western, caused it to be viewed as a buffer state in the region that could stand up to communist infiltration, as well as keep the Arab-Israeli conflict from widening. Jordan officially declined American offers of aid extended in accordance with the Eisenhower Doctrine, but the kingdom's general policies were sufficiently pro-Western to convince the Eisenhower administration that Jordan was worthy of American investment.

A BRIDGE BETWEEN THE ARABS AND THE WEST

International efforts to solve the Arab-Israeli conflict peacefully had not yielded positive results by the mid-1960s. The refugee problem and the issue of borders remained sticking points that precluded real negotiations, let alone a successful conclusion to the conflict. Arab states would not recognize the existence of Israel without negotiating first over borders, while Israel would not negotiate without first being accepted as a state. Nor would Israel acknowledge its responsibility for the refugee problem, and it repeatedly refused to abide by United Nations General Assembly Resolution 194, which required the repatriation of those refugees who wished to go back to Israel. To the Israelis, the return of refugees would constitute the liquidation of the state of Israel, at least in demographic terms, and would constitute a blow to the raison d'être of Zionism: a Jewish state.

Such was Jordan's state of affairs when the 1967 Arab-Israeli War erupted. The war was catastrophic for Jordan, which entered the conflict because of domestic and Arab pressure even as King Hussein realized that the Arabs could not win. Israel captured the West Bank from Jordan and, with it, East Jerusalem. Many Palestinians who lived in the West Bank now streamed into the East Bank. The massive influx of people severely strained Jordan's meager resources and again profoundly altered the demographic composition of the East Bank. The war was also disastrous for other Arab states: Israel seized the Sinai Peninsula from Egypt and the Golan Heights from Syria and destroyed Arab military capacities.

Nonetheless, the 1967 War also transformed Arab-Israeli relations by putting Israel in control of Arab lands that could, in theory, be traded for peace in the future. Now President Nasser's Egypt, hitherto hostile to Jordan, came to appreciate the role that Jordan could play in returning Arab territories through diplomatic means, using the good offices that King Hussein held with the West. Nasser explicitly asked the king to do so, and thus Jordan played a key role in formulating and passing UN Security Council Resolution 242 of November 1967, which called on Israel to withdraw from the territories it had occupied in the war as a quid pro quo for peace. Ever since, land for peace has been the cornerstone of Jordan's regional peace policy.

To Jordan, the combination of UN Resolution 242 and Egypt's tacit approval of it presented an opportunity to recover the West Bank and

Jerusalem. Two months before the passage of Resolution 242, the Arab Summit in Khartoum had adopted what became known as the "three no's": no to peace, no to negotiations, and no to recognition of Israel. This posed a particular dilemma to King Hussein, who felt a heavy personal responsibility over the loss of the West Bank and Jerusalem. Thus, despite the resolutions of the Khartoum Summit, Jordan reached an understanding with Egypt to use Resolution 242 to recover the occupied territories and reach a comprehensive peace in the Middle East as the optimal guarantee of Jordan's survival and prosperity. The old notion of wiping Israel off the map was deemed unrealistic not only by Jordan but also now by Egypt. But in any event, Israel was not yet ready to negotiate: in the West Bank it vigorously pursued a repressive security policy to stymie resistance and employed economic incentives to encourage pacification of the population.

Jordan's role began to evolve as a bridge between the West and the Arab world. Jordan had to walk a tight rope in this regional political minefield. As a result, Jordan's foreign policy on the Arab-Israeli conflict became one that adopted a strategy for peace that was based on Resolutions 242 and, later, 338, in order to secure an Israeli withdrawal from the occupied territories, including East Jerusalem, in exchange for a permanent, just, and comprehensive peace. At that time, the land for peace formula had not evolved into a resolution of the conflict based on a two-state solution involving an independent Palestinian state. Indeed, Resolution 242 does not mention a Palestinian state, and no consensus on the establishment of a Palestinian state existed among Arab states, in Israel, or in the international community.

Other international and regional factors undermined progress toward a peace settlement. The superpowers' global rivalry had engulfed the Middle East, which became an arena of competition and proxy war, particularly when U.S. administrations saw the Middle East through the prism of the Cold War.[3] The ascendance of the "Israel first" school of thought in American foreign policy vis-à-vis the region had also contributed to immobility in the peace process that began after the October War in 1973.

In the meantime, Palestinians in Gaza, the West Bank, and the diaspora, including Jordan, had not been standing still. An organized Palestinian nationalist movement had been cohering since the mid-1960s.

The Palestinian Liberation Organization (PLO) had been a marginal player on the regional scene until the 1967 War, but its credibility as a representative of Palestinian interests grew in tandem with the collective failure of the Arab states, Israel, and the international community to restore Palestinians' internationally recognized rights and alleviate their suffering. The PLO's call for armed resistance against Israel and its claim to represent Palestinians everywhere resonated among the refugees and dispossessed from the Arab-Israeli wars, as well as among Arabs everywhere who sympathized with the Palestinians' predicament. After 1967, the Jordanian government allowed the PLO to establish an official presence in Jordan. But several Palestinian factions started operating like a state within a state, openly carrying arms and often clashing with the Jordanian army. They also carried out attacks on Israel from Jordanian territory, inviting punitive Israeli retaliatory attacks. Matters came to a head when a radical faction of the PLO hijacked three Western planes and, after releasing the hostages, blew up the planes in a desert field in Jordan. The PLO and the Jordanian army began a military confrontation that lasted for two weeks in September 1970. Even though the Arab League brokered a cease-fire, it did not hold, and the PLO was driven out completely from Jordan in 1971. The trust between the two sides, particularly between King Hussein and PLO leader Yasser Arafat, was never really restored after that. Their mutual suspicion frequently derailed their work toward common objectives, in particular the goal of ending the Israeli occupation of the West Bank. The PLO's claim to represent all Palestinians was also in conflict with that of Jordan, which not only hosted but had given citizenship to millions of Palestinians. When Arab states recognized the PLO at the 1974 Rabat Summit as the "sole, legitimate representative of the Palestinians," Jordan had little choice but to accept this consensus, even though King Hussein felt he was better suited to broker a peace deal than the Palestinians were. The Rabat decision resulted in considerable constraints on Jordan's maneuverability in attempts to seek a diplomatic solution to the Arab-Israeli conflict. The ascension of the PLO ultimately transformed Jordan's view on the optimal solution to the conflict.

Starting in the mid-1970s the oil boom furthered Jordan's reliance on Arab funding and restrained Jordan's efforts to bring about a recovery of land occupied in 1967, given the division among the Arabs regarding the best way of solving the Arab-Israeli conflict. The split between those who advocated that all Arabs should move forward together and others who thought each state should pursue its own interests was highlighted by Egypt's defection from the Arab fold to sign a peace treaty with Israel in 1979, restoring the Sinai Peninsula to Egyptian control.

A second but perennial obstacle to Jordan's ability to push forward a settlement was Israel's position. In the first decade of occupation, the Labor-led government in Israel was sharply divided on the disposition of the occupied territories. The doves advocated territorial compromise with Jordan in return for a peace treaty between the two states. But hard-liners in the Labor Party, led by Moshe Dayan and Shimon Peres, threatened to bolt the government should the prime minister pursue a territorial concession. Israel rejected Jordan's suggestion of a disengagement agreement similar to the ones signed with Egypt and Syria. Instead the Labor Party adopted what came to be known as the Jordanian Option, based on the Allon Plan. The Allon Plan envisioned an Israeli withdrawal from the populated areas of the West Bank and the annexation of the most strategic areas and Jerusalem within the framework of a peace treaty with Jordan. Allon also suggested that Israel build settlements in strategic areas.[4] In an article published in *Foreign Affairs,* Yigal Allon, the plan's architect, delineated his concept of what he termed Israel's "defensible borders."[5] Although the government never adopted the Allon Plan, it constituted the basis for the first wave of settlements built in the occupied territories as a way to create irreversible facts on the ground once a peaceful settlement would require Israel to give up territory it held because of the war.

From Jordan's perspective, the Allon Plan was a nonstarter. As far as King Hussein was concerned, the only Jordanian Option was one that returned the West Bank, including Jerusalem, with minor border modifications on a reciprocal basis. This remained Jordan's position in all the clandestine meetings held with Israelis from the early 1960s.[6] But given Israel's complicated domestic political dynamics, no Israeli prime minister was either willing or able to agree with Jordan's peace proposal. The Jordanian Option became little more than a Labor Party slogan raised whenever the government needed to appear to have a peace policy less extreme than that of the Likud, which favored the wholesale annexation of the West Bank.

Internal developments led to a political hurricane within Israel in 1977. The Labor Party lost its twenty-nine years of dominance in Israeli politics, and Menachim Begin led Likud to a decisive electoral victory in the general elections and formed the first right-wing government in the history of the Jewish state. Soon after assuming power, Begin announced plans to intensify settlement activities in the occupied territories. To Likud, there was a need to fill the West Bank with settlements everywhere possible to lay the groundwork for annexation. This was a considerable departure from Labor's settlement policy, which was confined to areas deemed necessary for Israel's security. Jordan, which closely observed Israeli politics, did not view this development with comfort.

The settlement policy was much in keeping with Likud ideology, which viewed the West Bank and East Jerusalem as the heart of the biblical land of Israel. Settlements were thus a conscious policy not only to lay claim to those territories, but to preempt Labor's already limited ability to trade land for peace in the future. More worrisome for Jordan was the emergence of a new, alarming discourse from influential voices within Likud, including those of Ariel Sharon and Yitzhak Shamir. In an article published in *Foreign Affairs* in 1982, Shamir wrote that Jordan was Palestinian in everything but name. He proposed that the Arab-Israeli conflict therefore be solved by allowing a Palestinian takeover of Jordan. "The state known today as the Kingdom of Jordan," he wrote, "is an integral part of what once was known as Palestine (77 percent of the territory); its inhabitants therefore are Palestinians—not different in their language, culture, or religious and demographic composition from other Palestinians. . . . It is merely an accident of history that this state is called the Kingdom of Jordan and not the Kingdom of Palestine."[7] Likud's "Jordan is Palestine" mantra became known in Jordan and beyond as the "alternative homeland" conspiracy—a conspiracy to establish a Palestinian state outside the Palestinians' historical homeland in the West Bank and Gaza—against Palestinians' wishes and at Jordan's expense.

Under the pretext of the attempted assassination of the Israeli ambassador in London, Israel invaded Lebanon in June 1982 to dislodge the PLO, where the PLO had established its base of operations following its expulsion from Jordan. The invasion resulted in the PLO's expulsion to Tunisia and other Arab states and had a cumulative effect on the Palestinian approach to peacemaking, moderating its position and bringing it closer to the Jordanian approach. Two rounds of talks between Jordan and the PLO, designed to advance a peaceful solution to the Arab-Israeli conflict, were held in Amman. These efforts paid off in February 1986, when Jordan and the PLO signed what was known as the Amman Accord. The PLO had moderated its policy, indicated by its willingness to accept UN Resolution 242 as a basis to end the conflict, to make it eligible as a partner in any prospective peace negotiations. But due to internal PLO politics, Arafat backtracked from his earlier agreement with the king, and the accord collapsed.

At the heart of Jordan's foreign policy since 1967 had been the idea of mediation between the Arab side on one hand and the West on the other. Consistent with this mode of thinking, Jordan's foreign policy since 1967 had been to create an Arab consensus and an environment conducive to peacemaking based on Resolution 242 and to enlist international support for implementing the relevant UN resolutions. Hence, Jordan's foreign policy in the 1980s advocated convening an international peace conference attended by all parties to the conflict and the five permanent members of the Security Council. Jordan dedicated a great deal of effort regionally to help the Arabs agree to such an idea. The talks with the PLO should be seen within this perspective. After considerable persuasion from King Hussein, the Arabs agreed to the idea of an international conference. Yet this enterprise was thwarted by both the Americans and the Israelis. The Americans feared that an international conference might give the Soviet Union a channel through which to exercise influence in the Middle East.[8] Further, the Americans formed one voice with Israel in objecting to the PLO's participation in a peace conference before the organization would meet three conditions: recognize Israel, accept Resolution 242, and renounce violence and terrorism.

In any event, Israel was also unwavering in its opposition to an international conference out of fear that the international community could impose a solution that demanded territorial withdrawal, insisting instead on direct, bilateral negotiations.[9] The idea of an international conference became anathema to every right-wing government in Israel.

In 1987, King Hussein reached a deal in London with then foreign minister Shimon Peres in Israel's national unity government that would

lead to an international conference where the Palestinians would participate under a joint Jordanian-Palestinian delegation. But Peres could not
convince Prime Minister Shamir to accept the accord, and the deal fell
through.

The Arab-Israeli conflict was entering its fortieth year in 1987. The
community of Palestinian refugees and displaced persons now numbered in the millions, and Palestinians in the West Bank and Gaza Strip
had lived under Israeli occupation for two decades. Palestinians in the
occupied territories had grown increasingly fed up with life under occupation and Israel's relentless confiscations of what was left of Palestinian
land for settlement building. Seeing no other obvious solution on the
horizon, Palestinians in the West Bank and Gaza Strip took matters into
their own hands in December 1987: a civil revolt erupted against Israeli
occupation. The Palestinian Intifada, or uprising, raged for five years.

Jordan's objective of convening an international conference was laid
to rest in 1988 after the Americans abandoned the idea and Israel's hard-
line prime minister Yitzhak Shamir formed a new government. Protest-
ing Palestinians had also expressed a clear desire to pursue their future
independently not only of Israel but of Jordan, too. Fears were genuine
that the Intifada would spill over to Jordan. King Hussein concluded that
for all these reasons, the Palestinians themselves should assume responsibility for the future of the occupied territories, and he thus announced that Jordan would sever its legal and administrative ties with
the West Bank.

This was a turning point in the history of the conflict and represented a fresh approach to try to break the stalemate. Jordan's decision
that it would not speak for the Palestinians was a clear message to the Israelis that the Jordanian Option was off the table. It was also a message
to the PLO's leaders that if they wanted to lead Palestinians in the West
Bank, they would have to make serious decisions about peacemaking
and could no longer pass the buck to Jordan when and if things went
wrong. Indeed, the PLO's decision few months later to accept UN Resolution 242 and renounce violence positively contributed to the new policy of direct negotiations between Israel and the Palestinians that Jordan
was now advocating.

Given the abovementioned inter-Arab and Israeli politics, Jordan's
strong efforts did not yield the desired outcome: a comprehensive and

lasting peace. Nevertheless, the end of the Cold War in 1989 and the subsequent military campaign to drive Iraq out of Kuwait brought about a revitalized American willingness to work actively toward a resolution of the conflict, leading to the Madrid Peace Conference of 1991.

Jordan immediately capitalized on this opportunity. For one thing, Jordan had long championed the idea of an international conference. For another, settling the Arab-Israeli conflict peacefully had been a cherished Jordanian objective at least since 1967. Jordan also hoped that participation in peacemaking would help end the regional and international isolation imposed on it because of its position in the Gulf crisis of 1990–1991. (Jordan had opposed Iraq's occupation of Kuwait but had also opposed the presence of the coalition forces in the region and had attempted to work out a diplomatic solution.)

Recognizing Jordan's role in any peace settlement and in regional stability, the administration of George H. W. Bush reversed its attitude toward the kingdom, and Secretary of State James Baker conducted talks with King Hussein to attend the international peace conference.

Jordan's role was crucial in making possible Palestinian participation in the peace negotiations at Madrid. Jordan offered the Palestinians an umbrella under which to participate, agreeing to form a joint delegation with the Palestinians to help them talk directly to their Israeli counterparts and granting a Jordanian passport to a prominent Palestinian Jerusalemite, Dr. Walid Khalidi, to ensure the presence of a delegate representing Jerusalem. This was the only way to press Shamir to agree to talk to the Palestinians. I was appointed Jordan's spokesman to the peace talks and was a member of the negotiating team that went to Madrid in October 1991. The year before I had served as the director of the Jordan Information Bureau, the public affairs arm of the Jordanian embassy in Washington.

Madrid was a watershed in the history of the Arab-Israeli conflict. The conference was the sum of decades of efforts by the moderate Arab countries and the international community to negotiate a peaceful settlement to the conflict. It also vindicated the moderate position against the more radical positions on both sides: a radical Arab position that called for the return of all of historic Palestine to Arab hands and a radical Israeli position that sought to keep control over every inch of "Eretz Israel."[10]

The conference was somewhat daunting from a personal standpoint. I was dispatched there a week before the rest of the delegation to prepare for the meeting. Although I had acquired significant experience in dealing with the Western press through my work in Washington, particularly in the wake of the Iraqi occupation of Kuwait and the Gulf crisis, Madrid offered a challenge of a totally different scale. Almost six thousand reporters were covering the event, and I had to establish the Jordanian press center with no technical help. One morning, I received a call in my hotel room at 6:30. King Hussein was on the other line. Word had reached him that I was working alone, and with his customary graciousness, he assured me that help was on its way. The next day, four members of his press staff arrived, and they did a wonderful job in helping me handle the slew of reporters wanting information or interviews.

Madrid was also a turning point for the Palestinians in that the world saw them for the first time not as a group of terrorists but as a people yearning to live free of occupation. Hanan Ashrawi, the able Palestinian spokeswoman, illuminated the human dimension of the Palestinian story, hitherto unseen to the world, with her eloquence, poise, and integrity. The head of the delegation, Dr. Haidar Abdel Shafi, a soft-spoken, dignified, seventy-year-old physician, also gained the Palestinians much-deserved respect throughout the world. Perhaps most important, the imposing presence of the Palestinian delegation buried an old Israeli adage first uttered by Prime Minister Golda Meir: that the Palestinians did not exist, and hence there was no Palestinian problem to solve.[11]

Despite the momentum that had been building, Israel was still governed by the most inflexible government in its history, and Israeli participation in the Madrid peace conference was not genuine. Shamir was buying time to build more settlements in the occupied territories, as he himself made clear in an interview he later gave to the press.[12] The Bush administration took a strong stand against such settlement building, withholding loan guarantees to Israel equivalent to amounts spent on settlement building, thus contributing to the downfall of the Shamir government. For the peace process to yield positive results, Israel's domestic politics needed to change.

The electoral defeat of Shamir and the victory of Yitzhak Rabin in 1992 was thus a very positive development for the peace process. Unlike

Shamir, with his "not one inch" policy, Rabin was willing to seek a solution based on land for peace. There was finally a meeting of minds between Jordan and Israel. The peace process was revived and led in September 1993 to Israel and the PLO signing the Oslo Accords. The accords marked the mutual recognition of the PLO and Israel, with Israel willing to offer a territorial compromise directly to the Palestinians.

THE EMERGENCE OF THE TWO-STATE SOLUTION

Through the decades two schools of thought had formed within the Jordanian political establishment concerning the state's policy toward the conflict and toward Jordan's relationship to the West Bank. One school advocated a key role for Jordan in the West Bank and Gaza to prevent the emergence of an independent Palestinian state in the territories occupied by Israel since 1967. This school justified its policy on a straightforward security rationale: its advocates believed that a Palestinian state would be radical and irredentist and would thus constitute a threat to Jordan. This mode of thinking reflected the history of mutual mistrust and competition between Jordan and the PLO, and opposition to a Palestinian state was most pronounced within the country's security establishment.

The second school of thought believed that the emergence of a Palestinian state in the West Bank and Gaza would be a positive development not only for the Palestinians but for Jordan. A Palestinian state distinct from Jordan would bury, once and for all, the Israeli Likud traditional argument that "Jordan is Palestine," which could be used to justify the expulsion of West Bank Palestinians to Jordan and the creation of a Palestinian state on Jordanian national territory. Preventing Israeli implementation of the "alternative homeland" was thus of paramount importance to advocates of this school of thought. This school further stressed that a Palestinian state would help develop a healthy Jordanian national identity by defining once and for all who is a Palestinian (resident of the new Palestinian state) and thus who is a Jordanian. Within this second school, there were two subschools in terms of how they viewed the Jordanian national identity. The first was represented by many East Bank Jordanians, for whom a Palestinian state represented not only the death of the "alternative homeland" option but a chance to reinforce the country's Jordanian identity, which, they believed, had been diluted and obscured by the presence of Jordanian citizens of Palestinian origin. They hoped to weaken the "Palestinian component" in the evolving Jordanian national identity by having Palestinians move back across the river whenever possible. The other subschool sought two states but strove to realize a Jordan that was inclusive of all citizens regardless of their origin. The Palestinians in Jordan had been awarded Jordanian citizenship more than four decades earlier, and since then relations between East Jordanians and Jordanians of Palestinian origin had grown more complex at every level—social, economic, and familial.

Although the two lines of thinking were well known, the status of Palestinians in Jordan had never been publicly debated, nor was public consensus ever reached—mostly because the absence of progress toward conflict resolution had made the debate unnecessary as well as, for a number of reasons, politically unacceptable among large sectors of Jordanian society. King Hussein's announcement that Jordan would sever legal and administrative ties with the West Bank, however, changed all that.

The disengagement was controversial and has been intensely debated ever since. But King Hussein was clear on one point: the decision would not affect the rights of Jordanians of Palestinian origin. In announcing the disengagement on July 31, 1988, he explicitly stated that the measures "do not relate in any way to the Jordanian citizens of Palestinian origin in the Hashemite Kingdom of Jordan. They have the full rights of citizenship and all its obligations, the same as any other citizen, irrespective of his origin. They are an integral part of the Jordanian state."[13]

King Hussein's convictions on this issue were not enough to quell the groundswell of debate about who belonged to Jordan: the disengagement threw the doors wide open to discussion, and in the absence of progress in the peace process, the public in Jordan has yet to arrive at a consensus. Whether by default or by design, the disengagement also ultimately transformed Jordan's approach to the land for peace policy and its regional role.

The Madrid peace conference and process prompted Jordan to take a closer look at its interests and to decide what was best for the country. Israel had not recognized the PLO until then as the representative of the Palestinians, and it insisted that the Palestinians attend the Madrid conference under the umbrella of Jordan, in a joint Jordanian-Palestinian delegation formula, despite the disengagement decision. Realizing that this was the only way to get Israel to go to Madrid, Jordan was willing to provide such an umbrella while insisting that the Palestinians should represent themselves, and Jordan was keen not to act or appear to act as the Palestinians' custodian. In fact, following Madrid, Jordan and the Palestinians insisted on conducting negotiations in two separate tracks: Jordanian-Israeli and Palestinian-Israeli.

The signing of the Oslo Accords on September 13, 1993, was a turning point for Jordan. The initial Jordanian reaction to the announcement of the PLO-Israel accord was apprehension, due in part to the element of surprise and in part to Amman's perception that the Palestinians and the Israelis might be cooking up something against Jordan's interests or that they had defined a role for Jordan without its consultation. The Jordanian delegation to the peace talks, of which I was a member, was then in Washington, and we were taken completely aback. We met with the Palestinian delegation, headed by Dr. Haidar Abdel Shafi, only to find out that he himself was both surprised and angry at not being informed of the secret channel in Oslo. Abdel Shafi was apologetic and seriously considering resigning from the delegation.

We did not know how to react. On one hand, the delegation felt that after Jordan had given the Palestinians an umbrella under which negotiations with Israel could take place, the least it could expect was to be kept informed that another channel had been established where "real" negotiations were taking place. We also were not sure what impact this would have on negotiations between Israel and Jordan or indeed how Jordan would fare after these sudden developments. Once emotions settled, however, and following a long debate, we reached a consensus that acknowledged the importance of the Oslo Accords not only in providing direct negotiations between Israel and the Palestinian leadership—an objective Jordan worked for since the disengagement decision of 1988—but also in creating new opportunities for Jordan's negotiations with Israel. The Oslo Accords essentially transferred responsibility for negotiating the thorniest issues of peacemaking from Jordan to the PLO, making Jordan's negotiations with Israel far less problematic than they might otherwise have been. The emerging view among the delegation also was that Israel's recognition of the Palestinians would be in Jordan's interest and would help put to rest, once and for all, the Israeli right's notion that "Jordan is Palestine."

King Hussein listened to both arguments but kept his options open. The king was not sure of Israel's intentions and whether Rabin wanted to bypass Jordanian interests in any future deal with the Palestinians. He was also skeptical of the PLO's intentions, fearing that the PLO might be conspiring with Israel against Jordan. He worried that on such issues as East Jerusalem, the loss of which for him was a matter of personal responsibility, or Palestinian refugees, more than 40 percent of whom were Jordanian citizens, Israel and the Palestinians might arrive at a solution that would be unfair to Jordan. Another fear almost certainly must have been that the Palestinians, being the weaker party, would cut a poor deal that could only lead to a small and weak state that, to save itself, would look eastward. It thus became clear that the implementation of the accord and the emergence of a viable and independent Palestinian state were in Jordan's national interest. But King Hussein also began to realize that the accords had placed the territorial issue where it belonged: on Palestinian soil. Further, the identity crisis that many Jordanians of Palestinian origin experienced could not be resolved except by the creation of a Palestinian state.

The king had to make sure of Rabin's intentions. The immediate period after the signing of the Oslo Accords and the agreement on an agenda for the talks between Jordan and Israel on the following day—a period extending from September 1993 to May 1994—brought no significant progress in Jordan's negotiations with Israel. The king felt that the Israelis were giving priority to negotiations with the Palestinians over those with Jordan. Finally, he decided to meet with Rabin to ensure that Jordanian interests were protected. The two met secretly in London in May 1994, and the king was assured that Jordanian interests, particularly concerning Jerusalem and refugees, would be taken into consideration. This meeting led to the first public meeting between Rabin and the king in Washington on July 25, 1994. The Washington meeting culminated in the Washington Declaration, in which Israel recognized Jordan's special role in safeguarding the holy places in Jerusalem and stated that final status negotiations on refugees would not take place without Jordan's involvement. This set the stage toward resolving other pending issues between Jordan and Israel—borders and water being the most prominent—and the signing of a peace treaty in Wadi Araba between the two countries on October 26, 1994.

As soon as King Hussein was confident that Jordan's interests would be protected, the argument that a Palestinian state would be in the national interests won the day. Even though many within Likud and the Israeli security establishment claimed otherwise—some even to this day—Jordan's position was cemented.[14] The king from that point on became more vocal in his support of a Palestinian state, repeatedly emphasizing the need to consider Jordanian interests in any agreement to resolve the Palestinian-Israeli conflict.

The king first articulated these interests in a letter to Prime Minister Abdel Salam Majali in December 1997. King Hussein wrote that the time had come "to recall and identify clearly the bare facts of the well-known Jordanian position vis-à-vis the ongoing peace negotiations between the Palestinians and the Israelis." He described Israeli claims that a Palestinian state threatened Jordanian and Israeli security as "baseless" and said that he "categorically and unequivocally" disagreed with them. The letter explained that Jordanian interests in any settlement centered around seven issues: Jerusalem, refugees, borders, settlements, water, security, and sovereignty. Jordan's position toward the West Bank had made a dramatic turnabout: from outright opposition to an independent Palestinian state to full support for such a state as a Jordanian strategic interest. Jordan's quest for a two-state solution had begun in earnest.[15]

THE EMERGENCE OF AN EFFECTIVE ARAB CENTER FOR PEACE

Although Jordan held one of the most moderate positions on the peace process in the Arab world, its ability to push forward that position was limited by its relatively junior status in that world. Throughout much of the Arab-Israeli conflict, Arab consensus, although at times influenced by Jordan, was forged through an informal alliance of three states: Egypt, Saudi Arabia, and Syria. These three countries regularly coordinated their positions and made sure that they were generally in tandem. But the different nature of the three states prevented forward movement on the peace process. Syria maintained a hard-line position regarding the issue. Egypt's Nasser took an equally hard line, and Egypt moved toward a proactively moderate position only after the 1973 War under Anwar

Sadat's leadership. Saudi Arabia, which was not a confrontational state, advocated a cautious policy and was unwilling to risk taking the lead on peace initiatives.

When Egypt signed a peace treaty with Israel in 1979, the Arab world viewed this development not as a move toward comprehensive peace in the region but rather as a treacherous act that weakened the Arab bargaining position in any solution of the Palestinian-Israeli conflict. Almost all other Arab countries now hardened their positions on the question of peace with Israel (and ostracized Egypt from the Arab fold). The Arab public, which views Palestine not just as a Palestinian issue but as an Arab interest, would not tolerate further abandonment of the Palestinians. This situation persisted until Madrid. By that time, the Egyptian-Israeli peace process had gone little further than ending the state of war between the two countries. In that, the treaty did not differ much from the objectives of UN Resolutions 242 and 338, which did not mention peaceful relations among countries of the region.

Madrid provided a new framework whereby the declared position of Syria, Jordan, Lebanon, and the Palestinians paralleled that of Egypt in pursuing peace with Israel through a negotiations process based on UN Resolutions 242 and 338 and the principle of land for peace. The Oslo Accords and the Jordan-Israel Peace Treaty gave further legitimacy to negotiations.

These events put Jordan at the forefront of regional peacemaking. Once King Hussein decided that a two-state solution was the only result that would serve its strategic interests and secure regional peace, Jordan used its international prestige to champion independent Palestinian statehood. Nevertheless, many other non-frontline Arab countries continued either to oppose the Madrid process or to support it from a safe distance. They preferred to await the outcome before taking a stance or engaging in the process, but for Jordan there was no turning back.

September 11 changed all that. The emergent threat of extremism illuminated a new, shared Arab interest and a challenge that could be met only by ending regional tension, beginning with the Palestinian-Israeli conflict, which lies at its heart. Saudi Arabia's decision to take a more active role in the process effectively created a critical mass of Arab nations with enough weight in the Arab and Muslim worlds as well as in the West. A new Arab core emerged. This new core was both moderate and proactive and enjoyed good relations not just with the international community in general but with the West and the United States in particular. The new troika of Egypt, Saudi Arabia, and Jordan, which replaced the old troika of Egypt, Saudi Arabia, and Syria, immediately started coordination to advance a two-state solution to the conflict through such efforts as the Arab Peace Initiative and the Middle East Road Map.

CHAPTER TWO

First Ambassador to Israel

PEACE BETWEEN JORDAN AND ISRAEL was in many ways a leap of faith for my country and its leadership. It was also thus for me. Although I consider myself a moderate, and certainly a champion of Arab-Israeli peace, I faced an extraordinary personal dilemma as I contemplated becoming Jordan's first ambassador to Israel. That dilemma largely reflected the difficulty of crossing the abyss that still exists between Arabs and Israelis.

On November 16, 1994, less than a month after Jordan and Israel signed the peace treaty, I received a call from Talal Hassan, minister of state for foreign affairs. "I need to see you at my house tonight," he said. Immediately I knew what it was about. A couple of weeks earlier, Abdel Karim Kabariti, chairman of the Jordanian parliament's Arab and International Committee, had told me that I might be picked for the job of Jordan's first ambassador to Israel. I had brushed the suggestion aside, thinking that King Hussein would opt for an older military man, probably from a large Muslim tribe.

I had been delegation spokesman as well as a member of the negotiating team since the peace process started in Madrid. I was a firm believer in the need to achieve peace between the Arab world and Israel, and I had crossed many psychological barriers in my dealings with Israelis. But to be ambassador, to actually go and live there, in Israel—that was a leap I was not yet ready to take.

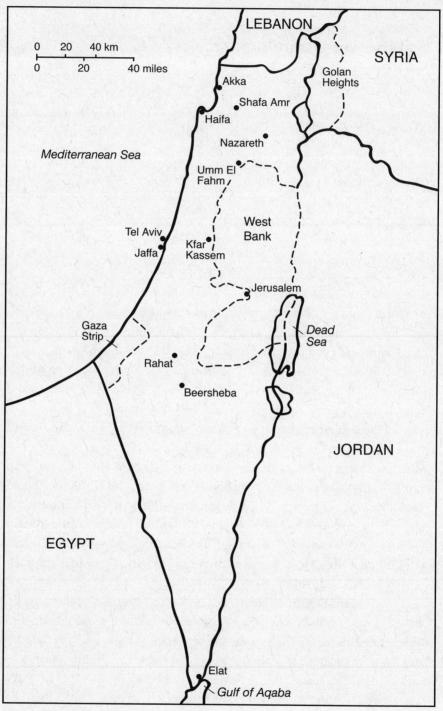

LEBANON

SYRIA

Golan
Heights

Akka

Shafa Amr

Haifa

Nazareth

Mediterranean Sea

Umm El
Fahm

West
Bank

Tel Aviv

Kfar
Kassem

Jaffa

Jerusalem

Gaza
Strip

Dead
Sea

Rahat

Beersheba

JORDAN

EGYPT

Elat

Gulf of Aqaba

0   20   40 km

0   20   40 miles

Israel and the West Bank

My worst fears were realized the moment I walked into Hassan's house. "His Majesty has chosen you to be our first ambassador to Israel. It is a great honor. Congratulations," he said, adding that he hoped he would be able to report my positive response to Prime Minister Abdel Salam Majali that very night. "I am not ready to answer yes tonight," I said. Hassan seemed taken aback and pushed for the answer he had expected. "Then my answer is no," I snapped. He asked me to think about it and give my answer the next day.

I returned home very troubled. This was something I certainly was not prepared for. I believed in peace. I knew it was the optimum option for Arabs and Israelis. But peace was not yet comprehensive and had not ended the Israeli occupation of all Palestinian and Arab lands. How would I feel if television screens were to show pictures of me socializing with Israeli officials one minute and Israeli tanks wreaking destruction in Palestinian cities the next? And yet, I worried that by refusing the job, I might be betraying my principles. Wasn't this job a real opportunity to build the peace we wanted? Couldn't I through this new position help convince the Israeli people that peace with the Palestinians was worth pursuing? Also in my thoughts were my family, the family of my wife, Lynne, and my friends. Many of them had not crossed the psychological barrier yet.

I immediately called Prince (then Sharif) Zaid Bin Shaker (1934–2002), head of the Royal Court and the man who had brought me into politics a few years earlier, appointing me as his press adviser in 1989 when he was prime minister. "I think you know why I am calling," I said. "I need to see you." He did know, of course, and asked me to visit him at his house the following morning. "I can't take this job," I told him when we met. I explained that I was not psychologically prepared for the task and that I needed to help look after the family business, my father having died a year earlier. Deep down, I felt that Bin Shaker sympathized with my predicament but could not say so openly. The king had chosen me, and it was Bin Shaker's job as a consummate diplomat, confidante, and loyal adviser to the king to convince me to take it. Bin Shaker, a towering figure, a distant cousin of King Hussein, and one of the most powerful men in the country, had been a military man for most of his life. He had risen through the ranks to become chief of the Joint Staff of the Armed Forces before being asked by the king to form a government in 1989. He was not known to be sympathetic to the Israelis, although he believed peace to be in Jordan's strategic interest. I asked him to arrange an appointment for me to see the king and added that I would avoid giving an answer to the government until I had a chance to speak to the king in person. He promised to arrange a meeting. I then retreated into my home, not answering the phone and not returning the many phone calls I received.

The next evening, I was at my mother's when the phone rang at about eight o'clock. Not thinking that anyone would be looking for me there, I answered. On the other end was the prime minister. "Where have you been all this time?" he asked, telling me to see him immediately. "Marwan, you are like my son, and when the king picks you to be his ambassador to Israel, you can't say no. I would give my own son the same advice." Still I wouldn't budge. For the next two days, I nagged Bin Shaker to arrange an audience with the king.

On Monday, November 21, King Hussein held a lunch to honor everyone who participated in negotiations with Israel, some two hundred people. Bin Shaker asked me to arrive early so that I could see the king. I came and waited, but to no avail. After the ceremony ended, people lined up to shake hands with the king. He had not said a word, and I began to feel I might be off the hook—until Bin Shaker whispered in my ear to remain after I shook hands with his Majesty.

Then, with his usual grace, King Hussein addressed me in front of all two hundred guests. "Marwan, I want you to become Jordan's first ambassador to Israel. I understand you have some personal issues, but we will work to address them together." I had no choice but to answer, "As you wish, Your Majesty."

Once the word got out, I endured the most difficult week of my life. Although my wife was opposed to the idea, to her eternal credit, she said she would accept and support whatever decision I made. My relatives were furious. I come from a large Christian family whose roots in the region date back to early Christianity and who have a strong public service record in Jordan. "You cannot make this decision on behalf of the Christian community in Jordan," said my cousin, a senator. He argued that, were I to accept, the entire Christian community in Jordan would be placed at greater odds with the Islamist opposition. The opposition, particularly the Islamists, might very well claim that the king could find no Muslim Jordanian to accept the post. My acceptance might suggest that Christian Jordanians were less loyal to the Palestinian cause than Muslims. My family and I might also face social isolation from many Jordanians who were not ready for a fellow countryman to live with the "enemy" on territory that once belonged to their compatriots. Adding to this, my father-in-law, a member of one of the oldest Christian families from Jerusalem, who once represented Jerusalem in the Jordanian parliament, could not fathom that his son-in-law would be ambassador to the people who drove him out of Palestine in 1948.

The burden was too heavy. I called Bin Shaker and said, "I cannot go. I am sorry." He could not believe it. "Do you realize that you said yes to the king in front of two hundred people? You cannot go back on your word now," he said. The news had leaked to the local press, and at home on Tuesday and Wednesday I must have received more than three hundred calls, answering none of them. Bin Shaker told me he was traveling to London and gave me his number there. "Think about it, and call me with your decision," he said, explaining that my political career would be over if I turned the king down.

For twenty-four hours, I locked myself in my house and received no one. I told my wife I wanted to come to a decision on my own. The idea of saying no bothered me, but not out of concern for my political career. "Why accept being the spokesman of the negotiating team with Israel but then refuse to be ambassador?" In the end my decision hinged on the answer to this question: Would you be able to live with yourself knowing that you chickened out of a difficult assignment, even this one? I immediately knew the answer: I could not. I told Lynne. She said that even though she was opposed to the idea, it was more important to her that I was at peace with myself. I called Bin Shaker in London. Despite the difference in age and experience, I knew he cared for me as a son. I had made one of the most important decisions in my life. There was no looking back.

THE TWILIGHT ZONE

It would be a few months before I assumed my post in Israel, since differences in opinion between Prime Minister Yitzhak Rabin and Foreign

Minister Shimon Peres obstructed agreement on an Israeli ambassador to Jordan for some time. I was sworn in by King Hussein on February 27, 1995. He gave me general directions and emphasized the importance of the communications channel established with the prime ministry (as opposed to the Israeli foreign ministry). King Hussein had never trusted Peres, preferring to deal with Rabin, whom he considered a man of his word. By contrast, the king felt that Peres was more of a dreamer and often did not regard peace with Jordan as a top priority. The king emphasized the need to build relations both with the 1948 Palestinians and those of the West Bank and Gaza. He wished me luck and did not revisit the subject of my reluctance to accept the job.

On March 12, I traveled to Israel with Lynne unofficially for a three-day visit to look for offices and a residence. Arriving in Israel was like stepping into the unknown—a twilight zone. Although I had been to Elat and Lake Tiberius during the negotiations, this was the first time I had truly visited and slept in an Israeli city, Tel Aviv. It felt so strange to step into a society so culturally different from my own and yet so close geographically. This city had existed for more than fifty years, so near—a mere hundred miles from Amman—and yet so far away!

In Tel Aviv I felt like a spectator. My first impression was that Israel was certainly more developed than Jordan but was by no means a superpower. The Israeli myth in my mind was being checked, for the first time, by reality. Tel Aviv looked like a mixture of old Beirut or Cyprus with a European city. The people were a strange combination of European businesspeople and Middle Eastern merchants. The young looked eccentric with a liberal sense of fashion. The city was not especially clean, with a lot of modern construction coexisting alongside old, seemingly abandoned structures dating to before 1948. But the most striking realization was this: even though this was historical Palestine, which had had a predominantly Arab culture, Arab architecture, and Arab way of life, the place I was visiting bore little resemblance to the romantic image of Palestine nurtured in my mind. Before me was a different culture, with people who spoke a strange language and architecture that looked more European than Middle Eastern, even with what remained of pre-1948 Arab houses and buildings. I could not help but wonder how the Palestinians who left in 1948 would feel if they had a chance to visit. The experience would indeed be bitter.

CROSSING INTO THE UNKNOWN

From the outset, I made a conscious decision to not be a "protocol" or a "celebrity" ambassador, such as the Egyptian ambassador in Israel seemed to be. I was determined to focus on the issues. Jordanians would not have looked favorably at an ambassador who brushed aside the difficult issues or opted for a comfortable diplomatic life instead of pressing for a just resolution to the unresolved issues of the peace process, such as the status of Jerusalem and the refugees or a just settlement of the territorial issues. I was determined to speak about these issues candidly but not in a spirit of confrontation. Rather, I wanted Israelis to know that peace with Jordan could not substitute for a permanent agreement with the Palestinians and that all the problems with the Arab world had not been solved. Therefore, I emphasized the importance of a comprehensive peace. In an interview with the *Jordan Times* published on the day I crossed to Israel, I stated, "If peace is to be permanent and comprehensive, the citizens of Jordan must feel that the Palestinian track is going in the right direction and that the Palestinian component of the Arab-Israeli conflict is being tackled in an acceptable manner. Short of that, it is difficult to perceive a peace that develops from the official level to the popular level. Peace at the people's level will take a much longer time than that at the government level. That is normal."[1] This theme that I repeated over and over would later land me in trouble.

I officially crossed the Sheikh Hussein Bridge in the north as Jordan's first ambassador to Israel on Thursday, April 6, 1995. My wife and our two children had stayed behind so that the children could finish the school year before joining me.

The first order of official business was presenting a copy of my credentials to Foreign Minister Shimon Peres on Friday. But I also had a personal matter to attend to.

MY MOTHER'S HOUSE

My mother is a Palestinian from Jaffa who was driven out in the 1948 War and came to Jordan, where she met my father. She had often told me about her life in Palestine, but I had never had a chance to see where she spent her childhood. Because she left in haste during the war, she had few mementoes of her life in Jaffa except for an old picture of her house. Her mother had kept the house key with her until her death, hoping, as have many Palestinians, that one day, she might return home.

I had always wondered if I would see where my mother had grown up. Now the opportunity had arrived, and I wasted no time seizing it. On Saturday, April 8, armed with that picture and the name of the street she lived on (King Faisal), I asked the embassy's driver to take me there. Jaffa, a thriving Mediterranean port city for the better part of its history, had become almost a suburb of Tel Aviv, which itself began as a suburb of Jaffa settled by immigrant Jews early in the last century. There was one problem, though. There was no longer a street in Jaffa called King Faisal. The Israeli municipality had changed all the Arabic names to Hebrew ones. The driver pointed out that an outlet selling sandwiches belonged to an original inhabitant of Jaffa, who might be able to help. Sure enough, he told us that King Faisal Street had become Yehuda Hayamit. We went there, driving slowly, until I found myself standing directly in front of my mother's home, which had hardly changed. The house was on the third floor, with the street-level floor having been a factory, as my mother told me. I looked up at the windows of that third floor, trying to imagine my mother as a young girl, perhaps doing her homework. Looking at the house where she lived almost half a century ago, gazing on the same scenery she once did, and somehow feeling that part of her spirit was still there engulfed me in a mix of emotions that I can hardly describe in words. Who was living there, I wondered. Do they know to whom the house belonged? I considered knocking on the door, but then thought twice: as Jordan's first ambassador to Israel, I would be making an inopportune political statement.

PRESENTING MY CREDENTIALS
I presented my credentials on April 10, 1995, to President Ezer Weizman. I was extremely nervous, knowing that Jordanians, Palestinians, Israelis, and the whole Arab world were watching. The knowledge that all eyes were on me set a pattern for everything I did. I learned to consider how each of these audiences would perceive every word I uttered.

The ceremony began at the King David Hotel, where I was accompanied by Mariam Shomrat, chief of protocol at the Israeli foreign ministry. Martin Indyk had just come back to the hotel from presenting his own credentials as the U.S. ambassador to President Weizman. I had known Indyk from my days at the Jordan Information Bureau and his days as the director of the Washington Institute for Near East Policy, but it was not until our concurrent terms in Israel that we forged a strong relationship.

We drove to West Jerusalem to the president's residence, where an Israeli band played the Jordanian and Israeli national anthems. I reiterated the same theme that a comprehensive peace needed to be translated into peace between people, not just governments.[2] I wondered how the picture of my toasts with the Israeli president would play in Jordan. The ceremony marked the beginning of a delicate balancing act I had to perform throughout my stay.

My first meeting with Yitzhak Rabin came the next day. I told him that Jordan sought full peace with Israel, but that peace would depend on political progress on the Palestinian track and on whether Jordanians perceived that peace would bring economic relief. Jordan had been suffering from an acute economic crisis: its currency had lost half its value a few years earlier following the loss of Arab aid. Jordanians hoped that the peace treaty would help in partly alleviating their economic problems through increased foreign aid and investments. Rabin said that he was disappointed that the Americans had been less forthcoming than expected in terms of providing debt relief to Jordan. (Congress later that year did vote on a debt relief package for Jordan.)

We also discussed the Syrian track. The *Jerusalem Post* had run an article the day before, quoting Rabin as telling his ministers they should not expect to start negotiations with President Hafez Assad on conditions less than those with President Sadat—who achieved full Israeli withdrawal from the Sinai after signing a peace treaty with Israel in 1979. Interestingly, Rabin reiterated this to me. He said he was aware that Assad felt that he could not accept any less than what had been given to Egypt—in Syrian terms, a full withdrawal from the Golan Heights—but, he added, this did not mean that Israel accepted these conditions.

At this first meeting with Rabin I was most struck by the combination of shyness and resolve that he possessed. He had a clear vision of where he wanted to go and spoke with determination and confidence. But he was not a man of small talk.

SETTING THE TONE: VISIT TO THE ORIENT HOUSE

Although I had no previous diplomatic experience, I was determined to be a serious, candid ambassador who spoke directly to the issues. I believed the best course to advance the Jordanian-Israeli relationship was to make the Israelis aware that there were still serious problems to be resolved and that peace with Arabs could not be compartmentalized. Progress, or the lack of it, on one track directly affected public opinion on other tracks. In addition, there were a large number of Jordanians with property lost in Israel—refugees who became Jordanian citizens—whose interests I needed to pursue.

I thus decided to appear on Israeli Arabic television for a half-hour interview just three days after I began my ambassadorship. I set the tone on all the above issues. The interview had a big impact in Jordan. Many groups, whether progovernment or in the opposition, suddenly began to see that I could be candid about the issues and that being an ambassador in Israel did not demand that issues be swept under the carpet. Bin Shaker called to say he was very pleased.

My first real test, however, was my visit to Orient House, a stately mansion built by the late Musa al-Husseini, mayor of Jerusalem in 1897. Over nearly a century, Orient House had become a political symbol of the Arab presence in Jerusalem and of a Palestinian national identity. After Israel occupied Jerusalem in 1967, Orient House became the Palestinian national gathering place in Arab East Jerusalem, and since the Madrid peace process had started, it served as the headquarters of the Palestinian negotiations team. I had received a telephone call from Faisal Husseini, grandson of Musa al-Husseini and son of Abdel Qader Husseini, who was a renowned Palestinian fighter in the 1948 War and whom I knew from the negotiating days in Washington, inviting me to visit Orient House. Husseini was using the mansion as his headquarters in Jerusalem. It seemed an excellent opportunity to reaffirm Jordan's position on Arab Jerusalem as well as an opportunity to demonstrate to the Palestinians that Jordan would use its newly founded relationship with Israel to help rather than hurt their cause. Prime Minister Bin Shaker and Foreign Minister Kabariti approved the visit.

After notifying the Israeli foreign ministry of my intended visit, I received a note verbale one day before the visit, "reminding" Jordan that the Oslo agreements with the Palestinians stated that the offices responsible for carrying out the powers and responsibilities of the Palestinian National Authority were to be located in the Gaza Strip and Jericho Area and that any attempt to exercise these powers in Orient House was a breach of these agreements.

I went anyway. On April 25, two weeks after I presented my credentials, I was received at Orient House by Faisal Husseini, the internationally known Palestinian spokeswoman Hanan Ashrawi, and Sari Nusseibeh, another prominent Jerusalemite academic. Husseini showed me around Orient House. The visit was widely covered by the press. I stood at the steps of the historic building and declared that East Jerusalem was "part of occupied Arab land and should return to Arab sovereignty."[3] Afterward, we all strolled through the city under the gaze of Israeli border police before having lunch at the National Hotel in East Jerusalem. There, we had a candid and useful discussion on the Jordanian-Palestinian relationship, particularly as regards Palestinian fears that Jordan had designs on the West Bank and hoped to restore its rule there in an eventual settlement with Israel.

The visit to Orient House more than any other act changed the attitude of many Jordanians toward the presence of a Jordanian ambassador in Israel. Even the most skeptical among them had started to see the value of raising the thorny issues through a newfound diplomatic channel. Many members of the opposition in Jordan sent me congratulatory messages. The Palestinians of course were elated.

The Israeli government was not pleased by the visit but let it pass. Beyond the note verbale, it did not pursue the issue. Though Moshe Peled, a member of the Likud opposition in the Knesset, called for my expulsion that day—the first of many instances when members of the Likud would reiterate that demand—I strongly felt that I could not be the Jordanian ambassador in Israel and not show sensitivity to the Palestinians and to their presence in Jerusalem.

MY BRUSH WITH AMMAN

The morning before my visit to Orient House, I had addressed the Foreign Correspondents Association in Tel Aviv, stating that East Jerusalem was the sole responsibility of the Palestinians. I went on to say that Jordanian support for the Jewish state was lukewarm at the popular level because the core of the conflict—the Palestinian issue—remained unresolved, as did issues concerning Syria and Lebanon. I explained that Jordanians had consequently taken a wait-and-see attitude. The challenge, I went on, was to have this government-to-government peace trickle down to the average citizen. This was a theme I had stated on several other occasions. My intention was certainly not to belittle the achievement of the Jordan-Israel peace treaty but to point out to Israelis that we were still at the beginning of the road to a full, lasting peace with which the average citizen could feel comfortable.

Sheikh Hassan Nasrallah, leader of the Lebanese Hezbollah group, seized on my statements, quoting me out of context and fiercely attacking the peace treaty between Jordan and Israel, declaring that even the Jordanian ambassador in Israel had claimed that peace was only between the two governments.

King Hussein was furious. Bin Shaker called to ask about my statements and diplomatically suggest that I not show up in Amman for a while. Bin Shaker was trying to protect me from the king's anger, even though my statements had been manipulated by the leader of Hezbollah. The whole episode was soon forgotten, however, with no ill feelings on the part of the king.

THE FIRST CRISIS: THE LAND EXPROPRIATION ISSUE

Weeks after I arrived, the Israeli government made a decision to expropriate 134 acres of land in East Jerusalem to build Jewish settlements. Although the Oslo Accords deferred the issue of settlements to final status negotiations, Palestinians and Arabs fully expected Israel not to take any measures, including building new settlements, that would affect the outcome of final status negotiations, particularly since the Oslo Accords specifically committed the parties against taking measures that would prejudice the outcome of final status talks. Since 1967, Israeli settlement building in the West Bank has continued apace against the will of the international community and in contravention of the Fourth Geneva Convention, which forbids an occupying power from transferring part of its population to the occupied territory. By 1993, when the Oslo Accords were signed, more than 265,000 Israeli settlers were living in East Jerusalem and the West Bank.

The decision, made on April 28, 1995, was Israel's first major expropriation of land since the signing of Oslo. On top of the fact that

Jordan—and most of the international community—has always regarded these settlements as illegal and an obstacle to a permanent solution to the conflict, the decision was a huge embarrassment to Jordan,
coming so soon after the establishment of diplomatic relations between
Jordan and Israel. Kabariti denounced the decision as a "breach of international conventions and the spirit of peace" and instructed me to follow
the issue persistently with the Israeli government.[4]

I first demanded to discuss the matter with the Israeli foreign ministry. I met with Deputy Foreign Minister Yossi Beilin and explained that
the decision had put Jordan in the unsavory position of appearing to defend the Israeli position on Jerusalem. I warned that the reaction would
be strong and would affect bilateral relations. I also urged him to take
our position very seriously into consideration.

Beilin, a fine man to whom I grew close later on, admitted to me
that he opposed this "legal but unwise" decision. He meant that from
the Israeli point of view, this was a legal decision, although, of course,
the international community did and still does consider the settlements
illegal.[5] He also expressed his appreciation that we had taken up the issue through diplomatic channels with the Israeli government. He said
that there was still room to maneuver and promised to take Jordan's concerns to his superiors.

On May 1, the new U.S. ambassador to Israel, Martin Indyk, invited
me to a dinner in honor of the visiting U.S. permanent representative to
the United Nations, Madeline Albright. Prime Minister Rabin also attended. Albright was obviously disturbed about the land expropriations and
asked Rabin about them. Rabin said that these lands were an extension of
Jewish neighborhoods, that Palestinians would be "compensated" for
them, and that Israel had already given "thousands" of building licenses to
Palestinian Jerusalemites, a statement that defied the facts. In fact, his entire response was an obfuscation of an Israeli policy—clearly being
implemented—to empty Jerusalem of its Palestinian residents and to isolate it from the West Bank by surrounding it on all sides by Israeli settlements. I intervened to tell Rabin and Albright that the expropriations were
not a matter of financial compensation but a political issue that would
stand in the way of a negotiated solution to the conflict. Rabin, never one to
mince his words, answered abruptly that the Jordan-Israel peace treaty confined matters of concern about Jerusalem to religious issues.

The Jordanian parliament, which was out of session, met informally in mid-May to condemn the Israeli decision and in fact raised the possibilities of abrogating the treaty with Israel and expelling the Israeli ambassador in Amman. Not long after, the Arab League announced its decision to host a summit at the foreign ministers' level to discuss the issue.

Foreign Minister Peres wrote a letter to Foreign Minister Kabariti on May 15 telling him he had listened attentively to my arguments raised with Beilin and assured him that "neither the substance nor the timing of these decisions were intended to have any bearing upon our mutual relations." Dismissing the decision as "a routine process," Peres's letter was merely an exercise in public relations that did nothing to address the Jordanian concern.[6]

During a meeting with Uri Savir, director general of the foreign ministry and someone with whom I developed a strong relationship, I emphasized that the decision had seriously jeopardized a series of pending laws in the Jordanian parliament to end the boycott of Israel. I also repeated my warning to Beilin that Jordan would strongly oppose this decision. Attempting to give the obvious crisis a patina of legitimacy with a silver lining, Savir argued that Jordan should look positively on the decision, since the Israeli government took a decision to stop such future expropriations. (Israel has never adhered to its declared commitment to end the expropriation of Palestinian land, and the practice continues today.) Savir contended that the government could not reverse its decision because of domestic considerations. We each agreed to talk to our respective government and then meet again to try to find a solution.

On May 21 I met Peres and explained in detail Jordan's diplomatic campaign to solve the problem. During the meeting, I also relayed to him a proposal by Kabariti to send an Arab delegation to Tel Aviv in return for an Israeli reversal of the decision and an agreement to start final status negotiations on Jerusalem.

Peres said that the Arab states' decision to hold an extraordinary summit on this issue had put Israel in a difficult position when the problem could have been solved otherwise. I reminded him that Jordan had tried to do just that, with no positive reaction from the Israeli government, adding that the Jordanian parliament and the government were in full agreement on the issue of land expropriations and that forcing a confrontation between the government and the parliament over the issue of Jerusalem would endanger the peace process. (The parliament was threatening not to amend several Jordanian laws pertinent to the peace treaty, including lifting the boycott against Israeli products and repealing legislation that discriminated against Israeli nationals.)

Peres would not budge, and had no authority to do so anyway, telling me that the Israeli government also had to consider public opinion and that, for domestic reasons, Israel could not rescind its decision. He suggested an "informal" way out; a petition to the Israeli Supreme Court to stop the decision brought by the Arab residents of Jerusalem. A legal battle, he contended, would delay the implementation of the decision while a diplomatic resolution was pursued.

I had feared all along that our position was not being taken seriously and that the Israeli government had counted on a difference of positions between the palace, the Jordanian government, and parliament—and perhaps believed that the Jordanian objection was the work of an overenthusiastic Jordanian foreign ministry. I told Peres that Rabin would soon receive a letter from King Hussein on the issue.

The UN Security Council met to discuss the issue on May 17, but a U.S. veto prevented the adoption of a resolution condemning the expropriation.

King Hussein, who had just returned from a trip abroad, penned a letter that day to Rabin and is published here for the first time (see Appendix 1). It was five pages long, unusual for an official correspondence between two principals. The king emphasized the importance of Jerusalem to Jordan and affirmed the Jordanian position that "in the context of peace East Jerusalem should become the capital of the Palestinian entity." He indicated his deep concern over this issue "for pre-1967 East Jerusalem has a very special place in my heart and conscience as it does all Jordanians." Although diplomatic, the letter was extremely candid. "I am thus completely at a loss to understand why now the government of Israel should contribute to [a loss of confidence between the Palestinians and Israelis,] further deterioration by unilateral action in Jerusalem and the confiscation of even an inch of Arab land. With all due respect, my friend, this should not stand and we seek your wisdom, courage, and far-sightedness to reconsider urgently and fully the action and repercussions and to act accordingly, recent events at the Security Council

notwithstanding. Your government and the Palestinians, as per your earlier agreed schedule, can then negotiate a mutually satisfactory, balanced
and just solution to the issues of respective territorial rights in
Jerusalem, rather than dealing with some of them now in a unilateral
way and thus further damaging the credibility of both sides and seriously threatening the Peace Process."

The next day, May 22, Rabin suspended the expropriation decision.
Although his decision was certainly affected by an internal crisis loom-
ing in the Knesset over the issue with the Arab MKs (members of the
Knesset), there can be no doubt that the letter from King Hussein was a
major factor. Many people have since confirmed my belief, among them
Moshe Shahal, minister of the police, Uri Savir, and Martin Indyk.

The expropriation issue was an important milestone in the relationship between Jordan and Israel. Until then, the Israeli street in general,
and Rabin in particular, had had the perception that either Jordan would
not be vocal on issues related to the Palestinian track or that the personal
relationship between King Hussein and Rabin could solve all problems.
Rabin quickly learned that Israel's relationship with Jordan was far more
complex than his own relationship with the king, that the monarch's
view on this issue was in keeping with the Jordanian national consensus,
and that Jordan would not hesitate to confront the matter head-on when
it came to such important matters as Jerusalem. In the end, Rabin understood the importance of the relationship with Jordan, and he chose
not to undermine it through this decision. From then on, Rabin and the
Israeli government would take Jordan much more seriously.

The crisis also highlighted the importance of the newfound diplomatic channel with Israel that Jordan made full use of to diffuse a highly
explosive situation. In a phone call on May 25, Abdel Wahab Darawsheh,
an Arab MK and leader of the Arab Democratic Party, conveyed to me Israeli Arabs' appreciation for the Jordanian position, calling it the most
outspoken of any Arab government, including that of the Palestinian
National Authority.

ABSENTEE PROPERTY IN ISRAEL

The subject of absentee property in Israel became one of the most explosive issues I followed in Israel during my ambassadorship and was
a prime example of Israel's unwillingness to come face to face with its

obligations under international law as well as its own laws governing conduct with Arab countries at peace with Israel. I felt then and still believe that Israel has not dealt with this issue in good faith.

On July 4, I sent the Israeli foreign ministry a note verbale officially inquiring "as to the exact status of any rights of Jordanians to buy land and/or property in Israel, in addition to the status of property owned by Jordanians prior to the signature of the Jordan-Israel treaty of peace."[7] The inquiry was instigated by two recent developments. The Jordanian parliament was debating the annulment of the anti-Israel boycott laws and the extension of the right to buy property in Jordan to Israeli nationals. Parliament asked for assurances that Israel would reciprocate by extending the same rights to Jordanians.

But this was not all. The property of many Jordanians of Palestinian origin, abandoned in 1948 during the first Arab-Israeli war, had been seized by Israel and, under legislation known as the 1950 Absentee Property Law, placed under the administration of a "custodian" with broad authority to lease, sell, and administer all such property. The law stipulated that a trust was to be set up whereby proceeds of the management of such property would be held in escrow until such property ceased to be absentee property, "and any right a person had to it immediately before it was vested in the Custodian shall revert to that person or his successor."[8]

Jordan was concerned that according to the law affirming the implementation of the peace treaty between Jordan and Israel and passed by the Knesset in early 1995, Jordanians would still be regarded as absentees before November 10, 1994, even though a peace treaty had been signed between the two countries.[9] Jordan felt that this was a direct violation of the terms of the peace treaty, in particular article 7 (2) (a), in which the parties agreed inter alia to remove all discriminatory barriers to normal economic relations; article 8, in which they agreed to alleviate problems of refugees and displaced persons arising on a bilateral level; and article 11 (1) (b), in which they undertook within three months "to repeal all adverse or discriminatory references in their respective legislation."[10]

Jordan's argument was both legal and logical. If Israel would not lift the absentee status from Jordanian citizens after a peace treaty was signed between the two countries, when would it ever do so? We felt that

Jordanians' absentee status should have been rescinded by Israel once the state of war between the two countries was officially ended and since the peace treaty forbade the existence of laws in either country that discriminated against the citizens of the other.

According to Uzi Vexler, then director of the Israel Land Administration, about 95 percent of all land in Israel is state land that cannot be bought by any person, Israeli or foreign, but can be leased to Israelis on a long-term basis and in very limited cases to foreigners. Absentee property was part of such land. When we spoke, Vexler estimated that absentee property accounted for about 8 percent of all land in Israel. Most of this had already been sold for "development purposes." Vexler confirmed that the proceeds were being kept in a trust to be returned to owners of such property once they were no longer regarded as "absentees."

On July 19, I received an official note from the Israeli foreign ministry stating that "in principle, Jordanians are allowed to own real estate in the State of Israel. Relating to privately owned real estate, there are no legal limitations to the acquisition of such property by Jordanians." The note ignored the official inquiry about the status of property owned by Jordanians before the signing of the Jordan-Israel peace treaty.[11]

When I pressed the Israeli foreign ministry for an official answer, I was told that Israel preferred to deal with property rights "unofficially." Foreign ministry officials asked why Jordan was raising an issue that would be addressed in final status negotiations. My argument was simply that Jordan did not view the question of absentee property as part of the refugee issue but as a legal and financial matter relating to the rights of Jordanians to their property. The Israelis responded that absentee property would be dealt with when a comprehensive solution to the conflict was reached. When Jordan countered that it had not signed a comprehensive peace treaty but a bilateral one with Israel, the Israelis responded that Jews had also lost property in Arab countries. However legitimate that claim may be—and Israel was free to raise it—there was not a single Jewish household in Jordan, so the quid pro quo, we believed, could not possibly apply.

Surely, if there was a trust in which these proceeds were kept, its value would be in the billions of dollars today—and in an open economy such as Israel's, surely this would be recorded. A request to meet with the custodian was ignored. My requests to know the value of this trust were also disregarded. In fact, it appears that despite the Absentee Law of 1950, most Arab property had been sold, no such trust exists, and Israel has routinely violated its own law regarding absentee property.

I met on September 4 with Eli Dayan, deputy foreign minister, to present him officially with our note articulating Jordan's position on the issue. The note stated that the Israeli law on the implementation of the treaty was inconsistent with the treaty of peace signed between the two states. Written in legal language, the note registered our objection to the legislation passed in the Knesset approving the peace treaty but maintaining Jordanians' absentee status. It officially requested the government of Israel to remove this inconsistency from its legislation.[12]

Dayan told me that just before negotiations between the two states concluded at the Hashemiah Palace in Amman in October 1994, it had been decided that negotiations on the refugee question would be postponed until final status negotiations with Palestinians began. Again, I countered that Jordan did not view the questions of refugees and property as related issues. I explained that our legal adviser, Awn Khasawneh, was present at those negotiations and had drafted the legal note presented to the Israeli foreign ministry. Our objection still stood, I said. Dayan replied only that the Israeli government would study the issue and send us an official answer soon.

Such an answer was never forthcoming. Shimon Peres came to Jordan in October 1995 to attend the Amman MENA (Middle East and North Africa) conference. In a meeting with Crown Prince Hassan, Peres asked that the issue be postponed until final status negotiations, stating that Israel was not in a position to address it at that point. A full year and a half later, in February 1997—by which time I had left Israel to become Jordan's minister of information—when Israeli prime minister Binyamin Netanyahu led a delegation to Amman to discuss bilateral relations and pending issues—we raised the issue of absentee property yet again and pointed out that Jordan was still waiting for an official answer to the note sent in September 1995. The Israeli delegation denied any knowledge of the existence of such a note (Appendix 2 reproduces the note).

JORDANIAN PRISONERS

Jordan felt that with the signing of a peace treaty, the issue of Jordanian prisoners who had committed security offenses against Israel should be revisited. When these Jordanians committed their offenses, Israel was officially considered an enemy state. Some sentences thus needed to be commuted and, in many cases, prisoners released. Effectively and justly addressing this issue was central to mobilizing public opinion and building public confidence in the treaty.

I sent the first official note on the issue to the Israeli foreign ministry on July 4, 1995, to inquire about the "exact status of all Jordanians in Israeli prisons, including their names, the charges against them, the sentences and jail terms."[13]

The ministry sent its reply on July 20 acknowledging the presence of twenty-seven prisoners with their names and places of detention.[14] The information did not correspond to Jordan's records but did include the name of the most famous Jordanian prisoner, Sultan Ajluni, who was arrested, tried and jailed for killing an Israeli soldier in 1990. We pressed the issue further, inquiring about the charges against all Jordanian prisoners and their jail terms.[15]

Six days later, the foreign ministry sent a more detailed note on the prisoners' status.[16] The list now included the names of nine more prisoners, for a total of thirty-six. Jordan believed that a majority of them, twenty-five, had not taken up arms and were therefore eligible for release. Five people were on our prisoners' list but not included in Israel's. I subsequently met with foreign ministry officials on this issue. They told me that out of the list sent, twenty-three people could be released within a month but that the rest had "blood on their hands" and would not be released. Not until 2007 did Israel, after lengthy negotiations with Jordan, change its position somewhat and release a group of such prisoners, including Ajluni, through an agreement that would have them serve up to an additional eighteen months in Jordanian prisons. Indeed, the first group of six Jordanian prisoners was released on February 29, 1996, less than a month after my return from Israel.

THE PALESTINIAN ARABS IN ISRAEL

Palestinian Arabs in Israel, who inhabited the land for centuries and who constituted more than 95 percent of the population before massive Jewish immigration at the turn of the twentieth century, would become a group in which I took particular interest. Even though I spent less than a year in Israel, I forged a strong relationship with this group that would endure after my departure. I realized almost immediately that this group, with its firsthand knowledge of both Arab and Israeli culture, is a natural ally of the Arab Center, one that can be a bridge between Arabs and Israelis and help both sides overcome the abyss that separates them. Unfortunately, both the Arab world and Israel treated them with suspicion, with Arabs looking at them as traitors and Israel viewing them as a fifth column inside the Jewish state. I concluded that I could play a role in helping bridge that misunderstanding between them and the Arab world, starting a series of visits that took me to many of their cities, villages, and communities.

In 1948 Palestinians in what became Israel numbered about 900,000. Of these, only 160,000 remained in Israel after the 1948 War. The rest, including most of the political and economic leaders, left or were forced out of Palestine to neighboring countries. Those who remained were economically devastated and viewed as a threat by the new state of Israel. For eighteen years, they would be placed under military rule, unable to leave their villages after dark and treated as second-class citizens. In succeeding years, their access to funds, education, and work opportunities was seriously and purposely curtailed, with deliberate attempts to isolate them from their Arab cultural roots.[17]

Shamefully, the Arab world treated them no better. Even though they refused to leave their land and endured hardships because of their steadfastness, they were denounced as traitors by Arabs for accepting Israeli nationality, whereas the Palestinians who left were glorified as heroes. Because of this convoluted logic, the Palestinian Arabs in Israel were ostracized in the Arab milieu, denied entry to other Arab countries, refused admission to Arab universities, and denied access to Arab funds. Shunned by both Israel and the Arab world, one might have expected the Palestinian Arabs to wither away, surrendering their Arab heritage and melting as best they could into the larger Israeli society.

But they did not. They persevered, and though they had to start from scratch, with little economic power and no political leadership, they fought back. By the time I went to Israel, the Arabs of Israel were represented by eight Knesset members. Although Arabs first entered the Knesset through the Israeli communist party, they later formed their own parties, as well as dominating the communist party (not because of any communist tendencies but rather because the party advocated a moderate position on the peace process and favored equal rights for the Palestinian Arabs of Israel).

These Palestinian Arabs in Israel (as they like to be called, versus 1948 Palestinians or Israeli Arabs, for example) were thirsty to reestablish their cultural roots with the Arab world. They have accepted Israel's creation, become citizens of Israel, pay taxes, and speak Hebrew; Israel has yet to accept them as full, equal citizens. Constantly regarded and treated as different by Israeli Jews, the Palestinian Arabs never forgot their Arab roots—even had they wanted to. Their "otherness" constantly reinforced their Arab identity. They rebuilt their economic power and fought to have their communities recognized as cities eligible for state funds.

When Egypt signed a peace treaty with Israel, the Palestinian Arabs in Israel saw a chance to reestablish contact with the Arab world. But Egypt was somewhat remote, with no large Palestinian community, and Egyptians continued to treat them with suspicion. The peace with Jordan was different. Jordan was geographically much closer, and many of its people had come from pre-1948 Palestine. To them, Jordanians were family, and they were eager to embrace their cousins at last. They also saw in the treaty a vindication of their position for the past forty-seven years, refusing to leave their land and fighting for equal rights within the Jewish state.

Welcoming telegrams from leaders of their communities arrived even before I set foot in Israel. Both King Hussein and Foreign Minister Kabariti felt they were a social and political force that could not be ignored and encouraged me to forge strong relations with them.

During my first few weeks in Israel, the small offices of the Jordanian embassy located in the Dan Hotel in Tel Aviv were flooded with the many delegations representing the different Arab communities that had come to welcome me to Israel. Their reception was overwhelming and made me feel at times as if I was their ambassador to the Arab world as much as I was the Jordanian ambassador to Israel. And I quickly found out that I wanted to be that.

I wanted to establish good relations with all the political and social forces of Arab society in Israel. Although nearly all the leaders came to visit me in my office, including MKs Abdel Wahab Darawsheh, Talab Sane', Saleh Tarif, Walid Sadeq, Nawaf Masalha, Chairman of the

Committee for Heads of the Local Arab Communities and mayor of ShfaAmr Ibrahim Nimr Hussein, and others, the first visit to an Arab community I made would be to the Bedouins of the Naqab (Negev) on April 27. This group has many relatives in Jordan and feels particularly close to the kingdom. I would be treated that day to many plates of Bedouin-style *mansaf* (a traditional Arab dish consisting of rice, yogurt, and meat, eaten by hand) at every stop I made!

My first political visit, though, was to the Arab Democratic Party of Abdel Wahab Darawsheh, then the largest Arab party in Israel, at its headquarters in Nazareth. I addressed a crowd of more than a thousand people that night, May 17, telling them that Jordan wished to make up for all the lost time in not keeping contact with Arabs in Israel. Their response was overwhelming. I stood for an hour, shaking hands with every person there, touched by the expression of joy on their faces that came from knowing they had finally reestablished a much-awaited bridge to their roots.

Next on my list was Hadash, the communist party that had been dominated by Arabs. Although I had visited MK Hashem Mahamid, leader of the party's bloc in the Knesset, relations between the party and Jordan were not good for historical reasons, since Jordan had taken a strong anticommunist stand in the 1950s, and Mahamid was naturally reserved. I decided to break the ice. The opportunity arose when the party held a large gathering to commemorate the first anniversary of the death of its leader, Tawfiq Zayyad, who was also mayor of Nazareth and a highly respected and popular nationalist. I had not received an invitation to the event but decided to invite myself. I called Mahamid and told him I wished to come and pay my respects to this great man. The organizers were taken aback but still received me, seating me in the third row (as the Jordanian ambassador in Israel, I was treated as a VIP and always given the seat of honor in any event I attended). Just as the event ended, Nazareth's new mayor, Ramez Jarayseh, himself a Hadash member, and Zayyad's widow, Naila, approached me with an invitation for dinner, which I readily accepted.

Later that summer, Fakhry Jdday, a pharmacist from Jaffa and an original inhabitant of the city (most original Jaffa Palestinians left in 1948), held a dinner in my honor at his home. The evening was a moving experience. His house, built by his grandfather more than a hundred

years earlier, was an artifact fit for a museum, with its high ceilings, dec-
orated floor tiles, and distinctive Arab architecture. He took me to the
balcony after dinner and showed me the abandoned houses of several
prominent Jaffa families. "Next to our house is the Rocke family house,"
he would say. "Over there, the Garghours, and there, the Dajanis." These
were all families I knew, families now living in Jordan. Some of their
children had attended school with me. Other descendants were friends
or colleagues. I was gazing at their families' houses, something they
probably had not had the chance to do. It was surreal and in many ways
painful. I later asked my mother if she knew Jdday. "Of course I knew
the Jdday family," she said. "They had a pharmacy on the main road."
"Mother, it is still there," I said. I could not tell whether the look on her
face was astonishment or pain.

All summer, I visited almost every Arab community in Israel, large
and small. I traveled to Nazareth, Jaffa, Akka, Haifa, Lydda, ShfaAmr,
Sakhnin, Umm Al-Fahm, Rahat, and many others. I was hosted by the
famous Palestinian poet Samih Kassim in his village, Rama, and was
treated with Lynne to a beautiful lunch with his extended family among
thousands of olive trees. In Lydda, I was shown where the Israelis gathered the townspeople in 1948 and ordered them to leave, on foot, after
shooting some of them. I fell in love with the land and with the people
who persevered. I admired their resolve, their determination to stay on
their land, and to rebuild their lives after being abandoned by friend and
foe. Everywhere I went, they made two requests: assistance from Jordan
to facilitate their hajj—the pilgrimage to Mecca, required by Islam of all
able Muslims—and scholarships for their children to attend Jordanian
universities. Their thirst for education and their strong will to preserve
their Arab culture were unmatched by anything I have seen in any other
Arab community.

In August, I visited the leader of the moderate faction of the Islamic
movement in Israel, Sheikh Abdullah Nimr Darwish. He lives less than
half an hour's drive from Tel Aviv in the village of Kfar Kassem, very
near the Green Line, the 1967 border between the West Bank and Israel.
I was struck by how little the village seemed to have changed since 1948.
The street names were all still in Arabic. Green flags (the flag of the Islamic movement) were everywhere, and there were few modern buildings or streets. Sheikh Darwish is a thoughtful, pragmatic leader who

advocates coexistence, democracy, and the pursuit of political objectives through peaceful means. He impressed me greatly, and I invited him to come to Jordan, which he did, lecturing there and appearing on Jordanian television. Sheikh Darwish advocated Arabs' participation in the Knesset elections so that their voices could be heard. The next elections were to be held in 1996. Arab participation in elections had always been somewhat lower than Jewish participation since they had been granted the right to vote, but considering that Arabs tended to vote overwhelmingly for pro-peace parties in the Knesset, their participation in 1996 was critical to advance the peace process within Israeli society. Opposing this position was Sheikh Raed Salah, the hard-line mayor of Umm Al-Fahm and leader of the extremist faction of the Islamic movement, who viewed participation in the Knesset elections as a form of giving legitimacy to the Israeli state.

I decided to visit Sheikh Salah in Umm Al-Fahm. Having received no invitation, I repeated the tactic I used with Hadash; I invited myself. When I called the sheikh to tell him I wanted to visit, he was taken aback and first pretended that he needed time to prepare the town for the visit. I told him I would meet him first and see the town later, which I did, a few days after my visit to Darwish. Sheikh Salah and I had a good, serious discussion attended by members of the city council. He would not budge on participation in the next elections, however, telling me that participation would weaken the Islamic movement by going against the wishes of its constituency and that he preferred to work at the local rather than national level.

During my many visits to the Arab communities of Israel, I often felt shame over how poorly the Arab world had treated them for the past fifty years, and I shared that sentiment with every community I visited. I always said that Jordan's aim was to try to compensate for the Arab world's misguided position and that Jordan wanted to be a bridge between them and their larger Arab environment. I have not stopped talking about their cause since. Although the Israeli authorities watched my visits closely and some members of the opposition in the Knesset called for my expulsion on grounds that I was interfering in Israeli internal affairs (one such call came after I visited the Nazareth municipality in December 1995), the Israeli government never lodged an official complaint.

RELATIONS WITH THE PALESTINIANS IN THE WEST BANK

The relationship with the Palestinians in the West Bank and Gaza was more complicated. On one hand, I was not accredited to the Palestinian National Authority, and given Yasser Arafat's sensitivities to any Jordanian activity in the West Bank and Gaza, out of his concern that Jordan still harbored ambitions for the West Bank, all contacts there had to be carefully considered to avoid causing alarm. On the other hand, ignoring the West Bank completely would have looked odd, especially to Jordanians. I had many friends from my negotiating days, not to mention many family members on Lynne's side. I also needed a break every now and then from the tense atmosphere I was living in. So I decided to make only social calls and not to engage in any political activity that might offend Arafat's sensitivities.

Indeed, I must say that the many Palestinian friends I made in Madrid overwhelmed me with their support. They extended countless invitations to dinners at their homes and meetings with their friends and made a genuine effort to make me feel at home. I am indebted to so many of them but must mention two people in particular. Hanan Ashrawi, my counterpart as spokesperson during the negotiating rounds, welcomed me many times into her home, where I always enjoyed a lively discussion about the peace process and the current situation in the Arab world. Ghassan Khatib, a member of the People's Party and a former member of the Palestinian negotiating team, was very helpful, supplying me with data and analysis from his center in Jerusalem.

The Palestinian National Authority greeted me with silence: with the exception of Faisal Husseini, no PNA official called me or extended an invitation during my term as ambassador to Israel. Even though I was a friend to many, they ignored my presence. Whether this treatment was ordered by Arafat I do not know, although I have always suspected it. At any rate, I respected their wishes and did not call them.

Almost every Saturday, our day off at the embassy, I would drive from Tel Aviv to Jerusalem, Ramallah, Nablus, or another West Bank city to visit friends or family or take a stroll in the Old City of Jerusalem. I had last visited the city in 1966, when I was ten and East Jerusalem was part of Jordan. Whether religious or not, one cannot be but awed walking in the alleys of the Old City, surrounded by its centuries of spiritual and historical importance. On many strolls there, I never took a driver with me, nor did I take my usual security guards. I never felt I needed protection. I was among family. Despite the often tense relationship between Jordan and the PLO, and despite the various attitudes toward the peace process among Palestinians, I think the West Bankers appreciated it. Stopping me for coffee or inviting me into a shop, I would often hear "Ahlan bi Safeerna" (Welcome, OUR ambassador!).

When I wished to visit Bir Zeit University, the president, Dr. Hanna Nasir, a first cousin of my father-in-law, a friend, and a fellow Purdue alumnus, was obviously reluctant and asked me to come after 5:00 p.m., presumably when most of the student body would be off campus. As we strolled on campus, a group of students approached. Hanna became nervous. "We would like to welcome you to our campus and invite you to a concert we are having on campus now," they said. I happily obliged and was warmly welcomed by the student body. Hanna also took me to the old dormitory rooms, where my own mother had stayed as a student. He pointed to an old stone doorstep, worn from decades of use. "Whenever people say there were no Palestinian inhabitants of the land before 1948, or no cultural life, all I do is point out this doorstep," he told me. "This is enough proof that we were here a long time ago."

My only visit to Gaza during my stay in Israel was in January 1996. I accompanied Abdel Salam Majali, who was heading a Jordanian delegation to monitor the Palestinian legislative elections. Together we went to see Arafat. Shortly after, I was recalled to Amman as minister of information, but my rendezvous with Arafat was just beginning.

PSYCHOLOGICAL BARRIERS: WALKING A TIGHT ROPE

As Jordan's first ambassador to Israel I faced many challenges and had to cater to a variety of needs, but the experience was also an exhaustive lesson in diplomacy. Among Israelis, I was an instant celebrity. They invited me to their homes, functions, events. "People invite the Jordanian ambassador because they want the Jordanian ambassador to be there, not because they want to listen to what he has to say," I told the *New York Times* in an article explaining my predicament. "And when you start focusing on the person rather than the issue, I get worried."[18] The Israelis looked at the peace treaty with Jordan as one proof that they could be accepted in the region, but they constantly sought reassurance. "How do you like us?

How do you like our country?" I was routinely asked. I often joked that Israel was the only country in the world where the Jordanian ambassador was more important socially than the American ambassador!

In fact, one of the first things that struck me in Israel was the deep sense of insecurity that the average Israeli felt. I had grown up in an Arab society that believed its security to be under constant threat from a regional power, a huge military machine that had resulted in the loss of Palestine, a lingering refugee problem, and the occupation of land belonging to three Arab states. Not until I went to Israel did I discover that the feeling was mutual. Israelis, too, felt a deep sense of insecurity from being in the middle of a "hostile" neighborhood. Each side shares a genuine fear about the other and harbors a profound sense that its personal and existential security is threatened by the other. Both sides also share another thing: an almost total lack of understanding of the depth of the insecurity they feel about each other. This alerted me to the fact that any sustainable solution to the conflict must seriously address the abiding security concerns of both sides.

On the other hand, I was determined to keep the focus on the issues. A high-profile, social ambassador was the last thing Jordanians—only a few miles across the borders and watching me closely—wanted. I was also being monitored by Palestinians and by the Arab world at large. Every move I made, every word I uttered, was thoroughly considered. I had to be on my toes twenty-four hours a day.

The first major test of my diplomatic skills came sooner than I expected. Less than three weeks after I arrived, Israel celebrated its independence. In any other country, this is a joyous occasion celebrated by the diplomatic corps. But to Arabs, particularly to Jordanians, this was the anniversary of the Nakba—the Catastrophe—when Israel won the 1948 War and most Palestinians lost their homes and land and became refugees. For Arabs, Israeli independence is no cause for celebration. President Ezer Weizman hosted a reception at his house in Jerusalem, as he did each year, for the diplomatic corps. I attended with great apprehension. Thinking that my face was still unknown, I "hid" behind the veteran Egyptian ambassador Muhammad Bassiouny and hoped to manage with a handshake with President Weizman and make a quick exit. But as soon as the president saw me, he raised his glass of wine and announced to the crowd his great joy that the Jordanian ambassador, for the first time in Israel's history, was present. Nearly twenty television cameras fixed on me; correspondents asked how I felt. I could not say I was happy because that would offend every Jordanian and Arab. And as ambassador, I could not say I was sad for fear of offending the Israelis. So I said that I hoped the day would come when all the peoples in this region could celebrate their independence. The moment passed, but the scene of how I was to behave was set.

Another moment occurred when Yitzhak Rabin invited Lynne and me to a dinner party at his apartment in Tel Aviv. It would be Lynne's first meeting with him. Rabin asked where Lynne was from. "Amman," Lynne answered. "No, I mean where are you originally from?" Rabin asked, his tone of voice suggesting that he already knew the answer. "My parents came from Jerusalem," she said. Rabin pressed on: where in Jerusalem, he wanted to know. "Well, I don't know what they call it now, but it used to be called Baqaa," Lynne said. "I know Baqaa," Rabin said. "I lived there for ten years. Unfortunately, when we went to Baqaa in 1948, there was no one there," he claimed. Lynne's blood pressure was shooting through the roof. "Please don't make a scene," I whispered, and to her credit, she did not.

Lynne and I both had to think twice before doing something that, anywhere else in the world, would be completely normal. We constantly asked ourselves: Is it okay to go to the movies? Take a stroll at the beach? Attend an apolitical event?

My stay in Israel was short, but I learned a great deal from it. Expecting a totally Western culture, I was surprised that half the Israeli population came from Arab nations and that their Arab origins were reflected in Israeli culture. In the course of one day, one can easily encounter the two extremes of Israeli culture: one very high-tech, modern, and efficient, the other archaic and bureaucratic enough to rival the worst administration of any Arab country. I was shocked at first to hear Arabic songs whenever I walked in an Iraqi-Jewish neighborhood or to see the picture of the late King Muhammad V in almost every Moroccan-Jewish house I visited. So numerous were these apparent anomalies that whenever I heard the often-repeated concern in the Arab world that Israel would culturally overwhelm it, I just laughed. After living in Israel for few months, I was convinced that, if anything, it would be the other way around!

I found Israelis to be very defensive, aggressive, confirming their international reputation. They tend not to take no for an answer. They even have a name for it, this national disposition: *sabra* (cactus flower), which, in their opinion, is rough on the outside but sweet on the inside.

I, of course, tended to befriend the "liberal" Israelis, whether on the political or social level, although I also dealt with the political opposition—then the Likud. But Israeli liberalism does have its limits, and Israelis can be as impenetrable as a brick wall. The overwhelming majority of Israelis, even those who firmly believe in a two-state solution, cannot face the fact that many of them are living in houses that once belonged to other people—Palestinians. Whenever a conversation veered in that direction, my Israeli interlocutor would immediately direct it elsewhere. This issue was taboo for most Israelis and still bothered them deeply after almost fifty years.

Many of the strong friendships I developed with Israelis have lasted to this day. Yossi Beilin, whom I regard very highly, deserves special mention. We established a strong working and personal relationship when he was deputy foreign minister and later when he joined the government of Shimon Peres after the Rabin assassination. Yossi always listened and was always keen to understand Arab culture and thinking and to take it into consideration. We had many discussions about that, and I truly appreciated his reaching out. I also tried to listen to his point of view as much as I could. We remain friends today. Another person I greatly respect is Uri Savir, who was then head of the Israeli negotiating teams with the Syrians and Palestinians. Uri was the contact person at the Israeli foreign ministry who always updated me on the Palestinian-Israeli track and the Syrian-Israeli track as well. But we also would engage in general discussions about Arab culture. Uri is another person who always listened.

Smadar Perry, the ever-energetic journalist from *Yed'iot Ahranot*, Israel's best-selling daily newspaper, also opened her home to us and was always helpful. Another journalist I developed a strong friendship with is Ori Nir, then working for *Ha'aretz*. Few Israelis possess a sharper insight into Arab culture than Ori.

ENCOUNTER WITH NETANYAHU

King Hussein was wary of Jordanian officials meeting with the opposition in any country, let alone Israel, where he did not want to anger Rabin. So

I was given instructions to delay requesting a meeting with the leader of the Israeli opposition, Binyamin Netanyahu. Almost three months after I arrived in Israel, Crown Prince Hassan called me to his office in Amman. Unknown to me, the prince had developed a relationship with Netanyahu. I was made to wait outside his office from 8:30 a.m. until 1:30 p.m. When he finally saw me, he treated me to a dressing down for failing to send my reports directly to him and for not yet meeting Netanyahu.

I met with Netanyahu almost a month later. For some reason, he set the meeting up in the Knesset cafeteria and brought with him several Likud members, including Zalman Shoval, the former and future ambassador to Washington whom I knew from my days as director of the Jordan Information Bureau. Netanyahu stressed the importance of building relations between the Likud and Jordan and went on to explain to me the importance of Jordan and Israel colluding against the establishment of a Palestinian state. "We have Palestinians in Israel, and you have Palestinians in Jordan," he told me, and opined that a Palestinian state in the West Bank and Gaza would radicalize the Palestinians in both countries. "We have a rather different point of view," I answered, explaining that neither the Palestinians in Israel nor those in Jordan were interested in being part of the new state, just in making sure that a state emerges so that decades of Palestinian suffering would end and that the Palestinians in the West Bank and Gaza would enjoy self-determination. "A Palestinian national identity is in the best interests of Jordan, because it would help the Jordanian national identity evolve in a healthier way and would end Jordan's fears that the conflict might be resolved at its own expense," I argued.

"Mr. Ambassador," Netanyahu assured me, "I think I understand the Jordanian position better than you do." "Regardless of where you got your ideas from," I shot back, "what I am telling you *is* the Jordanian position."

Netanyahu's arrogance would appear in many subsequent encounters, but the idea that Jordan's interests would not be served by a Palestinian state, an idea widely shared by the old Likud school, is repeated by many of its adherents today.

Netanyahu is a savvy politician, mindful of the sound bite, and always ready to use it. He tended to impress and befriend his interlocutors, often by stretching or hiding part of the truth. I had another difficult meeting with him as minister of information in 1996, dispatched by Prime Minister Kabariti to see him and urge him not to follow through on an Israeli decision to build more settlements in Jerusalem. His ability to win the trust of those who deal with him was very short-lived, as King Hussein and others would find out quickly after he became prime minister.

THE ASSASSINATION OF RABIN

After the signing of the Oslo Accords, which signaled the mutual recognition of the PLO and Israel, the Palestinians established their authority in Gaza and a small part of the West Bank. Negotiations between the two sides continued to agree on the next phase of the autonomy process. Oslo B, or Oslo II, was signed on September 28, 1995, in the White House and led to the dismantlement of the Israeli military government, the institution of civil administration in the West Bank, agreement on elections for a Palestinian legislature, and full or partial control by the Palestinians over 42 percent of the West Bank.

In October, after the Knesset passed Oslo B by a razor-thin majority (61–59), Rabin seemed to be in a difficult political position. For the first time in Israel's history, two Labor members of the Knesset voted against the government (Avigdor Kahlani and Emmanuel Zissman). Rabin was accused of being able to pass the agreement only with the support of the Arab parties. In fact, Oslo B struck a sensitive chord within Israeli society. The issue was no longer over security but over the philosophical argument of what kind of state Israel wanted to be. Rabin talked about a smaller Israeli state in which Jews comprised at least 80 percent of the population. Netanyahu, on the other hand, played on Israeli sensitivities when he accused Rabin of behaving as if Israel was a foreign invader rather than a landowner. "What would you say to Arafat and Sheikh Yassin when they start claiming the Galilee or the triangle, or when they start claiming to return to Jaffa, Akka, and the Sheikh Mou'nis village, on top of which the Tel Aviv University was built?" Netanyahu thundered in the Knesset.

For the first time since the creation of the state, Israeli society was facing its moment of truth. The settlers, who had grown in number and strength, were determined to fight the government in every possible way. Sit-ins were organized on highways to disrupt traffic. Outside his house Rabin was confronted daily by demonstrators calling him a traitor. Eitan Haber and Shimon Shevetz, two of Rabin's most trusted confidants, told me separately that they were worried about Rabin's short-term position.

In October, the second MENA conference was held in Amman, following the Casablanca conference in 1994. I went to Amman to attend it, as did a large Israeli delegation headed by Shimon Peres. While I was there, Marwan Kassim, chief of the Royal Court, told me that Peres had informed the king about a large peace rally being organized in Tel Aviv on the evening of Saturday, November 4, and asked that I participate on behalf of Jordan in that rally. The king agreed, and Kassim asked me to deliver a speech on that occasion.

After I returned to Tel Aviv from the conference, I received a letter from Zalman Shoval objecting to my participation in what he called a "partisan" event. We, of course, regarded it as a pro-peace rally rather than a rally for the Labor Party, and the king was determined that we would participate.

I arrived at the Kings of Israel Square and was shown to my seat on the platform erected for the rally, next to Rabin. I was seated to his right, and on his left were Peres and Muhammad Bassiouny, the Egyptian ambassador. Before the rally began, I saw Leah Rabin pacing back and forth, obviously concerned. I myself had thought that security was lax; the platform was accessible to most anyone. I went and exchanged pleasantries with her and told her that she should feel good about that night, with more than 250,000 people present, a big endorsement of her husband's policies amid the hostile atmosphere of the past few weeks. She was very warm and thanked me for coming, but I could tell she was terribly worried.

Indeed, the night was mesmerizing. A sea of people stood before the platform, chanting songs for peace, holding candles in their hand. Rabin was visibly happy, feeling that his policies were vindicated. The Egyptian ambassador, the head of the Moroccan liaison office, and I all spoke in support of the peace process and to show Israelis the benefits of peace with the Arab world. I had written the speech myself, and delivering it in front of all those people uplifted my spirits and gave a boost to my hopes that peace was indeed possible between the Arab and Israeli peoples. Rabin delivered an electrifying speech and then went on stage to sing a popular Israeli song from the 1960s, "The Song of Peace." His voice, low at first, slowly rose until he was soon not only singing the words but apparently doing so with joy. He was uncharacteristically relaxed, smiling broadly. Bassiouny and I were asked to join Rabin and Peres on the platform, and we did. Even though we didn't know the words to the song, it was truly a thrilling, uplifting experience. In a rare moment, Rabin and Peres, singing together, appeared as if they had finally made peace with each other.

As the rally was wrapping up, I suggested to Bassiouny that we leave a little early in order to beat the traffic. He agreed. We took the same flight of stairs down that Rabin would take a minute or two later. I was less than a minute away from home when a friend from Jordan, Makram Alami, and a diplomat at the embassy, Ramez Qussous, separately called. "They shot Rabin," Makram said. "Impossible," I said. "I was just there." Having confirmed the news from Israeli television, although neither the identity of the attacker nor Rabin's condition was known by then, I immediately phoned Prime Minister Bin Shaker in Amman. He was at a state dinner hosted by King Hussein for a visiting foreign dignitary. "I must speak to the prime minister," I urged the Royal Court operator. A few minutes later, Bin Shaker was on the phone. "They shot Rabin," I said. His first reaction was, "Who did it? An Arab or a Jew?" "I don't know yet," I said. Half an hour later, I called him again, telling him that Israeli television had just confirmed Rabin's death. Minutes later, the Royal Court operator phoned to tell me that Crown Prince Hassan wanted to speak to me. A voice came on the phone, and halfway into the conversation, I realized it was not the crown prince but King Hussein. "Do you plan to come to the funeral, Your Majesty?" I asked. "Absolutely," he said, without hesitation. The monarch instructed me to inform the Israelis and start the preparations.

The next two days were hectic. An advanced party from Royal Protocol arrived on Sunday with an armored car for the king. We spent Sunday and until 4:00 a.m. Monday arranging the king's attendance with the Israeli foreign ministry. King Hussein was the most senior head of state in terms of protocol, and thus his motorcade would be the last to arrive at the funeral, after President Weizman, and the first to leave.

The king landed at Ben-Gurion Airport on Monday, November 6, at 9:30 a.m. He was accompanied by a high-level delegation that included

Prime Minister Zaid Bin Shaker, Chief of the Royal Court Kassim, Foreign Minister Kabariti, and Senator Zeid Rifai. From there, we went straight to President Weizman's residence in Jerusalem. Of the foreign dignitaries present, President Bill Clinton, King Hussein, President Hosni Mubarak, Prime Minister Felipe Gonzalez of Spain, and Prime Minister Victor Chernomyrdin of Russia were to deliver speeches. King Hussein, as was always his habit when he felt strongly about an issue, spoke without a prepared speech. "I am determined to fulfill the legacy for which my friend fell, as did my grandfather in this very city," he told mourners at the top of Mount Herzl, where Rabin was buried.[19] It was the king's first visit to the Holy City since it had fallen to Israel in the 1967 War.

Later, the king held discussions with President Clinton and the new Israeli prime minister, Shimon Peres, at the King David Hotel. At 9:30 p.m., he and the Jordanian delegation left from Ben-Gurion Airport again. A new era had begun.

King Hussein would visit Israel only one other time during my tenure. In January 1996, two months after Rabin was assassinated, the king came to attend a ceremony at Ichilov Hospital to dedicate the trauma center in Rabin's name. He arrived in a military helicopter at a small airport in Tel Aviv, and I was there to receive him. The reception he received from Israelis was overwhelming, with people lined up along Ibn Gibrol Street, which had been closed to traffic.

Rabin's death was a severe blow to the cause of peace. A military man known for his toughness and concern for security, with a long and distinguished public service record, Rabin was trusted by Israelis to make the compromises necessary for a settlement with the Palestinians. It is hard to think of any other politician in Israel, then or since, who fit those qualities to lead his people. Rabin understood that achieving consensus was difficult among Israelis on the issue of peace, but he also refused to let the status quo dictate his policies, and he was not afraid to lead.

Many Arabs, certainly many Palestinians, could not forgive Rabin for his tough, bone-breaking anti-Palestinian policy during the first Intifada, when he served as minister of defense. But Rabin was an Israeli who took a leap of faith. He saw early on that Israel could not indefinitely claim it was democratic or Jewish while it continued its occupation of Palestinians. This early revelation would be followed years later by Israelis on the right, including Ariel Sharon and Ehud Olmert.

In many ways, the peace process has not recovered from his assassination. While peace cannot ultimately depend on visionaries such as King Hussein and Rabin, it is also true that such powerful leaders can serve as catalysts in bringing about a permanent reconciliation. Without them, the process of achieving peace will take much longer—and it has.

LEAVING TEL AVIV

Three weeks later, I went to Amman on a weekend to attend to some business concerning the Al-Aqsa Mosque guards in Jersualem. I was not to return. Over the weekend the government had changed, and the new prime minister, Abdel Karim Kabariti, asked me to become the minister of information. Even though my assignment in Israel was difficult, I felt that I could use more time there, since I was learning and observing so much. But I welcomed the opportunity to work with Kabariti, a lifelong friend and a like-minded liberal.

I am often asked whether I ever regretted going to Israel. I do not. Of all the complex assignments that would later be given to me, this was the most challenging. But I learned a great deal from my time as ambassador. When I reflect on my extreme reluctance to accept the position and the challenges I had to overcome, I am often reminded of the old adage, "What does not kill you makes you stronger." I consider myself one of a handful of people in the Arab world who had the chance to become familiar with the Israeli psyche and experience Israeli culture firsthand. The insights and wealth of knowledge I acquired about the country and its politics are immeasurable. Short as my ten months in Israel were, they were full of activity. I felt like a sponge, eager to learn as much as I could, traveling the length and width of the country, visiting almost every town, large or small, and witnessing what I before had only read about in books.

I got to know almost every Israeli major politician, whether from Labor, Likud, Meretz, Shas, or the Arab Israelis. Of course, there were exceptions. I could not meet Ehud Olmert, because he was then mayor of Jerusalem, and Jordan did not—and still does not—recognize his jurisdiction over all of Jerusalem. Nor did I encounter Ariel Sharon (I would meet him with King Hussein at the Wye River negotiations in Maryland, in October 1998). In the 1980s, Sharon was one of the principal authors of the "alternative homeland" policy, together with the "Jordan is Palestine" catchphrase that represented that policy. As such, he was hated by Jordanians. He later altered his position.

I was, and remain, proud of the relationship I developed with the Palestinian Arabs in Israel. To this day, I discuss their cause whenever possible, particularly with other Arab politicians. The Arab world has done them a terrible injustice, and it is about time that Arab states correct that wrong.

Whatever diplomatic skills I may have today were learned mostly in Israel, where I had to face tough situations daily, be firm but diplomatic, say no with a smile, and live under adverse conditions without letting them affect me. Whenever later attacks on me were mean or personal in the Jordanian press, I recalled my time in Israel. Being ambassador to Israel taught me how to brush such attacks aside, how not to get distracted by them but to keep focused on the issues, and how to push my way forward. After Israel, what seemed like difficult situations to friends or colleagues were for me a piece of cake.

The experience opened up my eyes to other issues as well. The Arab world tends to look at Israel in black and white—mostly in black, because of the Israeli occupation. There is no doubt in my mind that the occupation is wrong. No occupation is benign by definition, and the Israeli occupation of the Palestinian people is no exception. As all occupations are, the Israeli occupation of the Palestinian people and their land is both illegal and immoral. It should not and will not last. But not everything about Israeli society should be renounced. As an Arab, I had always viewed Israel from the outside, through the lens of the occupation. From the inside, I observed some admirable characteristics of Israeli society. One thing that strongly impressed me in Israel is Israelis' work ethic and determination to build a solid state and economy. Arabs tend to dismiss Israel's economic success by attributing it to the international aid it receives. No amount of aid, however, can account for the fact that Israel today, a country comparable in size of population to Jordan, has an economy ten times larger than Jordan's. There is a reason one does not see in Israel the multitude of luxury cars and hotels found in the Arab world. Israelis tend to spend their money on improving productivity. Although Israel is no doubt extremely undemocratic in its occupation of the Palestinians and in its treatment of Arabs inside Israel, there is also no doubt that there is real democracy within the Jewish part of Israeli society. That has meant more accountability, transparency, and creativity, which have all contributed to Israel's survival and well-being. If the Arabs are to catch up to Israel, they must start paying more attention to the values that shape not just Israeli society but progressive societies everywhere. Otherwise, when the occupation one day ends, Arabs will find themselves in stagnating countries, where censorship kills creativity and economic backwardness deprives them of a quality of life far less than they deserve and could, in fact, achieve if they muster the political will to do so.

As I write, comprehensive peace between Israel and Arab states remains elusive. But the peace treaty with Jordan opened both a diplomatic channel through which many problems related to the Palestinian track have been resolved and a rare insight into Israeli politics and way of thinking. Because of the Jordan-Israel peace treaty, Jordan has been instrumental in facilitating many Palestinian-Israeli agreements, including the Hebron agreement of January 1997 and the Wye River Accords in 1998. Jordan's increased international stature and exposure regarding the peace process after the treaty also facilitated several important initiatives, including the Arab Peace Initiative and the Middle East Road Map, both in 2002. Jordan used its relationship with Israel several times to help the Palestinians in their own relationship with Israel and with the United States.

Jordan's moderation has also affected Israeli public opinion positively on numerous occasions and has shown Israelis that comprehensive peace is possible—but contingent on the restoration of Arabs' internationally recognized legal rights. King Hussein never feared addressing Israeli public opinion directly; neither has King Abdullah II. Both have frequently spoken to Israelis through the Israeli media to explain the Jordanian and Arab positions, and my experience tells me that these appearances have had a tremendous positive influence on Israelis.

At the same time, the peace treaty with Israel has not prevented Jordan from taking a firm stand against Israeli actions or policies it views as detrimental to the interests of the peace process. One clear example of this has been the Jordanian position on the Israeli separation wall. Jordan believes that the barrier directly affects the prospect for a two-state solution and in 2004 challenged its legality before the International Court of Justice (discussed in Chapter 8).

Many years have passed since I went to Israel as Jordan's first ambassador in 1995. And the story of my time there is but one personal narrative that constitutes part of a broader national narrative. It is a story very much about leaps of faith and wise choices; both those taken and those not taken. Many taboos have since been broken, but so much remains to be done before Arabs and Israelis reach true and lasting peace.

Peace is not a prize that one state can win at the expense of another but a condition of being that must be enjoyed by all. Anything else is a recipe for ruin—for both Arabs and Israelis. Both must choose wisely, and both must abandon their idea that their national narratives are mutually exclusive. The thousands of years of history provide the Middle East with a rich heritage, but this alone cannot define its future. Indeed, this legacy stands in the way of such a future. We must choose wisely, and we must let go.

CHAPTER THREE

The Last Six Months of King Hussein's Life

The last time I spoke to King Hussein was on Friday, January 29, 1999, in Rochester, Minnesota. He had been flown there a couple of days earlier from Jordan after cancer had mercilessly reattacked his body. I entered his hospital room, where he was lying down. The tubes in his mouth prevented him from speaking at length. His doctors were not optimistic about his chances for survival. The sight of him in such a weakened condition and the thought that he might die saddened and unsettled me. King Hussein—after forty-six years on the throne—was the only king many Jordanians, including me, had ever known. I had had the privilege of working with him closely for the past seven years, had grown close to him, and now found the fact of his impending death hard to accept. Instead of my consoling him, he comforted me, a testament to the strength of his character. "I am at peace with myself," he told me. "My conscience is clear. I have done what is best for Jordan." It was almost the only thing he said. I stayed for two or three minutes and left him to rest.

KING HUSSEIN RARELY SPOKE DIRECTLY about major issues, except to a close circle of advisers. It was his habit to use language laden with symbolism, and Jordanians had grown accustomed to interpreting his meaning. I have little doubt that when he spoke to me at the hospital King Hussein was alluding to his dramatic decision days earlier to change the line of succession, appointing his eldest son, Prince Abdullah, heir apparent to the Hashemite throne. Abdullah replaced Prince Hassan, the king's brother, who had been crown prince for nearly thirty-four years.

The change in the order of succession was one of two of King Hussein's most prominent acts during his illness—the second being his facilitation of the Wye River Accord negotiations between Israelis and

Palestinians, which led to agreement on further Israeli withdrawals from occupied Palestinian territory. These two acts have never been given the scrutiny they deserve. The first has been trivialized as palace intrigue, the second dismissed as little more than a function of King Hussein's desire to shore up his legacy. In fact, they illustrate how strongly King Hussein aspired to cement a new regional order founded on a peace driven forward by the Arab Center and a new domestic order built on a comprehensive and inclusive reform process.

He made the succession announcement on January 25, only few days after returning from the United States, where he had been undergoing chemotherapy for six months at the Mayo Clinic. Several hours later, a Jordan Television anchor read aloud a letter from King Hussein to Prince Hassan. Jordanians were astonished at its harsh tone and the anger and frustration that seemed implicit in it. The letter referred to many instances of conflict between the brothers, including on the issue of succession itself, and openly discussed "parasites" that had poisoned the atmosphere in Jordan.

The apparent abruptness of the change and uncordial tone of his letter to his brother, who had served by his side for decades, seemed at first to confirm rumors about King Hussein's dynastic ambitions and palace intrigues during his six-month absence from Jordan while he underwent therapy. There has been much speculation in Jordan and abroad as to the king's motives, ever since the constitution—which defines succession according to primogeniture—was amended in 1965 to allow the king to designate one of his brothers as crown prince.

The amendment was made during the most turbulent era of contemporary Middle Eastern history, during which King Hussein survived numerous attempts on his life as well as a failed coup d'état. Prince Abdullah was then but a toddler, far too young to assume the challenges of monarchy. It is believed that King Hussein then sought the change in order to ensure that Jordan would survive come what may but had always planned to pass the crown to his son. Talk of the order of the succession was revived after the king's first bout with cancer in 1992 and intensified when he fell ill again in 1998.

When the change finally did come, many reports noted its apparent haste. Some suggested that on his deathbed the king had submitted to the natural inclination of any monarch to seek to be succeeded by his son; others suggested that the monarch acted in a fit of pique over intrigues involving Prince Hassan and his wife, Princess Sarvath, during the king's absence from Jordan. Still others have suggested that the two men's different characters had motivated the monarch.

King Hussein very likely did wish to pass the crown to his son, and events that transpired during his stay in the United States certainly may have been a contributing factor; in fact, they may have hastened his decision. It is also true that King Hussein and Prince Hassan were very different in upbringing, temperament, and worldview: the king was a military man, a populist, and a pragmatic leader; Hassan was an Oxford graduate, an elitist more comfortable with ideas than he was with people.

The king, however, was neither petty nor impulsive. It was his habit to act decisively but not rashly. My experience with King Hussein suggests that his decisions were thoroughly considered and strategic. Viewed through this lens, his motives can be brought into sharper focus. In fact, over the years, the character differences had led to conflicting opinions on questions of vital interest to the future of Jordan, beginning with the question of the succession but extending to other affairs of state, including the vital issue of Jordan's relationship with the Palestinians.

The question of the succession had, in fact, troubled the king for some time, as he indicated himself in his letter to Prince Hassan. In the letter, he said his first bout with cancer had focused his mind on determining Prince Hassan's successor. King Hussein had expressed his preference for a Hashemite family council to determine who would be most suitable to lead Jordan, but the two men could not agree on the necessity or efficacy of such a mechanism.

Despite the brothers' differences, the king did not change the succession then. The issue was secondary to regional threats to the kingdom from revolutionary regimes and schemes by some Israeli factions to make Jordan the alternative homeland for the Palestinians. The peace treaty signed with Israel in 1994 changed that calculus. Only then did the king feel that the existential threat to Jordan and the "alternative homeland" scenario to solve the Palestinian-Israeli conflict at Jordan's expense had subsided. That, in turn, had illuminated new challenges in the domestic arena. Reform, modernization, and consolidating a livable

state in a turbulent region became more crucial for survival and prosperity. One clear challenge was the economy. Jordan had begun an economic reform program under the aegis of the International Monetary
Fund in 1989. But by 1999, it had not gotten far. King Hussein appreciated the need for reform but did not take a robust interest in it; the deterioration in the peace process throughout the 1990s constituted a major
distraction. And having been raised in the school of realpolitik, the
monarch had little facility for the demands that an increasingly global-
ized economy was placing on the country. Consequently, successive governments haltingly carried out piecemeal reforms.

Putting Jordan's economic house in order was essential to minimiz-
ing Jordan's reliance on foreign aid and ensuring economic self-
sufficiency in a post-peace era. It was also crucial to coping with another
key challenge. By the time King Hussein died in 1999, half the country's
population was under age thirty—and unemployment was in the double
digits. The economy was growing nowhere near fast enough to employ
the country's youth. Jobs, jobs, and more jobs were needed.

At the same time, both King Hussein and Prince Hassan were easily
twenty and thirty years older than the majority of Jordan's population.
This generation gap was defined by the politics of the region: King Hussein and Prince Hassan were the products of regional conflict and rivalry to which development had been held hostage for half a decade. Although Jordan's youth had not exactly come of age in peacetime, most
had no memory of the terrible conflicts that marked their parents' generation. They had grown up in relative stability, were more exposed to
foreign cultures than their parents' generation thanks to satellite television and the Internet, and had entirely different expectations that deserved to be fulfilled. For many, the talk of armed struggle coming from
the rejectionist camp then seemed as much of an anachronism as censorship in the age of the Internet. They worried how they would pay for
higher education and whether they would be duly rewarded with jobs
that respected their intellect and talents and would advance their living
standards.

King Hussein must also have been alarmed by some new youth
trends. Though not on the scale seen in neighboring countries, some
younger people had moved toward more radicalized positions. Some,
particularly those who went to fight the Soviets in Afghanistan in the

1980s, came back with a new worldview regarding regional conflicts and relations with the West. This highlighted the need for another reform: cultural reform. King Hussein often challenged the call of going back to Islam with his famous call to "move forward" to Islam. For him, the big challenge amid fundamentalism at home and abroad would be how to reconcile modernity with heritage and good governance with security.

Another crucial issue was one that each of the three key players to the peace process faced: national belonging. As the process got under way in the early 1990s, Jordanians, Palestinians, and Israelis all had to confront a question that conflict had allowed them to avoid for far too long: Who belongs to the state? In Israel, Israelis asked: Who is a Jew? And who is an Israeli? Can a non-Jew ever be trusted to be a citizen of the state? In the West Bank and Gaza, Palestinians considered: Who had the right to rule? Those who had suffered under and resisted occupation? Or those who had returned from "outside" after the signing of the Oslo Accords in 1993? And in Jordan, the same question reared its head: Who is a Jordanian? Only those born on the East Bank? Or could Palestinian refugees and displaced people from Gaza and the West Bank who had Jordanian citizenship rightfully call themselves Jordanian? Was the distribution of power and resources among Jordanians equitable and justifiable? King Hussein had clearly stated on the eve of Jordan's disengagement with the West Bank that that act would be undertaken without prejudice to Jordan's citizens of Palestinian origin, but not everyone shared his sentiments about inclusiveness.

One cannot underestimate the importance of Jordan's signing a peace treaty with Israel, looking to the country's next phase of development, and determining who was best suited to lead it in the king's decision to change the succession. The removal of an existential threat meant a reordering of priorities and accordingly a reordering of leadership. Without taking anything away from Prince Hassan's abilities, Prince Abdullah, then age thirty-seven belonged to the next generation and was thus closer to the majority population. He was in a perfect position to turn his attention from the issue of Jordan's survival to building on the solid foundation King Hussein had laid and making sure that the state would thrive.

None of these challenges could be surmounted without driving the peace process toward a two-state solution and definitively ending whatever remained of the mistrust and hostility that had historically tainted relations between Jordan and the Palestinian leadership. And King Hussein's last public act of diplomacy was spent doing just that.

How this story played itself out is an affair I was one of few people to witness in my capacity as Jordan's ambassador to the United States when it happened. But as far as I can tell, the story itself is secondary to what the implications were for the king's decisions about Jordan's and the region's future.

The king was instrumental during his stay in the United States in 1998 in facilitating the Wye River Agreement between the Palestinians and the Israelis. To him, this was another step toward regional stability and consolidating the Arab Center. Despite his and Arafat's mutual suspicion, King Hussein felt that he was in a unique position to help the Palestinians achieve a settlement, and he spared no opportunity to do so. It was part of his vision to bring peace to the region and move beyond the policies of fear toward the policies of hope.

Thus, 1998 was a busy year from my perspective in Washington. I was then the Jordanian ambassador to the United States, having been asked to serve there by King Hussein in 1997 after resignation in March of the Kabariti government. The U.S. administration was actively working with the Palestinians and Israelis to achieve progress in negotiations. The United States was trying to convince Prime Minister Netanyahu to agree to an Israeli withdrawal from a further 13 percent of area C in the West Bank and transform them into areas B and A.[1] Netanyahu would commit to only 10 percent. The United States was keeping Jordan informed on the negotiations through U.S. Middle East peace envoy Dennis Ross. Jordan also tried to mediate between the Palestinians and Israelis much as it had ahead of the last Palestinian-Israeli agreement, the Hebron Agreement of 1997.

On the bilateral front, we were lobbying the U.S. administration and Congress to try to protect Jordan's levels of American assistance ($225 million in economic aid and $75 million in military aid). The economy had slowed, partly because of the king's deteriorating health, and we were in need of outside assistance. We also initiated talks with the administration on a debt relief package for Jordan.

In June, King Hussein visited Washington, meeting with President Clinton and Secretary of State Madeleine Albright. Clinton had come up with a specific proposal for the Palestinians and Israelis in March and was having a tough time selling it to Netanyahu. Clinton indicated to the king his frustration with Netanyahu's inflexibility, a frustration the king shared. In a later meeting, Dennis Ross pushed the king to outline Jordan's red lines in any final status negotiations between the Palestinians and the Israelis. "We need to know your parameters," Ross said. "We do not want to go along roads you don't want us to take."[2] This was not the first time the Americans had told us that, and it would not be the last. But the king felt it was premature to talk about this issue and continued to resist an open discussion with the Americans over it, preferring to wait until such negotiations actually started. He did not want to be seen as colluding with the Americans over the future of the West Bank or to be blamed for any bad deal reached with the Palestinians. Instead, he preferred that the Palestinians assume full responsibility for their destiny while he worked to preserve Jordanian interests.

In mid-July, my wife and children traveled to Jordan for their summer vacation. I had made plans to join them by the beginning of August, when Congress would be in recess. But I received an unexpected phone call from Ayman Majali, chief of royal protocol, telling me that King Hussein was coming to the Mayo Clinic in Rochester, Minnesota, for a checkup. This sounded strange to me. The king had been in the United States only a month earlier and had a checkup then. The king had been having bouts of unexplained fever since the previous November or December, but two examinations, one in the United States and one in London, showed no indication of cancer. I canceled plans to go to Jordan and hoped for the best.

The monarch left Amman for Rochester on July 14 and did not stop in Washington along the way. A few days later, I learned that doctors suspected he had cancer but that results were inconclusive.

On July 21, King Hussein sent a public letter to Crown Prince Hassan informing him that he might have lymphoma, pending further tests. The letter was subsequently published in local papers, provoking concern among Jordanians who were well aware that the king had had an operation to remove part of his urethra after suspicious cells that could have led to cancer were detected in 1992. A week later, on July 28, the king announced in a televised interview from Rochester that he indeed had a treatable form of cancer called large B cell lymphoma and that he had undergone the first of six chemotherapy treatments. King

Hussein rarely addressed the nation on television without a good reason, and when he appeared this time, his tone was optimistic though his
words were serious and direct. "There is life, and there is an end to life,"
the king said, adding that he hoped that when his life reached its end,
people would say that "this man tried and his family tried" to bring
about what was best for Jordan. He assured Jordanians that his disease
was curable, but his words nevertheless had a dramatic effect. For many
Jordanians, the king had become a father figure, and people were naturally very concerned about this development. This would also be the
king's first extended stay away from his country.

On August 6, the king arrived in Washington from Rochester, and I
received him at the airport. He had piloted his own plane, just as he always
did, and seemed in high spirits. The effects of chemotherapy were not yet
visible. That night, he and Queen Noor dined on the White House balcony
with President and First Lady Clinton. His situation at that stage did not
look that bad.

During this visit to Washington stories about goings-on in Amman
began to emerge from the king's entourage. I was told that the crown
prince's wife, Princess Sarvath, had asked for changes in the decor of the
Throne Room, where official functions were hosted at the Royal Court.
There were mumblings that the crown prince, acting as regent in the
king's absence, had begun to behave like a head of state, with intense
overexposure on Jordanian television. A number of articles also appeared around this time in the Western press, including *Newsweek,* that
were rather critical of Queen Noor and flattering to Princess Sarvath.[3]
Those close to King Hussein suspected that these articles were no coincidence but had been planned by a source feeding reporters with material. I wondered what he thought about it himself.

The king finished his second chemotherapy course on August 22
and returned to Washington, where the new prime minister, Fayez
Tarawneh, and the new chief of the Royal Court, Jawad Anani, met him.
We all convened at King Hussein's house in the suburbs on August 25. I
noted that the king's mind was not on the new government, the first during his reign that was formed in his absence.

Once the king had announced his health situation, many visitors
came from Jordan and other Arab countries to wish him well. He received the emir of Qatar in Rochester in August, and in September he

received Crown Prince Abdullah of Saudi Arabia and Sheikh Sabah Al-Ahmad Al-Sabah, foreign minister of Kuwait, at his house in Washington. Kuwait and Saudi Arabia had been outraged by Jordan's neutrality during the first Gulf crisis of 1990–1991, so much so that by 1998, the rupture between Jordan and the two Gulf states had not been mended. The two visits were thus highly significant as expressions of goodwill. King Hussein was visibly touched.

He would never show his visitors that he was weak, however. I experienced just how strong his will was firsthand, when on September 27 Queen Noor was participating in a Washington event to fight cancer, an event that included speeches by her and Vice President Al Gore. The king, although physically weak after his third round of chemotherapy, had insisted on attending. The day was hot, around 95 degrees Fahrenheit, and a tent had been erected so that the king could rest before the event. But he was too weak to appear, almost fainting because of his condition and the heat. His doctors decided that he should go home. As he was attempting to walk to his car, I ventured near him to assist him. He never uttered a word, but the look on his face clearly told me: "Don't you even dare look at me in this condition, let alone help me walk." That was all I needed to retreat. He was such a proud man, and many times after that, whenever a visitor would appear, I would see him summon all his scant energy to appear strong and jovial despite his obvious pain.

THE INCIDENT WITH THE ARMED FORCES

September, though, was an eventful month because of another incident. During that month, the king received the chief of staff of the armed forces Lieutenant General Abdel Hafiz Ka'abneh in Rochester. Ka'abneh brought upsetting news. According to members of the king's entourage, the general told the king that Crown Prince Hassan had asked him to retire some officers and promote others in the armed forces. Military affairs were strictly the king's domain. No one, including the crown prince, had ever been permitted to interfere in this realm. According to these sources, Ka'abneh told the crown prince that he needed the king's authorization before making such changes and at one point said that he would resign and let his second in command execute the orders rather than carry them out without the commander in chief's explicit order.

This account was later confirmed to the king by several officials who came to visit, including the director of the intelligence department Lieutenant General Samih Battikhi, according to these same sources. The king was furious. He sent the crown prince a letter instructing him not to make any changes to the armed forces leadership while he was away.

The king was also obviously unhappy about what he saw as excessive coverage of the crown prince on Jordanian television during this time. As minister of information two years earlier, I was well aware of the king's discomfort with extensive coverage of royal family members on Jordanian television. He had urged me many times before to limit such coverage, including of himself. The king had established a satellite link to watch Jordanian television from Rochester. He grew increasingly uncomfortable with the extensive coverage of the crown prince and subsequently instructed his chief of the Royal Court to ask the prince to limit his television appearances.

I remain convinced that the encounter with the armed forces chief of staff cemented the decision in the king's mind. I have no way of knowing this for a fact, nor do I know what process went on in the king's mind, a process that had probably spun in his head for years. But Prince Hassan had been crown prince for almost thirty-four years, and any move to change the succession was naturally not easy. The army incident and the events and developments that followed it convinced me, however, that it was the prime reason for what started the final countdown.

THE WYE PLANTATION TALKS

The Oslo Accords of 1993 had outlined a gradual peace process that would have the PLO and Israel reach a final settlement by May 1999. Indeed, Oslo B, signed in September 1995, gave the Palestinians full or partial control over 42 percent of the West Bank and led to a further redeployment of the Israeli army from the West Bank. A third redeployment was to take place while the two sides started final status negotiations. But the momentum created by the Oslo process slowed dramatically with the assassination of Rabin and the election of a hard-line government under Binyamin Netanyahu in June 1996. Netanyahu was opposed to Oslo and to a third redeployment from the West Bank. The peace process had been in virtual paralysis since January 1997, when with King Hussein's help the two parties signed the Hebron Agreement.

This was the situation when U.S. efforts to advance the peace process brought Arafat and Netanyahu to Washington in October 1998, and on October 15, President Clinton announced the immediate convening of a four-day summit at Wye River Plantation in Maryland to reach agreement on further Israeli withdrawal from the West Bank.

The king was in Rochester. He had finished his fourth chemotherapy round on October 12 and was resting in Minnesota when an article appeared in an Israeli newspaper claiming that unnamed American officials had told Israeli delegates to the Wye talks that the king's illness was advanced. Secretary of State Albright phoned Crown Prince Hassan and informed him that these reports about American leaks were inaccurate. A spokesperson from the Mayo Clinic also denied these reports about the king's health.

The Wye talks were not going well. The four-day period was extended, with no real hope of reaching an agreement. King Hussein flew into Washington on October 18 after President Clinton and Secretary of State Albright phoned him for help. On October 20, Clinton sent a helicopter to a small helipad near the king's residence in the Washington suburbs. I accompanied the king and Queen Noor from there to Wye Plantation, where the king was given a cottage where he could conduct talks and rest.

King Hussein had been weakened by the four chemotherapy courses, but he was determined to help the Palestinians and the Israelis reach an agreement. The future of the peace process clearly weighed heavily on his mind. That day, he met with Secretary of State Albright, President Clinton, Arafat and the Palestinian delegation, Netanyahu and the Israeli delegation, then Arafat again. Some of the sticking points were the number and type of Palestinian prisoners to be released from Israeli prisons, a meeting of the Palestinian National Council (PNC) to amend the Palestinian Charter that called for Israel's destruction and was a main Israeli demand, and whether a third-phase redeployment by Israel should be mentioned in the agreement (the Palestinians insisted that Israel commit to a third withdrawal phase, as stipulated by Oslo B, while the Israelis demurred).

A despairing President Clinton told the king that he had felt the day before that an agreement was impossible. "Both sides trust you, admire you," the president said. "I would appreciate anything you can do to help them put themselves in each others' shoes."[4]

Indeed, in the context of the peace process, empathy was one of the monarch's most prominent qualities, and of all the players in the Middle East peace process, perhaps no one understood better than King Hussein the importance of seeing things the way others saw them and addressing the fears and anxieties—be they political or personal—that emanated from their perceptions, no matter how distasteful, unfounded, or seemingly irrelevant they might be. He understood that even the smallest gesture could go a long way toward building trust. He acted on this principle often, such as when he went to console the families of the schoolgirls who were killed by a Jordanian soldier on the border or his attendance at Rabin's funeral.

At Wye, King Hussein told Clinton that an agreement to release a substantial number of Palestinian prisoners would help drive a deal forward, and Clinton asked him to find a way to impress on Netanyahu how important that would be, as well as to move the Palestinians toward accepting to convene a PNC meeting to amend the charter.

The king then met with Arafat, who was accompanied by Mahmoud Abbas, or Abu Mazen, who would become the president of the Palestinian Authority after Arafat's death, Ahmad Qurei, or Abu Alaa, Nabil Shaath, and Nabil Abu Rudainah. Although the relationship between Jordan and the PLO leadership had been contentious, the Palestinians' eyes welled up with tears when they saw King Hussein. They had come to respect him.

Arafat was pleased that Sharon, minister of foreign affairs, was part of the Israeli delegation. "He is a decision-maker, more so than Netanyahu," Arafat said. He then described the state of negotiations. Arafat felt that there had been progress on the suggested 13 percent redeployment from the West Bank and on language regarding a third redeployment. He also thought agreement on security arrangements was proceeding well. Arafat felt that the PNC meeting still presented a problem and indicated that if a meeting was held then, the PNC would reject the Oslo agreement outright. Arafat instead suggested a meeting of the more moderate Palestinian Central Council (PCC, 170 people). He also pleaded with the king for help with the prisoner issue. The king thought Arafat's suggestion regarding a meeting of the Central Council was reasonable, adding that the Israelis must agree to a meeting of the PNC "at the appropriate time." He also told Arafat that he was ready to help the Palestinians with any issue following the signing of the agreement, including security arrangements.

The king then met with Prime Minister Netanyahu. He was accompanied by Ariel Sharon, Natan Sharansky, and Defense Minister Yitzhak Mordechai. It was the first time I met Sharon. The king told Netanyahu he thought the Palestinians were acting reasonably and asked him to put himself in their shoes. He explained that a meeting of the PNC at this point would destroy Arafat and his people. "Leave it to take place at the right time," the king urged. He reiterated the Palestinian suggestion for the Central Council to meet now and urged flexibility on the prisoner issue.

Netanyahu thought that the PCC could meet then, followed at a later point by a meeting of the PNC after the second redeployment took place. He was not ready to be flexible on the prisoners, though.

The king met again with Arafat that day to brief him on the outcome of his discussions with the Israelis. King Hussein felt that progress had been made. Arafat expressed his appreciation and urged him to keep up his involvement on the thorny issues.

Once again, the king was too proud to show the leaders he met at Wye that he was tired. After each meeting, he would take an hour's rest, wrapping himself with a blanket and sitting in the warm autumn sun with Queen Noor, enjoying the beautiful grounds of the plantation. He would thus gather his energies and prepare himself for the next meeting. He would also give me instructions to go talk to the different delegations and brief him on the latest developments. Each night, we would head back to Washington by helicopter, where he would rest at his house.

Despite all the efforts to bridge the gap, by Thursday, October 22, the negotiations had reached a crisis. The Israeli delegation had packed their bags the night before and pretended they were leaving. I flew back with the king that noon from his home in Washington to see what could be done. Toni Verstandig, deputy assistant secretary of state, briefed me on what was going on. Secretary of State Albright was appalled, she said, at the Israelis' behavior. The issues of the third deployment, the PNC meeting, and the prisoners, among some others, were not solved yet. The security work plan had been agreed to and initialed, she told me. "We just don't know how to get through to this man, Netanyahu," she said, adding that the president and the secretary would "look to the king for help."

I then met with Nabil Sha'ath and the Palestinian representative in Washington, Hassan Abdel Rahman. The Israelis had refused to release more than 150 prisoners, out of 3,500, Shaath told me, and would not even commit to including this number in the text of the agreement. The Palestinians wanted at least 900 released. The issue of the PLC meeting was still being worked on in the negotiations. Abdel Rahman told me that Clinton had suggested that the Palestinians sign whatever had been agreed to, and then return in a month to resume negotiations. The other option was to announce failure to reach an agreement on Friday. Abdel Rahman added that the Palestinians were not interested in a "mini-package," and were ready to stay until agreement was reached.

In the afternoon, I briefed the king on these developments. By 10:00 p.m., the talks were on the verge of collapsing. President Clinton again appealed to King Hussein for help. The king, Queen Noor, and I went to the dining room, where the delegations were having dinner. When the Madrid peace process began, the sight of Palestinians and Israelis dining together, chatting, exchanging jokes, and even inquiring about each other's children, was something extremely odd to us Jordanians. In real-ity, while we in Jordan had been entirely distant from the Israelis, nearly thirty years of occupation had bred as much familiarity as contempt be-tween Palestinians and Israelis. In many respects, they knew each other well. Such scenes became de rigueur throughout the 1990s. This time, however, the tension between them was palpable; each delegation was at a different table. All in all, there were about thirty of us.

King Hussein rose and gave an impromptu pep talk. Addressing President Clinton, he said, "I have worked with many presidents, but never as closely as with you. No one has given more time, energy, dedi-cation to the peace process than you have." Then he addressed the Pales-tinians and the Israelis.

"We expect success, and hopefully tonight," he said. "You cannot af-ford to fail. This is an agreement not just for you, but for your children, and your children's children. Even if I was on my death bed, I would come to try to help."[5] It was a moving moment. Both Netanyahu and Arafat approached him separately, hugged him, and promised to give negotiations a fresh try.

Members of all delegations, American, Palestinian, and Israeli, later told me that the king's speech had been a turning point. The negotiating teams went back to work, and by 4:00 a.m. Friday, October 23, they reached an agreement. The king had returned to his residence in Washington after the speech to await the outcome.

I went to the king's residence that Friday morning only to learn that Netanyahu was threatening to call off the deal if an American national serving a prison term for spying for Israel, Jonathan Pollard, was not freed. The president was furious, and both he and Albright called the king to see if he could again ask for help. The king called Netanyahu from the house and tried to persuade him. Finally, Netanyahu budged, and the stage was set for the White House ceremony that afternoon.

THE SERIES OF MEETINGS THAT DECIDED IT ALL

One sentence during in the king's speech foreshadowed much of what was to come. "Many in our part of the world and different parts of the world have written me off," he said. Many understood that to refer to Prince Hassan. Unknown to most Jordanians, another series of dramatic events were unfolding that day. As soon as the king was done with his final contribution to the peace process, he turned his attention to changing the line of succession.

Many delegations were coming from Jordan to visit the king. That week several individuals and delegations arrived. Among them was Abdel Karim Kabariti, the former prime minister who had fallen out of grace with King Hussein over, among other issues, Crown Prince Hassan's role in affairs of state. During his tenure, Kabariti had been adamant about restricting the crown prince to the ceremonial role described in the constitution. Kabariti had not seen the king since his government had resigned a year and a half earlier. In addition, the chief of staff of the armed forces was there, heading a military delegation to a meeting of the joint U.S.-Jordanian military commission.

The king first summoned the military delegation to my office. In addition to Chief of Staff Ka'abneh, present were Prince Abdullah, the armed forces deputy chief of staff, Tahseen Shurdoum, and other senior military officials. The king asked that I remain in the room and proceeded to lecture the delegation about the importance of maintaining the military's unity and countering interference in its work. King Hussein rarely spoke explicitly, but the implication of his words was generally clear. That day, neither I nor any member of the delegation had any doubt that he was referring to the incident between the crown prince and General Ka'abneh.

The king then saw Kabariti alone after receiving him before us in an extremely warm manner. The ten minutes they spent together seemed like eternity to me. The king's warm and fatherly reception of Kabariti was not accidental. The relationship between the two men had soured over several issues, including Kabariti's combative relationship with Crown Prince Hassan a couple of years earlier. In the end, the king had dismissed Kabariti quite unceremoniously after Kabariti had written a much-publicized letter that had insinuated that his dealings with the crown prince reflected the king's directives.

Kabariti had been stunned by what transpired in my office and related what the king had told him. "I want you to leave that banking business of yours and come back to work with me," Kabariti recalled the king telling him. "What is happening in Jordan is not acceptable. I know Jordanians are worried about their future. I have big plans for Jordan when I come back, and I want you to help me achieve them." What the king was saying was clear. He had decided to change the line of succession.

THE JORDANIAN POSITION ON FINAL STATUS NEGOTIATIONS
Though Jordan had no interest in being at the table in final status negotiations between the Palestinians and the Israelis, such negotiations would bear directly on the kingdom, and thus Jordan was certainly interested in following them closely. One key issue was that of refugees, since 41 percent of all Palestinian refugees around the world live in Jordan and had been granted Jordanian citizenship. Jordan believed it was responsible for negotiations concerning their rights and had been keen to ensure that this was reflected in the Jordan-Israel peace treaty. The treaty stipulates that negotiations on those refugees should take place in tandem with final status negotiations between the Palestinians and Israel on the same issue.[7]

The Palestinians' view, by contrast, was that they were responsible for all the refugees, even those who held Jordanian citizenship. King

Hussein wished to avoid friction with the Palestinians over this issue. When Dennis Ross and Martin Indyk, now assistant secretary of state for Near East affairs, prodded us to define Jordan's interests in final status negotiations, the king would not answer, preferring to wait until negotiations started.

On October 28, I accompanied Chief of the Royal Court Jawad Anani to a meeting with Dennis Ross at his State Department office on final status issues. According to the Wye Agreement, these were to start in December 1998. Anani had worked with the crown prince for a number of years and was considered by the king to be Prince Hassan's man. Midway into our discussion, Ross requested a one-on-one meeting with Anani. Given my heavy involvement in the peace process and my relationship with the king, this request was highly unusual. Anani said nothing, so I left. This was disturbing. Ross was keen to discuss final status issues with us, but the king was reluctant to do so with him, and I could not imagine what Ross could possibly wish to discuss with Anani that could not be said in my presence. It was especially troubling since Ross was aware that I was more of a confidant of the king than Anani. King Hussein shared my annoyance when I informed him of the meeting. Later, Prime Minister Tarawneh suggested to the king that Anani travel to Jerusalem to meet with Netanyahu to discuss final status issues, but the king asked him to send me on the trip along with Anani "since our ambassador has been involved in the peace process since the very beginning."[8]

I traveled to Amman on November 6 with instructions not to be committal on any final status issues prematurely. Shortly after I arrived, we had a meeting at the crown prince's residence to discuss the trip to Jerusalem. Prime Minister Tarawneh, Anani, and other officials were there. During the discussion, sensing that it was moving in a direction that did not reflect the king's position on final status, I diplomatically made a point that did not meet with Prince Hassan's approval. "Let us listen to the proconsul here," he said derisively.[9] The mere use of this expression pointed to his tension with King Hussein, as well as to their difference of position regarding final status issues.

Anani and I traveled to Jerusalem on November 11 and met with President Weizman, Prime Minister Netanyahu, and Foreign Minister Sharon. Netanyahu was extremely angry at the United States for what he perceived as its hostile position toward his government and the pressure that the Clinton administration was exerting on him to ratify the Wye Agreement. He declared in our meeting that the U.S. administration might not be with Israel but the Israeli people certainly were. Sharon, well aware that it had been agreed that the Palestinian Central Council would convene first, followed by the PNC, emphasized that Israel could accept nothing but the convening of the PNC, and not just the Central Council. Sharon then shifted to a discussion on final status issues. He emphasized that Israel would not allow a Palestinian presence in the Jordan Valley and that it would ask for a 10-to-12-mile corridor—more than 750 square miles of the West Bank—along the Jordan River. This reflected Sharon's well-known concern to either prevent the emergence of a viable Palestinian state or control any such entity by surrounding it on all sides with an Israeli presence. It was also in line with Likud's traditional concern that a Palestinian presence in the Jordan Valley would threaten both Jordan and Israel, a concern that Jordan no longer shared.

Anani emphasized that final status negotiations were very important to Jordan because they would directly affect Jordan's interests. Although Jordan did not want to be part of the negotiations, agreement on a consultation mechanism—either bilateral or multilateral—was needed, Anani said. Both Netanyahu and Sharon wanted a bilateral mechanism, with no direct American involvement. Anani also emphasized the importance of the refugee issue for Jordan and informed Netanyahu of his chat with Dennis Ross, but without going into details.

The following day Anani and I met Mahmoud Abbas in Amman to coordinate our positions. Anani told Abbas about his meeting with Dennis Ross, who had expressed an American preference for bilateral discussions on final status issues between Jordan and the Palestinians, especially concerning the refugee issue, and again spoke about the importance of the refugee issue to Jordan. He also informed Abbas that Sharon was likely to be a key player in these negotiations.

Abbas agreed that Sharon would be important and indicated that he was planning to see him soon. He also said that during Dennis Ross's next visit to the region, the Palestinians would start coordination with Jordan. Anani then told Abbas that the Israelis were not keen on Ross's direct involvement. Abbas also said that the Palestinians were aware of Jordan's interests and that their policy was to coordinate with Jordan ahead of negotiations with Israel. Abbas understood Jordanian concerns, particularly on the issue of refugees, more than any other Palestinian official and genuinely sought coordination. It was doubtful, however, that he had a mandate from Arafat for such coordination. Indeed, despite Jordan's repeated efforts, then and ever since, to hold a serious discussion about the refugee issue with Palestinians, no such meeting has taken place. Arafat, who did not trust Jordan and in any case did not want to cede control over the issue, was probably the main obstacle.

THE SUCCESSION ISSUE TAKES CENTER STAGE

As of October 23, King Hussein began holding his meetings at my office in Washington and asked me to attend each one. He repeated a central theme to every visitor: Jordanians' concern about the future in light of the monarch's condition. He told almost everyone he met that he planned to make "major changes" when he returned to Jordan in order to reassure Jordanians about the future. Changes of government were almost annual, so when the king talked about major changes, they understood him to mean something much more significant. Unaware of the developments in Washington, Prime Minister Tarawneh issued a press release on November 4 stating that the succession issue was "not contentious."[10]

The king celebrated his sixty-third birthday on November 14 in Washington. The celebrations took place just six days after I had made a statement to the media announcing that after a fifth chemotherapy course, the king's body was free of cancer cells and that a six precautionary course would be administered. Many official delegations, members of parliament, family, and friends from Jordan were in Washington to wish him well, but I was struck by a meeting that had been arranged by Royal Protocol for the king with a delegation from the Jordan Press Association. The king met with them in my office on November 19 and reiterated his message about the "major changes" he planned to make once he returned home.

When the press delegation returned to Jordan, a reporter, basing his story on an account of the meeting told to him by one of the attending journalists, published King Hussein's words in the Arabic daily *Al-Hayat*. He was subsequently summoned for questioning by the General Intelligence Department. His editor called me from Amman. "Ambassador, you were present at that meeting. Did you understand the king's words differently?" he asked me. "Why would the Mukhabarat question our reporter on something that was said by the king?" This incident suggested that the king had not shared his decision with anyone, not even General Battikhi, the man at the head of Jordan's security services.

The king departed for Rochester shortly after that to receive a sixth chemotherapy round and to undergo a bone marrow transplant procedure to bolster his chances of being cured. The two chambers of parliament met in joint session on November 22, a measure required by the Constitution whenever the monarch is away from the country for more than four consecutive months. Parliament was briefed on King Hussein's condition, and President of the Senate Zeid Rifai wrote the king a letter to inform him of the meeting. In his reply, King Hussein would publicly reiterate, for the first time, the themes of change and confidence in the future. "I hope to contribute in eradicating any possibility of concern among every Jordanian, male and female, regarding the future, and in working to cement our solid achievements."[11]

King Hussein spent December in Rochester; the bone marrow transplant procedure and recuperation required total rest and isolation. At the end of the month, Crown Prince Hassan announced that King Hussein had been cured and that he was on his way to Washington. The king himself announced that the next checkup would be in March 1999.[12] Jordanians breathed a sigh of relief. Everyone, including me, felt that the king had successfully defeated cancer for the second time in less than a decade. Morale was high, and Jordanians prepared a grand homecoming.

THE LAST MEETING WITH CLINTON

General Battikhi arrived in Washington in early January 1999 to see the king and to accompany him to the White House for a meeting with President Clinton on January 5. In Washington, King Hussein congratulated Clinton on the "brave speech" he had given in Gaza in December at the Palestine National Council during a meeting in which the PNC finally amended its charter, removing from it clauses that called for Israel's destruction. Clinton had shown a lot of empathy with Palestinians in that speech, telling them that he knew that for many of them, the benefits of the peace process remained remote. "I understand your concerns about settlement activity, land confiscation and home demolitions," he said, calling on "Palestinians to recognize the right of Israel and its people to live safe and secure lives today, tomorrow and forever," and on Israel to "recognize the right of Palestinians to aspire to live free today, tomorrow and forever."[13] Israeli elections were then scheduled for May 1999. It was clear from the White House meeting that the Americans were not enthusiastic about Netanyahu's possible reelection, nor was the king. By then, he had lost hope that the Israeli prime minister was a reliable partner for peace.

The two leaders also discussed the situation in Iraq and the U.S. aid package to Jordan. As a result of Wye, the administration was submitting a supplemental aid package in Congress for Israel and the Palestinians and wanted to add an amount to help Jordan. The administration was thinking of two hundred million dollars, but we were lobbying both the administration and Congress for more.

Clinton was extremely warm toward the king and displayed both an understanding of Jordan's economic problems and a willingness to help. After the meeting, Queen Noor and Hillary Clinton joined the two leaders for a half-hour private talk.

We went back to the hotel for a snack lunch. The king was in high spirits, talking about the future with confidence. "I like this small delegation meeting," he told Battikhi and me, in reference to the many previous meetings where he had been accompanied by a large delegation. He determined then and there that in the future, "I am going to only bring a small delegation with me." To me, that was an indication that the king felt he had successfully fought the cancer and was planning for the future.

The following day, Tuesday, January 6, the king departed for London for a period of rest before returning to Jordan. Martin Indyk called me on January 8 to let me know that President Clinton had agreed to add another hundred million dollars to the supplemental package for Jordan. Albright had argued that it was unusual for the king, who usually shied away from directly asking for assistance, to talk about aid and that his doing so must be reciprocated with a positive response. The president agreed.

The crown prince flew to London to pay a surprise visit to his brother on January 8. He saw him for few hours and returned to Jordan.

That seemed to subdue the rumors about the succession, at least publicly. The crown prince returned thinking that the issue had been settled in his favor. However, the king had sent a letter detailing the arrangements he wanted of his return home, specifically that Crown Prince Hassan not be first in the receiving line but rather assume a position in the line according to his family seniority—an arrangement that would place his older brother, Prince Muhammad, ahead of him.

On January 16, the king addressed Jordanians through a televised speech from London, where he again talked about "the need for a comprehensive review of our national march soon."[14] By now, the clues were too numerous and too obvious to be ignored. Jordanians waited impatiently to hear what the king had to say.

The king finally returned to Jordan on January 19 to a tremendous welcome by Jordanians, who had lined the streets of Amman to greet him, even though it was a cold and rainy day. Protocol arrangements left little doubt in Jordanians minds that a change of succession was imminent. In statements to the media, the king reiterated his earlier statements that "the next phase needs some studying to arrive at the appropriate decision so that citizens can feel confident and secure about their future."[15]

Less than twenty-four hours after his return, the king appeared on CNN in an interview with Christiane Amanpour, to whom he declared that his principal concern was to assure Jordanians about the security of their future. When Amanpour asked him directly about the succession, he gave the clearest response that the issue for him was not personal but had to do with the country's future. "There is no personal greed or ambition as far as I am concerned. The best is what concerns me. (Amanpour: For your country) . . . and people living happily, and people living together, and not a group coming to try to destroy what the previous one has done but to add to it."

Then, on January 25, the king appointed his first son, Prince Abdullah, crown prince. That night, Jordan Television announced that a letter from the king to his brother would be forthcoming during the eight o'clock news bulletin. At the embassy in Washington, we waited impatiently to hear what King Hussein would say. The eight o'clock news came and went with no information; indeed the delivery of the letter was inexplicably delayed for five hours. Later we learned that the king's temperature had been rising for a few days and that initial checkups in Jordan revealed that cancer cells had returned to his body in massive numbers. His rapidly deteriorating health had demanded his return to the Mayo Clinic and prompted swift action. In her memoirs Queen Noor explained the delay in delivering the letter as the result of the fact that the king spent more than six hours drafting the letter while taking breaks to rest.[16]

When the JTV news anchor finally read the letter at almost 1:00 a.m., Jordanians were astonished by its tone and the anger and frustration that it seemed to contain. The letter referred to many instances of conflict between the brothers and openly discussed "parasites" that had poisoned the atmosphere in Jordan. Although Jordanians were aware of some of these issues, this was the first time the king brought them so starkly to public attention.

BACK TO THE MAYO CLINIC

Having done what he could for peace, consolidating an Arab Center he helped create, and preparing Jordan for the next phase, King Hussein had to tend to his deteriorating health, knowing by now that he had little time to live. The account of his last six months might very well be about peace, coexistence, and a brighter future for the region, but it is also very much a human story of courage and vision. No account would be complete without telling it.

One day after that dramatic change of succession, I received a call from Colonel Hussein Majali, the monarch's military aide-de-camp, announcing King Hussein's return to Rochester. He was calling from aboard the royal plane, which had left Amman only hours earlier. I was shocked. "Please assure me things are okay," I said, fearing his answer. "Unfortunately, I cannot," he replied. Majali refused my offer to meet the plane in Rochester, telling me that there was no reason for me to do so. "I'll call you when we arrive," he said.

I was devastated. That the king was returning to the United States so soon after having arrived in Amman was certainly not good news. I simply could not stay in Washington. I went to my office and arranged to fly to Rochester the following day. Majali called me later that night to tell me that the king had been admitted to the hospital, where a chemotherapy course was immediately administered. I told Majali I was coming, regardless, because I felt that as the only Jordanian official in the United States, I ought to be there. Majali then gave me another shock. "Do you happen to have a large Jordanian flag at the embassy? Can you bring it with you?" The implication of his question was clear.

I arrived in Rochester on Wednesday, where I met Queen Noor, the king's physician, Dr. Samir Farraj, and Colonel Majali. The situation was serious. Even before the king had left Amman, his doctors had believed that his chances of surviving the flight were slim and that a stop in Shannon, Ireland, en route would be needed to administer a blood transfusion. By the time I arrived in Rochester, a powerful chemotherapy course was being administered, but it was largely experimental—such a strong treatment had never been given to a man of King Hussein's age so soon after completing a chemotherapy regimen. The doctors wanted to attempt to kill all the cancer cells in a procedure that required another bone marrow transplant and would bring the king's immunity to zero. It would take around ten days before the new marrow would start functioning and his immunity would return, during which there was a considerable chance of vital organ failure from the massive doses of chemotherapy. The doctors' prognosis was that his chances of survival were no more than 10 percent.

This was grave news, but none of us wanted to believe it or to give up. I quickly settled into a routine: I arrived at the hospital each morning around eight o'clock and stayed at the king's wing, where a special waiting area had been set up. There, I spent time with Dr. Farraj, Colonel Majali, and Queen Noor's press secretary, Nadine Shubailat. Queen Noor and Prince Hamzah, Queen Noor's oldest son, rarely left the monarch's bedside. Few visitors were allowed into the king's room because of his reduced immunity. I brought my laptop so that I could work, communicating from the hospital with Washington and Amman and making a daily statement to media organizations, including the Jordanian press.

We would have lunch either in the wing or at the hospital's cafeteria, and we then stayed all evening at the wing until about eight or nine o'clock. We would then have a small bite and retire for the day. Our small group developed a special bond, giving each other support while hoping for the best.

After my final meeting with the king at his hospital bed, I announced that yet another new round of chemotherapy was being administered and that the treatment would last around days.[17] I followed it with another statement the following day announcing that the chemotherapy course was over and that a bone marrow transplant would take place the following Tuesday and Wednesday.[18]

The king's situation was critical, and we all knew that his chances of survival were slim. Jordanians needed to be prepared. As the only official attending the king, the task fell to me. Thus, on Tuesday, February 2, Jordan Television organized a live interview with me from Rochester, and I explained to Jordanians the treatment process the king was undergoing and discussed the complications of the operation. My heart was heavy as I spoke, and those who viewed that interview in Jordan later told me that my tone, expression, and body language had told them everything they needed to know about King Hussein's situation: Jordanians knew that their monarch was not likely to recover.

As ambassador to the United States, I also had to familiarize members of Congress and other decision makers in Washington with the new crown prince. I asked Rania Atalla, director of the Jordan Information Bureau in Washington, to send me draft letters to 180 such individuals giving some background about Prince Abdullah. Signing those letters in the hospital wing was one of the most painful experiences of my diplomatic service.

THE FINAL JOURNEY HOME

The events that unfolded beginning on Thursday, February 4, 1999, were unforgettable. I walked into the hospital wing at eight o'clock as usual, where the doctors were already meeting. King Hussein's body had rejected the bone marrow transplant, and although his vital organs were functioning, medicine could do nothing more at this point. King Hussein had made his last wishes known: if it ever became clear that he could not recover, he should be returned to Amman. He wanted to die in Jordan.

Arrangements had to be made to set up the necessary medical equipment inside the royal plane. The king had to be put on a respirator, which requires induced unconsciousness. Doctors estimated that the monarch had thirty-six hours to live. I called Toni Verstandig to inform the State Department. "We are going home, Toni," I said before choking up.

The plane took off around midday on Thursday. On it were Queen Noor with her four children, Prince Hamzeh, Prince Hashem, Princess Iman, and Princess Raya, in addition to Princess Haya, King Hussein's daughter from Queen Alia, who had died in a plane crash in 1977. No one was in a mood to talk. We all knew how sad this journey was on both personal and national levels. Queen Noor, who was a pillar of strength, went around the plane and shook hands with everyone on board. We numbered about forty or fifty. Then she entered the king's room, where he lay unconscious, and spent most of the flight there. As the plane took off, two U.S. Air Force F-16s escorted us out of American airspace. We were all overcome with grief.

The king's five children entered his cabin intermittently, sitting near him and reciting the Koran. The rest of us just sat in our seats, barely uttering a word during the long flight.

Shortly before the plane landed on Friday morning, Queen Noor asked if anyone wished to spend few moments with the king. We all lined up and went into the room one by one. She was by his side, holding his hand. We took turns spending a few moments with him to say good-bye. The scene will be imprinted in my memory forever.

From the airport I went straight to my parents' home to rest before Rania Atalla and I started helping with the hundreds of international reporters who had descended on Jordan. For the first time in months, I was observing the scene not from Washington but as an average Jordanian. One could feel grief in the air; it engulfed the country. Jordanians were preparing for the death of a leader who had ruled with dignity and maturity. Because he had ruled for forty-six years, most Jordanians had grown up knowing no other leader, and King Hussein was the common bond running through every citizen regardless of socioeconomic, religious, or ethnic background.

The illness or death of long-serving rulers inevitably invites speculation about the security and stability of the countries over which they preside, and Jordan was no exception. The international media was awash with stories about Jordan's social, political, and economic dynamics and the potential for its destabilization, to which the change in the line of succession had introduced a new twist. Thus, after King Hussein's return from the Mayo Clinic, I spent the next two days at the press center set up in a hotel in Amman, trying to answer questions from the media and assure them of Jordan's stability.

I was at the Intercontinental Hotel in Amman on Sunday, February 7, talking to reporters with Rania Atalla, when a close friend of ours walked in. "Jordan Radio just announced it," he said quietly. "King Hussein has died."

KING HUSSEIN'S LEGACY

King Hussein had good reason to be at peace with himself. Since the country's foundation in 1921, historians and analysts had regarded Jordan as an artificial entity that could not possibly withstand the many threats to its survival. Many believed that Jordan lacked the necessary components, such as natural resources or thriving urban centers, to support a modern state and that Jordan's survival rested solely on the character and personality of the ruler. It was often said, in fact, "Jordan is the king and the king is Jordan." Such predictions were de rigueur especially after King Hussein assumed the throne at the young age of seventeen at a time when radical ideologies had taken center stage in a region struggling to adjust to the postcolonial era and Arab states were competing for regional influence.

But Jordan did survive, and today the country enjoys a standard of living, a level of development, and a degree of security not attained by many of its wealthier neighbors. Although his reign may have been controversial for many, few can dispute that these conditions exist in Jordan today thanks largely to King Hussein's leadership.

He strove to forge good relationships both with key states in the Arab world and the West that served the country's political and economic interests well. Foreign aid from the Arab world and the West was always a key factor that helped the country overcome the challenges to its existence and contributed to the country's development. Peace was a similarly strategic objective for him, as it ensured Jordan's political survival and promised it greater economic prosperity.

But Jordanian policy established during his era—and which persists to this day—was not motivated solely by realpolitik. The Arab-Islamic modernity, moderation, and centrism for which King Hussein stood were also borne of fundamental conviction. He was always aware of his

Hashemite legacy, being a direct descendant of the Prophet Muhammad, which influenced his work and thinking. Perhaps this explained why he strove for objectives beyond his immediate personal interest. He was open to all groups, and he was in turn respected by adherents to all the different brands of Islam.

He fundamentally believed not only that Jordanians would benefit from regional peace but that all people of the region deserved to live in peace and security. He willingly put his credibility on the line to seek peace and cooperation among all peoples of the region. At no time was this more apparent than when he left his sick bed to intervene at Wye. He was the region's most energetic champion of peace and envisioned a peace that would satisfy the aspirations of all people of the region by addressing their political, development, and security concerns. Jordan has carried on in his absence, but it does seem that the peace process has never recovered from his death: regional peace today seems to be as distant a dream as it was several decades ago.

His legacy is a country that had developed against all odds into a modern state that is home to one of the most enlightened, open, and tolerant societies in the most troubled region of the world. His decision to change the line of the succession has to be seen in the light of his vision for Jordan's future. Under King Hussein, Jordan withstood the years of postcolonial turmoil and regional rivalry and the Arab-Israeli Wars of 1948 and 1967. By the time he died in 1999, Jordan was a country of institutions sufficiently developed to shift its focus from mere survival and state building to economic well-being and political development. That required a new generation of leaders, unburdened of the historical baggage that had bogged his generation of leaders down and able and flexible enough to further open up and adopt policies that would usher it into the twenty-first century.

Perhaps the most eloquent words summing up the reign and character of King Hussein came from President Clinton. "During the Wye Summit, when the talks were not going so well, he came out within a few short minutes and changed the tenor of the meeting. Though frail with fighting for his own life, he gave life to the process many felt was failing. The smallest man in the room that day was the largest; the frailest was the strongest. The man with the least time remaining reminded us we are working not only for ourselves, but for all eternity."[19]

POSTSCRIPT

The first two years of King Abdullah II's reign would prove King Hussein's vision right. The new monarch, with a peace treaty with Israel that was holding despite all the challenges, could and did focus his attention on the economy. Plans to privatize state-owned entities, encourage foreign investments, downsize the bureaucracy, and end subsidies, for example, had languished for years but were rapidly implemented after 1999, and among the notable results of reform has been Jordan's integration into the global economy through such institutions as the World Trade Organization and the free trade agreement with the United States. King Abdullah II robustly pursued expanded trade and financial exchanges with Jordan's Arab neighbors that had long been stifled in part by regional political rivalries. He championed new initiatives that would have a qualitative effect on the country's youth, introducing the Internet and computers to all public schools starting in first grade. He also supported the development of new sectors for the economy, notably the information and communications technology sector, with impressive results.

King Abdullah II has sought to nurture a more cooperative relationship with the Palestinian leadership. Today the monarch and other Jordanian officials not only routinely announce Jordan's support for a viable, independent Palestinian state; they have also actively championed a Palestinian state as the cornerstone of regional peace on the international stage. Within a year, he had ended the presence of Hamas in Jordan, which had been a source of friction for years with the Palestinian leadership. And crucially, he sought to allay Palestinian concerns that Jordan had lingering ambitions for the West Bank by announcing that Jordan would surrender its custodianship over the holy sites in Jerusalem to a sovereign Palestinian government once its rights in the holy city were recognized by Israel. And then he returned to the business of readying Jordan for the demands the twenty-first century.

It seemed then that the Israelis were readying to turn a new page with the Palestinians, too. Three short months after King Abdullah II's ascension to the throne, the Israeli public elected a new government, with Ehud Barak as prime minister. The peace process was suddenly injected with new life, and political negotiations resumed between the two sides—this time with a much better atmosphere.

The honeymoon was brief. Within the first two years of his reign,

King Abdullah II found himself back in the thick of the process, with the collapse of the Camp David and Taba talks, the election of a new Israeli government under the premiership of Ariel Sharon, a new U.S. administration under George W. Bush, and September 11. As we shall see, Jordan would again play a crucial role in developing a more effective Arab political center to address the challenges posed by these developments.

CHAPTER FOUR

The Arab Initiative

My mood was light as I boarded a commercial plane at 8:40 a.m. on Tuesday, September 11, 2001, from Dulles International Airport. I was traveling to Houston to meet King Abdullah II, who was arriving that day from Amman. Although the peace process had been in crisis for more than a year, recent events had suggested that the United States—which had been absent from the peace process during that time—was preparing to reengage. I looked forward to the king's meeting with President George W. Bush and felt that we could make headway with him.

The plane was flying to Houston via Jackson, Mississippi. Passengers were unaware of the events unfolding in New York City, Washington, DC, and Pennsylvania. Just before the plane prepared to land, the pilot announced that an airplane had plowed into one of the World Trade Center towers in New York, another had hit the Pentagon, and U.S. airspace had been closed. Everybody on the plane sat silently in shock. Who could believe such news? As we began to register the magnitude of what had happened, another airplane slammed into the second World Trade Center tower.

I was outraged. I could not comprehend how or why any human being could commit such savagery against other human beings. When I finally got through to the king's advance team in Houston, his plane had turned around in midflight and was being redirected to London. I called my wife to make sure that all was well at home.

I had no idea who could have conceived such a horrific attack, and along with everyone else I waited impatiently for the details to unfold. I also prayed to God that the perpetrators were not Arabs. For Arab involvement would deal a severe blow not only to the cause of peace but also to the overall image of Arabs in the United States. Moderation, tolerance, and improved mutual understanding between the Arab world and the United States were at stake, I thought. Reports that Al-Qaeda had been involved confirmed my worst fears.

For the next two days, I was stranded in an airport hotel room, unable to find transportation back to Washington. I used the time to give back-to-back phone interviews with the media, denouncing the terrorist acts and explaining that no sane person in this world could justify these acts. I finally gave up hope of finding a way home and asked the embassy to send me a car with two drivers who took turns covering the sixteen-hour drive from Washington. They reached the hotel at 7:00 a.m. Thursday, September 13, and promptly collapsed in the backseat. I drove back, one hand on the wheel and the other clutching my mobile phone, which had not stopped ringing with requests for interviews. Finally, after three long days, I arrived in Washington not long after midnight on Friday. It was to be a Washington that was changed forever.

THE IMPACT OF SEPTEMBER 11 was no less dramatic in the Arab world. The attack was as much against Arabs—Muslims and Christians alike—as it was against Americans and other Westerners. For Al-Qaeda is an exclusivist group that claims to speak on behalf of all Muslims, although, in fact, its leaders and supporters belong to a deviant form of Islam that is violently opposed to the mainstream, as subsequent attacks on Muslims in a number of Islamic states have since demonstrated. Nevertheless, the entire Arab world had been tainted by Al-Qaeda's crime against humanity. The West sought explanations for how and why societies produced individuals capable of such mass brutality and identified authoritarianism and repression as key factors; democracy, the West believed, was the answer to this problem. The objective of the West to reform Arab societies was in fact not dissimilar to that of Al-Qaeda. For years, the extremist group had blamed conditions in the Arab-Islamic world on a lack of religiosity; Islam, they said, was the answer. As this ideological battle cohered between Western capitals and the mountains of Afghanistan, it quickly became clear to Arabs that unless they initiated change from within their own societies, change would be imposed on them by external forces according to formulas not necessarily of their liking.

Also, even though Al-Qaeda had never asserted the Palestinian-Israeli conflict as one of its priorities, the prevalent feeling in the region was that something needed to be done to address people's frustrations on this issue, which extremists could easily exploit for their own purposes. The Arab-Israeli conflict was and remains a principal cause of frustration in the region. No single regional factor has done more to deprive people of hope and drive them into the arms of those who promise them a better life in heaven. On September 11, the Arab-Israeli peace process had been ongoing for nearly a decade, with little achieved on a resolution to the core issue: the Palestinian-Israeli conflict. The parties themselves were too far apart to propose initiatives that might help. The new administration of George W. Bush was unenthusiastic about a sustained engagement that might break the impasse, after so many administrations had tried and failed, and the events of September 11 promptly further diverted U.S. attention from the peace process. It fell to the Arab Center to reclaim the initiative on the Middle East peace process.

EVENTS LEADING TO THE ARAB INITIATIVE

The personal relationship between King Hussein and Yitzhak Rabin and the king's satisfaction after the peace treaty that Jordan's interests had been taken into account paved the way for Jordan to move forward on the two-state solution with more confidence. Unfortunately, Rabin's assassination in 1995 helped derail the peace process. Rabin's successor, Shimon Peres, was fickle and failed to uphold Rabin's legacy, and his evasive style and tactics prevented him from capitalizing on the unprecedented public support for Labor following Rabin's death. In a dramatic turnaround, brought largely by a series of suicide bombings by radical Palestinian groups, the Labor Party under Peres lost power to a more hawkish Likud led by Binyamin Netanyahu. Netanyahu formed his government with Israeli radicals who had opposed the peace process since its inception: seven of the eight parties that constituted his government had opposed Oslo. Netanyahu himself made undermining the Oslo Accords a pillar of his candidacy. For this and other reasons, such as Netanyahu's abrasive personal style, it was difficult for King Hussein to develop a liking for him, let alone the personal rapport he had enjoyed with Rabin. Before long, King Hussein began to realize that Netanyahu was not a trustworthy peace partner. In a scathing letter addressed to Netanyahu in March 1997, the king accused the Israeli premier of undermining peace, turning it into a "distant, elusive mirage." The letter was uncharacteristically strong for a diplomatic exchange and reflected the king's deep frustration with Netanyahu's policies.

KING HUSSEIN'S PEACE PROPOSAL

When Rabin was assassinated, King Hussein felt he had lost a partner who understood Jordan's needs and who earnestly worked for a two-state solution. But he also realized that peace could not be made with one individual or party in Israel. For peace to endure, the king needed to work with the whole political spectrum in Israel. That is why, despite the Likud's traditional hard-line policies toward Jordan as well as the Palestinians, Jordan was the first Arab country to welcome Netanyahu's election in mid-1996 and to express its willingness to pursue peace efforts with the Likud-led government. Yet relations between the two countries, and the two leaders, quickly soured. Netanyahu's intensification and expansion of settlement activity, particularly in and around Jerusalem, his controversial opening of a tunnel under the Haram Al-Sharif compound, and his tough line with the Palestinians did not endear him to the monarch. Netanyahu was also someone who did not keep his word, and he often retreated on commitments made to Jordan without consideration for its delicate situation. It was almost inevitable that the relationship between the king and Netanyahu would take a nosedive. When Netanyahu ordered a failed Mossad operation to assassinate a Hamas leader, Khaled Mishaal, in Amman in September 1997, the king felt that Netanyahu had essentially spit on the Jordan-Israel peace treaty. Indeed, the incident almost caused the king to abrogate the treaty, and the relationship between the two leaders was irrevocably damaged.

Meanwhile, negotiations between Israel and the Palestinians, with the United States as mediator, were going nowhere. The peace process that started in Madrid had failed in three important respects: (1) there were insufficient incentives for Israel to make the concessions that a Palestinian leader could accept and still survive; (2) the Palestinians had nothing by way of incentives to offer Israel; and (3) the United States had neither the political will nor the ability to bridge the gap. King Hussein concluded that a durable peace would have to be comprehensive— *involving all Arab states,* which together held the key to Israel's security, rather than only the Palestinians. Thus, in 1998 King Hussein, frustrated and alarmed by Netanyahu's antipeace policies, and the threat this posed to the two-state outcome, devised a new approach to peacemaking.[1] He envisioned a peace initiative that was much broader than Madrid in scope: it would include all Arab states rather than only those neighboring Israel, and it would commit the whole Arab world to peace with Israel once Israel withdrew from all occupied Arab land.

His purpose was to offer an Arab peace plan dramatic enough to attract favorable international support, especially with the Israeli public and the U.S. administration. He believed that if Syria joined, Israel would have a hard time turning down such an initiative, and that if Iraq joined, it would dramatically alter the course of Middle East history, given Israel's security concerns, which went beyond its immediate neighbors. The proposal contained the following elementary provisions:

- Arab League members, individually and collectively, agree that, if and when, (1) a Palestinian state is established, with mutually agreed borders, a formula for Jerusalem, and a solution to the refugee problem is arrived at, and (2) the Golan Heights, with pre-June 1967 borders, are returned to Syria, and (3) the controlled territories in South Lebanon are returned to Lebanon;
- The Arab League states will:
  1. Establish diplomatic relations with Israel at the same time Israel establishes diplomatic relations with the Palestinian state;
  2. Open their countries to free trade with Israel on a reciprocal basis; and
  3. Sign a mutual, comprehensive defense/security pact with Israel, containing safeguards, verifications, and territorial guarantees.

I was ambassador to the United States at that time, and I was kept fully abreast of the evolution of this concept. Given Egypt's centrality in the Arab world, King Hussein was convinced that only President Mubarak could successfully sponsor such a proposal. As one of the smallest and poorest Arab states, Jordan's ideas, warnings, and initiatives have often gone unheeded within the Arab League. In addition, Jordan has often been regarded as too pro-Western, which has frequently cast doubt over the sincerity of its objectives and the credibility of its ideas—even when it has introduced initiatives and ideas that other larger countries such as Egypt, Syria, or Saudi Arabia appreciated. Jordan has often had to convince another Arab nation of the merits of an initiative and encourage it to introduce the idea as its own.

The king thus lobbied President Mubarak for Egypt's support for a pan-Arab peace initiative. Mubarak took the idea on board and announced his intent to call an Arab summit to adopt the initiative. Unfortunately, in 1998 Secretary of State Madeleine Albright launched an intensive round of "shuttle diplomacy" in 1998 and advised Mubarak that an Arab summit would undermine the American effort. Mubarak obliged Albright and withdrew his proposal. Subsequent events hindered the initiative's revival: King Hussein's deteriorating health and eventual death, the Wye River Palestinian-Israeli peace talks and agreement, and early Israeli elections. Another four years passed before a similar initiative, introduced by Crown Prince Abdullah of Saudi Arabia, would see the light. The Arab Initiative passed in Beirut in March 2002 by all Arab states contained the principles outlined above, although by then my role in its passage would be more than peripheral.

With the election of Labor candidate Ehud Barak as prime minister in May 1999, hopes of arriving at a two-state solution revived. President Clinton convened a summit at Camp David in July 2000 with Yasir Arafat and Barak to try to reach an agreement on final status. Although much progress was made, particularly on such hitherto untouchable issues as Jerusalem and refugees, the talks ended in failure. A few weeks later, Ariel Sharon visited Al-Aqsa Mosque in Jerusalem, provoking the eruption in the occupied territories of the second intifada.[2] The ensuing Palestinian-Israeli violence reached levels that dimmed all hopes of reaching a settlement. Clinton would not stop trying, however. In December, he called a Palestinian and an Israeli delegation to the White House and laid out what had become known as the "Clinton Parameters," a take-it-or-leave-it American proposal to bridge the gap between the two sides and reach an agreement (see Appendix 3).

Based on these parameters, which both sides found to form a reasonable basis for the resumption of negotiations, the two sides arrived in the Egyptian Red Sea resort of Taba in January 2001 for a last-ditch attempt to reach an agreement before Israeli elections, scheduled for February 6, 2001. Never before had the two sides come so close to concluding a historic agreement, but they nevertheless walked away empty-handed. The Israeli elections returned a Likud government to power, this time headed by Sharon. Political negotiations came to an abrupt halt and, at the time of writing, had not been resumed. By 2002, the prospects of a two-state solution seemed remote indeed.

None of this was good news to Jordan, where the violence in the West Bank and Gaza, coupled with the lack of a political process, were having a dramatic impact on public opinion. The new Bush administration, however, did not view the Palestinian-Israeli conflict as a priority, particularly after the strenuous efforts of President Clinton had failed. King Abdullah II dispatched Prince Zaid Bin Shaker, an ex-prime minister and a confidant of the late King Hussein, and his foreign minister, Abdel Ilah Khatib, to Washington immediately after the new U.S. administration took office in January 2001 to discuss the next steps in the peace process. Jordan argued that negotiations should be resumed where they had left off in Taba rather than be allowed to slide backward should Sharon win the Israeli elections. It also urged the United States to stay engaged so that a two-state solution could be achieved.

Neither happened. The Israelis and the Palestinians differed on where the negotiations had actually reached in Taba, and the Bush-led administration was clearly hesitant to tarnish its prestige by stepping into an apparent quagmire. The administration instead adopted a hands-off approach, and peacemaking efforts remained at an impasse. Meanwhile, the cycle of violence persisted, and the situation in the occupied territories rapidly deteriorated. This posed a challenge to all parties, especially Jordan. Alarmed by this tragic development, Jordan decided to work proactively first to end the bloodshed and then to move the process forward. Thus, in March 2001, Jordan and Egypt proposed a series of measures beginning with ending the crisis between Israel and the Palestinian Authority and followed by confidence-building measures that would lead to the rehabilitation of the negotiating process and preserve and build on all that had been achieved from November 1999 through the Taba talks in January 2001. The Israeli side, however, would not be swayed. On the contrary, the only movement Sharon was considering was making good on his pledge to the Israeli public to quell the intifada by force within one hundred days. Sharon belonged to a strand of Zionism that believed in the utility of force in international relations. The Jordanian-Egyptian initiative, therefore, fell on deaf ears. The Israeli government would accept no reference to the negotiations in Camp David and Taba and was unwilling in any case to talk about political negotiations at this stage. Meanwhile, the United States did little to press Israel on the matter.

In October 2000, a month after the intifada started, President Clinton formed a fact-finding committee, headed by former senator George Mitchell, to study the outbreak of violence. The committee's report, published in April 2001, included principles from the Jordanian-Egyptian initiative. It also asked Israel to "freeze all settlement activity, including the 'natural growth' of existing settlements"—the first such request by an official American body. That clause was critical from the Palestinian standpoint because the number of settlers had nearly doubled since the 1993 Oslo Accords. The Mitchell Report also addressed many security and confidence-building measures, but it carefully avoided making stringent political demands, advising only that "Israel must take steps to reassure the Palestinians on political matters in return for Palestinian reassurances on security matters."

The Bush administration accepted the recommendations of the Mitchell Report and announced the appointment of William Burns as special envoy to the Middle East peace process. The president dispatched him and CIA Director George Tenet to work on security arrangements that would pacify the boiling situation in the West Bank and Gaza.

All the efforts of the administration, however, were concentrated on addressing the security situation, with the aim of restoring calm and then moving slowly into confidence-building measures. This style of mediation failed to account for Palestinians' utter frustration and impatience at the lack of any political horizon. Resumption of a serious political process was not on the agenda. The general Arab consensus opposed the emphasis on security issues at the expense of political ones, and Arab states argued that a deadline needed to be set for the completion of final status negotiations that were already long overdue: under the terms of the Oslo Accords, they were to have concluded by May 1999.

Meanwhile, the security situation continued to deteriorate in the occupied Palestinian territories. In February 2001, Amnesty International released a report calling Israel's targeted killings of Palestinians part of a "policy of state assassinations." Between September 2000 and September 2001, 560 Palestinians and 177 Israelis had been killed. During the same period, an increase in the number of checkpoints in and closures of the occupied territories led to a total loss of $4.25 billion across all sectors of the Palestinian economy. In the West Bank alone 5,000 Palestinian residential buildings were destroyed.

Disillusioned by these developments, King Abdullah II decided to revive King Hussein's proposal of 1998. On September 8, 2001, he wrote to President Bush, arguing that incremental steps had not worked and that the time had come for final status negotiations, based on withdrawal of Israel from all occupied Arab land—Palestinian, Syrian, and Lebanese—in return for security guarantees for Israel from all Arab states, including the Palestinians.

I delivered the king's message to the president's senior adviser on the Middle East at the National Security Council, Bruce Reidel, on September 10, 2001. I told Reidel that the king wished to discuss this issue personally with the president during his impending visit to the United States. The king was scheduled to meet with the president on September 20 after a working tour that would start in Houston on September 11, 2001. Reidel, an experienced and thoughtful career official, encouraged me not to sugarcoat the message and felt that Jordan needed to speak candidly on the issue.

I had met with Prince Bandar, the Saudi ambassador in Washington, and Nabil Fahmy, the Egyptian ambassador, at the prince's house on September 9 to coordinate our positions. I briefed the two ambassadors on the contents of the king's letter to the president on the previous day. Prince Bandar in turn informed us that Crown Prince Abdullah of Saudi Arabia had also sent a frank message a couple of weeks earlier, appealing to the United States to play a more active and balanced role in solving the Arab-Israeli conflict. He also pointedly said that it had become clear to Saudi Arabia that the U.S. administration was working against Arab interests, and in a clear reference to oil prices, he wrote that Saudi Arabia would reciprocate by pursuing its own interests without consideration for American interests. In a written response dated August 29, President Bush replied that he intended to define the administration's position regarding the conflict, including acknowledging the Palestinians' right to self-determination and a state of their own, in an upcoming speech.

SEPTEMBER 11, 2001

My optimism at the thought that the United States was becoming attuned to the message from the Arab world and would soon declare its
policy was rapidly dissipated by the terror attacks of September 11. When
I heard that the attacks were the work of Al-Qaeda, my worst fears were
realized. But I was also determined to do everything in my power to prevent these terrorists from winning the battle of ideas.

Arab states had different views on how to respond to 9/11. Jordan's
response was prompt, with King Abdullah II unequivocally denouncing
the attacks. Jordan had always joined the international community in the
fight against terrorism as a matter of principle. "Some people are trying
to portray this as a clash of civilizations. We see it as a clash of civilizations *against* terrorism," I told the *Washington Post*.[3] Egypt and Saudi
Arabia joined Jordan in condemning the attacks. Syria and Lebanon, by
contrast, dissembled, demanding that terrorism first be clearly defined
in order to avoid a confrontation with the radical group Hezbollah. To
ask the Americans at such a time for a definition seemed to me insensi-
tive and politically incorrect.

The crimes committed on September 11, 2001, led the Americans to
ask, "Why do they hate us so much?" Jordan likewise thought the time
was ripe for the international community to reexamine one of the root
causes of terrorism and the prevalent anti-American sentiment in the
Middle East. Jordan, an ally and a friend of the United States, believed
that what we perceived as pro-Israel bias in American foreign policy was
the chief source of the Jordanian public's resentment of American policy
in the region. Jordan hoped that the American administration would see
the link between the persistence of the Israeli occupation of Arab lands
and anti-American sentiments in the region. Indeed, some twenty-seven
former U.S. diplomats sent the American administration a letter expressing that very point. Jordan therefore hoped that the United States
would have an incentive to be more closely engaged in conflict resolution between Arabs and Israeli and remove a major source of frustration
that Al-Qaeda and other fringe groups exploited to recruit its foot sol-
diers. But the days and months immediately following the tragedy of
September 11 were not the appropriate time to ask the United States to
work on two parallel tracks: one on terrorism and another on conflict
resolution.

Television images of a few Palestinian children dancing in the street in apparent celebration did not help either. Although they were clearly not representative of Palestinian society, the scene was played over and over again. Israel was quick to capitalize on the September 11 tragedy by equating Al-Qaeda terrorism and suicide bombing attacks on Israeli civilians as well as other violence in the occupied territories. The government of Israel has since meticulously and methodologically justified its policy of violent repression and occupation of the Palestinians by conflating it with the war against global terrorism and by qualifying all violent resistance against the occupation as terrorism. Unfortunately, the Palestinian Authority never quite seized the moment to seriously address and put an end to suicide bombings, which has allowed Israel to blur the line between suicide bombings and legitimate acts of resistance. Consequently, the Palestinian Authority was increasingly viewed by the U.S. administration as condoning terrorism. We repeatedly raised this issue with Arafat, to no avail.

The Americans' initial plan to outline their position on the Arab-Israeli conflict in a speech addressing the UN General Assembly, which had been due to start days after September 11, was thus postponed.

King Abdullah II's meeting with President Bush was rescheduled and took place on September 28, 2001. During their meeting, the king expressed his strong support for the fight against terrorism and Jordan's sympathy for all the victims and their families on that terrible day. The conversation then turned to the peace process. President Bush clearly stated his commitment to UN Resolutions 242 and 338. He even went so far as to criticize Sharon's attempts to evade further peace talks, telling the king: "Sharon told me he would go after Arafat while I go after Bin Laden. I said, 'No.'"[4]

At that point, what remained of the American focus on the peace process concentrated on implementing the recommendations of the Tenet Plan, which dealt mainly with security, and the Mitchell Report, which included confidence-building measures and a freeze on settlement activity. Both lacked any reasonable or serious plan to push the political process forward or to provide a political horizon for the Palestinians that would facilitate such an effort. The United States still favored the incremental approach. In any event, a strike against Al-Qaeda in Afghanistan eclipsed all other concerns in the U.S. administration.

The administration also felt at that point that Arafat was showing more seriousness in preventing the radical Palestinian groups from carrying out suicide bombing operations. We saw eye to eye with that assessment, and King Abdullah II asked Bush to encourage Israel to reciprocate Palestinian efforts to end the violence. The king stressed that Israel also needed to be forthcoming if the process was to move forward.

The Bush administration faced competing pressures at that time. King Abdullah II, other Arab leaders, and Prime Minister Tony Blair urged the U.S. administration to move the peace process forward. Meanwhile, the Israeli government and the pro-Israel lobby in Washington were campaigning against the inclusion of any Arab state in any international coalition against terrorism and arguing that any U.S. engagement in the peace process would be tantamount to "rewarding" terrorism. AIPAC (the American Israel Public Affairs Committee), the powerful American-Jewish lobbyist organization in Washington, was particularly active during this period in advancing this argument.

This all resulted in the U.S. administration's clear reluctance to engage. I had many discussions with U.S. officials during this period, urging them to announce their policy on the Middle East.[5] Only after many rancorous internal discussions within the administration did Secretary of State Colin Powell deliver his long-awaited speech at the University of Louisville in Kentucky on November 19, 2001. Powell was firm about Palestinians' need to address the security issue before moving to the next phase, particularly after the assassination of Israeli tourism minister Rahavam Ze'evi, who had been killed the previous month by a radical Palestinian group. (The assassination of Ze'evi followed Israel's assassination of the leader of the Popular Front for the Liberation of Palestine, or PFLP.) But Powell did refer—for the first time—to ending the occupation and stopping settlement activity. All previous administrations had danced around the edges of this issue, labeling settlements as an "obstruction to peace" and "unhelpful," but had never so clearly called for a halt to this clearly illegal activity. It was for us the first signal that the U.S. administration had finally begun to realize that the Palestinians needed a political horizon. Yet a trip to the region by Assistant Secretary of State William Burns and retired general Anthony Zinni almost a month later to seek agreement between the two parties on a security

plan and plan the next phase accomplished little. Against this background, violence persisted unchecked.

By the end of the 2001, the situation looked bleak. Arafat's credibility was at an all-time low in Washington, and security considerations still
dominated the Bush administration's thinking. Without progress in the
security situation, officials were reluctant to discuss political steps. In
any event, the war on terror was still the administration's number one
priority, and it was quietly starting to contemplate a move against Iraq.[6]

On November 28, *New York Times* columnist and former Middle
East correspondent Tom Friedman, a close friend, joined me for break-
fast at the Hay Adams Hotel in Washington. I discussed with him the
idea King Hussein had entertained in 1998 to have Arab states offer collective peace and security guarantees to Israel in return for total withdrawal for all Arab occupied land and a solution to the refugee problem.
I also told him about King Abdullah II's letter to President Bush on September 8. Tom was intrigued and clearly interested. Three months later,
he would play a key role in announcing to the world a similar effort by
Crown Prince Abdullah of Saudi Arabia, much to my pleasant surprise.

FOREIGN MINISTER

Several weeks later, I was having lunch at a Washington restaurant with
my wife, Lynne, and some family relatives who were visiting from Amman when my mobile telephone rang. The prime minister was on the
line, asking me to become the foreign minister in his new government.
I was so taken aback that I was only able to tell my wife about this development three hours later. Another new era had begun for me.

By the time I assumed the foreign ministry portfolio in January
2002, the situation in the occupied territories was grave. Arafat had
been under siege in his half-destroyed headquarters in Ramallah since
December 3, 2001, and Israel was rigorously pursuing its policy of "targeted" assassinations. The Israeli army had attacked and killed several
Palestinian leaders with missiles or helicopter attacks, often unapologet-
ically killing scores of innocent people in the process. Suicide bombings
were also nearly routine.

In short, the security situation was disastrous. Adding to the tensions,
on January 3, 2002, Israel seized the *Karin A,* a Palestinian ship that was

carrying arms from Iran and attempting to smuggle them into the Palestinian territories. Israel fingered the Palestinian Authority and demanded that Arafat hand over the Palestinian officials suspected of organizing the operation. It quickly became evident that Arafat had known of the operation and approved it, which further eroded his credibility with the Americans. Days later, he arrested three Palestinian officials accused by Israel of having masterminded the affair.

I had been back in Amman for just a few days when I accompanied King Abdullah II to Washington on a scheduled visit. We found the Americans in a somber mood. During the king's meeting with Secretary of State Powell on January 31, 2002, Powell expressed Americas' disappointment in Arafat's inability to rein in those elements that planned suicide bombings. Powell felt that the weapons-smuggling incident had killed the momentum that had been building since his Louisville speech and Zinni's subsequent efforts. He maintained that the United States was also talking to the Israeli side about its policy of targeted assassinations and the demolition of houses belonging to relatives of suicide bombers. The king repeated Jordan's position that the Palestinians needed a political horizon that would give them hope and that a detailed plan that specified both sides' security obligations was required. The monarch also said that Egypt, Saudi Arabia, and Jordan were ready to help adopt a moderate position during the upcoming Arab summit but that they needed something to work with. He also stressed the importance of Israel allowing Arafat to attend the summit and return to Ramallah afterward. Israel was already making an issue of this and was not willing to guarantee Arafat's return to the West Bank should he choose to leave Ramallah.

During King Abdullah II's meeting with President Bush the next day, Bush expressed anger with Arafat over the *Karin A* incident and said that he wanted to exert pressure on Arafat to rein in the extremist elements in the West Bank and Gaza. The president plainly had been persuaded by Israel's argument that its war against the Palestinians was part and parcel of the global war against terror. "We can't be hypocrites about terror," Bush told the king. "Terror is terror. I have a vision which goes beyond Afghanistan. We have to react to it consistently."[7] The monarch felt that he made headway with the president only in convincing him to show public empathy for the plight of the Palestinian people.

We left with a clear understanding of Washington's bottom line: if the Bush administration was to engage seriously in the peace process, Arafat needed to take demonstrable measures to curb suicide bombings. It was also obvious that despite the flagrancy with which Israel violated international law with its policies of targeted assassinations and house demolitions, Bush was starting to view the Palestinians as a source of terrorism rather than as a people living under the boot of occupation and resisting it in hopes of eventual freedom. The situation was sliding into chaos and destruction.

CROWN PRINCE ABDULLAH'S PEACE PROPOSAL

Several weeks after Tom Friedman and I had discussed the king's idea of collective peace and security guarantees for Israel in return for total withdrawal for all Arab occupied land and a solution to the refugee problem, Friedman published a column on February 6, suggesting that the twenty-two members of the Arab League offer Israel full diplomatic relations, normalized trade, and security guarantees in return for Israel's total withdrawal to the June 4, 1967, lines. Days later, the *New York Times* published an interview by Friedman with Crown Prince Abdullah of Saudi Arabia, during which Friedman had presented the idea to the crown prince. Abdullah reacted with astonishment, mockingly accusing Friedman of "having broken into [his] desk." The crown prince said Saudi Arabia had been considering a scheme in which the Saudi kingdom would consider normalizing with Israel and persuading the Arab world to do likewise if Israel would reciprocate with a full withdrawal from the occupied territories. "Full withdrawal for full normalization of relations," is how he framed it.[8]

I was elated. A "major" Arab state was in sync with Jordanian thinking on the key regional issue. We had initially sought to encourage Egypt, the largest Arab country, to take the lead on this initiative. But Saudi Arabia brought another important credential to the table: if, as the leader of the Muslim world, Saudi Arabia took the lead in offering collective peace with Israel in return for full withdrawal and a Palestinian state, the chances that the whole Arab world and most of the Islamic world would follow suit would be greatly enhanced. I spoke immediately with the king, and we agreed that Jordan would not only welcome the initiative but champion it.

Thus, the Jordanian public reaction was swift. The foreign ministry issued a statement to the Jordan News Agency, Petra, on February 20, putting forth the country's position: "The ideas of Crown Prince Abdullah are very positive, and we hope they will contribute to breaking the stalemate in the peace process. The Saudi proposal represents a clear political vision for solving the Arab-Israeli conflict in a manner that would serve all parties. On the one hand, it calls on Israel to withdraw from the occupied lands in the West Bank, the Golan Heights and the Lebanese lands, and on the other hand it guarantees the security of all the region's countries, including Israel."[9]

MY FIRST VISIT TO ARAFAT

I paid my first visit as foreign minister to Arafat in his besieged headquarters in Ramallah on February 19. We felt it was important to relay to Arafat what we had heard from President Bush and what we believed was needed to move forward.

I made the trip by a Jordanian army helicopter—a twenty-five-minute flight from Amman to Ramallah. The view from the air of the West Bank was devastating: everywhere I looked there was destruction. I was even more frustrated at having been delivered to Arafat's headquarters by an Israeli army convoy. The streets leading to Ramallah were all dirt, the asphalt having been ripped up by Israeli tanks. I could not help but remember my earlier visits to Ramallah when I was ambassador to Israel, visiting friends or relatives of my wife or taking my son to eat ice cream at a popular hangout. The streets then were bustling with people, an indication of the optimism that had initially accompanied the peace process, which had offered hope and brought some relief to Palestinians living under occupation for far too long. In 2002, the streets were deserted. Ramallah had become a ghost town. It was a truly painful sight and left a strong impression on me.

Arafat was notorious for putting on a public show in front of others, and true to form, during my expanded meeting with him, which included several Palestinian officials, he said nothing of substance. He would repeat this practice later. Arafat tended to be more focused in private meetings, however, and in our one-on-one meeting, I candidly told him that he had a tremendous credibility problem with the Americans. I explained to him that Bush was not like President Clinton: he had no facility for nuance and instead tended to see things in black and white. I emphasized that he needed to rebuild his credibility with the Americans—by arresting those responsible for the *Karin A* incident, by being consistent in his public statements, and by arresting Ze'evi's assassins—before the United States would help him with the Israelis. I added that he was running short on friends in the U.S. administration—that the one person willing to give him the benefit of the doubt, Secretary Powell, would lose faith if Arafat failed to deliver. Arafat was long on understanding and willingness to move on all these issues but terribly short on practical details to make those things happen.

Crown Prince Abdullah had told visiting EU High Commissioner Javier Solana that he intended to present the initiative at the Arab Summit in Beirut. This transformed the ballgame. The Saudi thinking had been that the idea should be kept simple. Too many details could rob it of its power. Now that the initiative was public knowledge in the Arab sphere, the struggle would commence with Arab states that would either insist on loading the initiative with many details, such as Syria and Lebanon were likely to do, or reject the whole concept of collective peace, likely to be the stance of Libya and Iraq. King Abdullah II decided that Jordan should immediately start consultations with as many Arab countries as possible to achieve consensus.

The king met with Solana and the EU special envoy on the Middle East, Miguel Moratinos, on February 28, just after Moratinos had visited Egypt and Saudi Arabia. Solana told us that the Saudis were now thinking of drafting a simple text and presenting it to the Arab Summit for endorsement. He also said he thought the Egyptians were now on board, after displaying an initial lack of enthusiasm, in large part because they had not initiated the idea.[10]

PREPARATIONS FOR THE SUMMIT

If we—Jordan, Saudi Arabia, and Egypt—could get the Palestinians on board, then we would constitute a solid block of Arab support for the initiative ahead of the Arab Summit. The king and the prime minister instructed me to work toward that objective.

On March 2, Sa'eb Ereikat, the Palestinian head negotiator and a confidant of Arafat, arrived in Amman, where we both jointly announced Jordan and the Palestinian Authority's support for the initiative. Momentum was building when on the second day Syrian president Bashar al-Assad gave a statement in Lebanon that was implicitly critical of the initiative. Assad stated that regional peace must be based on all UN Security Council Resolutions and must rest on UN General Assembly Resolutions 194, 242, 338, and 425 (regarding Lebanon).

So we turned our attention to Syria. Prime Minister Ali Abu Ragheb and I traveled there two days later to see the Syrian president in Aleppo. President Assad said he had three points of concern:

1. Syria did not feel comfortable with the term "full normalization." Instead, Assad wanted to use the word "normal relations."
2. Syria wanted to make sure that full withdrawal to pre–June 4, 1967, lines was guaranteed. This, of course, was a longstanding Syrian demand, one that led to the collapse of the negotiations with Israel during Clinton's term when Israel wanted to retain a few yards along Lake Tiberias to prevent the Syrians from laying any claims to the lake's waters.
3. Syria also insisted that the right of return had to be explicitly mentioned, mostly in solidarity with the Lebanese, who were—and remain—adamantly opposed to the resettlement of any Palestinian refugees on Lebanese territory for fear that refugee resettlement would upset the country's delicate sectarian balance.

Assad said he would travel to Saudi Arabia to seek clarifications on these points before Syria took an official position regarding the initiative. In general, we felt that the meeting was positive and that Assad was flexible. I generally found Assad to be always more reasonable in private. Even while delivering the Syrian "party line" on issues, he generally did so in a mild manner, and he listened to opposing arguments with attentiveness and a desire to understand other points of view. His apparent habit of pontificating in public was abandoned in private settings, especially when other Syrian officials were not present. Still, my impression of him is that he lacked informed analyses of the various positions in the international community, particularly the United States, and, despite having lived in Great Britain for two years, did not often display an informed exposure to the outside world.

In spite of the Syrian reservations, momentum did start to build toward a collective endorsement of the initiative. I phoned Prince Saud after we returned from Syria and briefed him on the Syrian position. We agreed to meet in Cairo on the sidelines of an Arab foreign ministers preparatory meeting so that other Arab countries could agree on the text. I also phoned Sa'eb Ereikat and briefed him on our efforts.

King Abdullah II visited Bahrain and the United Arab Emirates on March 5. Their support was immediately forthcoming, and shortly after that, President Assad announced his support for the crown prince's idea.

In spite of Assad's announcement, Arab League secretary-general Amr Moussa remained concerned about the position of the Syrian foreign minister, Farouq Sharaa, as well as that of Libya. He had visited Libya and found Muammar Qaddafi opposed to giving Israel security guarantees and to normalization with Israel. We agreed to sit down in Cairo and try to come up with a text that would be acceptable to Libya but still be new and, perhaps more important, acceptable to Israel and the international community. Without comprehensive acceptance, the effort would be meaningless.

Mindful of American and Israeli thinking, and wanting to present a simple and powerful formulation that would capture the needs of all parties, I thought the best approach would be to write the initiative in English; that is, with the international community in mind. I thus attempted such a formulation ahead of the Cairo meeting. The offer had to have the following major components, expressed in the simplest terms possible:

1. Full Israeli withdrawal from all Arab land to the 1967 borders.
2. Full normalization with Israel by all Arab states
3. Security guarantees for all states of the region, including Israel.
4. A solution to the refugee problem that would preserve Palestinian rights while not scaring Israel into thinking that the Arab world was insisting that four million Palestinians would return to the Jewish state.
5. A clause ending the conflict, which I felt would be central to assuring Israelis that once a Palestinian state was established and the refugee problem was solved, there would be no further claims by any party. This was mostly meant to assure Israelis that Palestinians would not make future claims on any part of pre-1948 Palestine once a treaty was signed.

I drafted a resolution in English containing all these points. Finding language on the point about refugees that would be acceptable to all was a struggle, however. United Nations General Assembly Resolution 194 states: "Refugees wishing to return to their homes and live at peace with their neighbors should be permitted to do so at the earliest practicable date, and that compensation should be paid for the property of those choosing not to return," effectively requiring return and/or compensation to the Palestinian refuges. However, even though the vast majority of Palestinians are not likely to want to return to a culture and country that is no longer theirs, judging by the results of all polls on this issue, any mention of Resolution 194 or the right of return might give the impression that Arabs still insisted on the return of *all* refugees to Israel. This would kill the initiative.

I tried to summarize the positions of all concerned. The Palestinians understood the impracticality of all refugees returning and wanted those who wished to do so to return predominantly to the new Palestinian state in the West Bank and Gaza. Yet they still wanted to preserve the right of return, even if in principle, coupled with a nominal return of several thousand Palestinians to Israel proper. The right of return remains a big psychological factor among Palestinian refugees, especially among those generations who were literally driven off their land and who want to bring fifty years of suffering to a close. Even if they understand how impractical the exercise of this right may be or indeed may not wish to exercise their right, they do not wish to surrender it, particularly before an overall settlement to the conflict is achieved.

Israelis, on the other hand, fear that the right of return is a conspiracy to destroy the Jewish character of the state—and thus the state itself—by introducing four million Palestinians to Israel, a country of five and a half million people, more than a million of whom already are Arabs. Both publics have dealt—and continue to deal—with this issue from a purely emotional perspective instead of seeking rational solutions that would satisfy the needs of two peoples.

Additionally, Arab countries such as Lebanon, which hosts anywhere between two hundred thousand and four hundred thousand Palestinian refugees living in camps with no citizenship and limited working rights, understand Resolution 194 to mean the full return of all Palestinian refugees in Lebanon. They want the refugees to leave, even if they choose compensation over return. The Lebanese argument is that the refugees, mostly Sunni Muslims, would disrupt a delicate balance that exists among the different religious sects in the country: Sunnis, Shiites, Druze, Maronites, Greek Orthodox, and several other smaller denominations.

In the last round of peace negotiations in Taba, a number of practical solutions were tabled: an unlimited exercise of the right of return in the new Palestinian state; a symbolic return to Israel proper, largely for family reunification purposes; compensation for all refugees; citizenship in refugees' countries of residence; repatriation to third countries; and return to those lands that might be swapped with Israel in any final agreement.

Any formulation would have to satisfy all these different concerns. Since the solution needed an agreement among all sides for it to be acceptable, and since negotiations on this issue made significant progress on reaching such an agreement, I believed a formulation along the lines of "an agreed solution to the refugee problem consistent with UN resolutions and the sovereignty of all states concerned" should satisfy all. The word "agreed" would assure Israel that refugees would not return in numbers enough to affect the demographic nature of the Jewish state, while the reference to UN resolutions would satisfy the Arab side. The reference to the sovereignty of all states concerned would satisfy both.

Prince Saud confirmed to me in a phone call on March 6 that the right of return was a sovereign Palestinian decision and added that he was still trying to persuade the Libyans to change their minds. The Egyptian foreign minister, Ahmad Maher, said the Saudis had not approached him yet, but he was ready to sit down on March 8 with all of us and work on a draft.

Prince Saud is an impressive man by any standard. A graduate of Princeton University, he is well versed in English and French. He has a habit of quoting Shakespeare by heart and is extremely witty. He had been Saudi Arabia's foreign minister since 1975. Vast experience and a princely but humble demeanor have made him the doyen of Arab foreign ministers. When Prince Saud speaks, other Arab foreign ministers listen. He used his status and his lineage (the son of King Faisal, a very popular man in the Arab world) to build Arab consensus on any issue debated. In contrast, I was the newest addition to the Arab foreign ministers' club and to Arab politics in general. When we met on March 8 in his suite for an introductory meeting, I liked him immediately. His humility and sharpness of mind impressed me.

I was honored by his words welcoming me to the club: he said that my appointment represented a qualitative addition to the foreign ministers' club with my knowledge of the peace process and my exposure to the West. A very close working relationship would develop between us over the next three years. Prince Saud had already worked on a draft for discussion with a few Arab ministers. I showed him my draft, but his view was that the initiative needed to be written in Arabic. Although I understood his motives for writing an Arab plan in Arabic, I believe to this day that the proposal's impact would have been significantly greater had it been written in simple, plain English rather than being translated into English from the flowery language of Arabic. At any rate, Saud liked the idea about having the word "agreed" in the formulation on refugees and immediately adopted it.

Farouq Sharaa discussed Syria's concerns and wanted to change "full normalization" to "full peace." Saud agreed. Although the foreign ministers of the key countries had talked about the final text, no formal discussions had been held. A formal discussion had been postponed until a meeting of the Arab foreign ministers in Beirut just before the summit. But the general outline of the initiative was being crystallized, and we continued to work to build consensus.

On March 11, I accompanied King Abdullah II to Damascus to see President Assad and found him more relaxed about the initiative. He reiterated Syria's support for the effort on that day. A day later, Vice President Dick Cheney came to Jordan, one stop in a tour of several Middle East countries to talk about Iraq. He found that everyone's focus was on the Middle East peace process. That day, Israel launched the largest military offensive against the Palestinians in the West Bank since 1967, killing thirty Palestinians in one day.

Also on March 12, the United Nations passed Security Council Resolution 1397, drafted by the United States, supporting for the first time the establishment of a Palestinian state. Syria, then a Security Council member, abstained on the grounds that the resolution demanded "the immediate cessation of all acts of violence, including acts of terror, provocation, incitement and destruction," without referring to Israel as one of the perpetrators of violence.

Prime Minister Abu Ragheb and I traveled to Saudi Arabia and Egypt for final consultations with Crown Prince Abdullah and President Mubarak ahead of the Beirut Summit. Mubarak was still piqued that the initiative had not come from Egypt but lent his lukewarm support.

Meanwhile, we in Jordan were pushing the Americans for a strong endorsement of the initiative once it was formally endorsed in Beirut. The Americans were weary of the thorny details that they feared would "weaken" the initiative in their judgment so would only commit to "a strong endorsement of the initiative as a basis for negotiation, not implementation."[11] Their two major worries were the clauses on "full withdrawal" and on refugees, which were not finalized yet.

MY FIRST TRIP TO LEBANON SINCE COLLEGE

Against this string of successes, it was becoming obvious that the Lebanese position, which exceeded the demands of UN Resolution 194, would threaten the initiative. Instead of remaining a simple, powerful statement that could break the impasse, the initiative was getting bogged down in details that addressed Lebanon's problems rather than those of the Palestinians. King Abdullah II sent me to Beirut on March 20, three days ahead of the Arab foreign ministers meeting, to talk to President Émile Lahoud, firmly in the Syrian camp, and Prime Minister Rafiq Hariri to see if their position would be swayed.

This was my first visit to Lebanon since I had been a student there thirty years earlier, at the American University of Beirut (AUB). I had left Beirut in 1976 during the height of the civil war and had not returned since but for a brief visit in 1977. I had spent four years in Beirut as a student, and my return after so many years induced a wave of nostalgia.

I had arrived in Beirut only the night before my meetings but decided I could not pass up the opportunity to pay a visit to my alma mater. So I woke up early, slipped past my security detail, and headed for the university. When I explained to the guard at the gate that I had been an AUB student and was now the foreign minister of Jordan, he promptly let me through AUB's main gate. As I passed, I glanced at the inscription on the gate, from John 10:10, which every AUB student knows by heart, "That they may have life, and have it more abundantly."

For an hour, I devoured every sight of the campus I had lived on and loved. Beirut had changed a lot since the 1970s. The downtown area, which had been completely ravaged by the war, was almost totally rebuilt by Hariri. But the university campus had not changed much. Even my old mailbox, now of course belonging to another student, was still there. I remembered its number and location, and once I got there, I stood in front of it for a few minutes and traveled back to a time when I was a carefree student and the mailbox was my lifeline to family and friends at home in Amman.

AUB represents the best of what America can offer in our region. Contrary to the hostility most Arabs feel toward American policies in the region regarding the Arab-Israeli conflict, the American University of Beirut is highly regarded. It has offered first-class education for the region since it was established in 1866 by American Protestant preachers. Its emphasis on critical thinking and on the dangers of subscribing to an absolute truth made it a rare institution in the Arab world. Many of the region's top politicians, economists, business leaders, and writers are AUB graduates, and all feel a special bond to it. It is no coincidence, therefore, that despite all the destruction the civil war had brought on Beirut, the AUB campus was left largely intact by all warring factions.

I returned to the hotel an hour later to find our ambassador in Lebanon frantically searching for me. After I calmed him down, we headed to meet the Lebanese foreign minister, Mahmoud Hammoud, who accompanied me to meet President Lahoud. Lahoud had adopted an inflexible position on the refugee issue and was not receptive to any arguments. He was also backed by Syria, which had exercised heavy influence on Lebanon's politics since 1976, when the Syrian army entered the country to help end the civil war there. Syria's intelligence services, operating freely and openly in the country, made sure Lebanon's policies were in line with its own hard-line stands on regional issues. From that meeting, I went into a working lunch with Prime Minister Hariri, Hammoud, and several other Lebanese officials at Hariri's house. Again I tried to explain why the Lebanese position on refugees exceeded the requirements of Resolution 194 and why insisting on such a position would undermine the initiative. Hariri would not budge. He stuck to the position I heard earlier from Lahoud. Once we finished lunch, Hariri, a very warm and personable man, asked me to take a cup of coffee with him on the balcony. Once we were alone, he turned to me and said, "Please tell His Majesty that I understand where he is coming from, but my hands are tied by an unreasonable president." The encounter was a sad commentary on Lebanon's situation: the prime minister could speak frankly only in a private encounter out of fear that others, particularly the Syrian intelligence, might hear.

DELIBERATIONS ON FORMULATION

In spite of that apparent setback, we were determined that the Saudi initiative should succeed. If we did not capitalize on the momentum, we might never have another chance to break the stalemate. Starting on March 24, a small group of Arab ministers started discussions on a final text that would be acceptable to all. It was not going to be easy. The regional atmosphere was tense. Israel was essentially refusing to let Arafat leave Ramallah to attend the session by refusing to guarantee that it would facilitate his return to the Palestinian territories. Libya had taken a firm stand against the initiative, and Syria and Lebanon were insisting on loading it with details that might kill it. Iraq was also against the initiative but wanted to appease the Arab world as it braced for a showdown with the United States over American accusations that it was concealing weapons of mass destruction. The rest of the Arab countries had no strong position on the formulation but supported the initiative. Jordan, Egypt, Saudi Arabia, the Gulf States, Tunisia, and Morocco formed a solid block that wanted to keep the formulation simple and general, defining the overall framework for a settlement while leaving the details for later.

The Syrians set up the first hurdle. Foreign Minister Farouq Sharaa entered the meeting with a new demand: Syria was no longer satisfied with the phrase "full peace" and instead wanted to replace it with "normal peaceful relations." Prince Saud, obviously increasingly frustrated by the Syrian position, agreed. The first hurdle had been passed.

The foreign ministers' preparatory meeting was my first encounter with Sharaa. Different in every aspect, we were destined to clash early on. Sharaa was a product of the doctrine of the Syrian Arab Socialist Baath Party, which translated Arab nationalism into a walled ideology instead of following a policy of political inclusion. This doctrine adopted a rigid approach to diplomacy and assumed positions that were stuck in

the Cold War era rather than adapting to the current geopolitical realities. Further, it also believed that Syria was the heartland and patron of
the Arab world and as such was deserving of the fealty of other Arab
states. Despite his tenure as Syria's ambassador to Italy from 1976 to
1980, Sharaa displayed no serious understanding of the outside world
and acted as if Syria was at the center of all issues. His personal character did not help either; he was often sour and seldom smiled. If he had a
sense of humor, I was not privy to it. In addition, our two countries had
very different approaches to the peace process, methods that were
largely reflected in our two personalities.

Since everyone agreed that in return for peace, Israel must fully withdraw from all occupied Arab territories to pre–June 1967 lines, that
clause faced no opposition. The Palestinians understood that it mainly
applied to the Syrian case, as their own negotiations with Israel had already come close to a territorial agreement, with minor modifications to
the 1967 line necessitated by the presence of large settlement blocks on
the green line dividing Israel from the West Bank. Still, that clause was
important to emphasize the point that any modifications to the 1967
border should be minor and reciprocal, even though the initiative itself
did not address that point in detail.

The only major sticking point was the refugee issue. Two operative
paragraphs listed both Israel and the Arab states' obligations:

Israel's obligations
2. Further calls upon Israel to affirm:
Full Israeli withdrawal from all the territories occupied since
1967, including the Syrian Golan Heights to the lines of June
4, 1967, as well as the remaining occupied Lebanese territories
in the south of Lebanon.
   i. Achievement of a just solution to the Palestinian
     refugee problem to be agreed upon in accordance with
     UN General Assembly Resolution 194.
   ii. The acceptance of the establishment of a Sovereign In-
     dependent Palestinian State on the Palestinian territo-
     ries occupied since June 5, 1967, in the West Bank and
     Gaza Strip, with East Jerusalem as its capital.

Arab States' obligations
3. Consequently, the Arab Countries affirm the following:
    i. Consider the Arab-Israeli conflict ended, and enter into
      a peace agreement with Israel, and provide security for
      all states of the region.
    ii. Establish normal relations with Israel in the context of
      this comprehensive peace.

Lebanon, wanting to emphasize its wish that all Palestinian refugees living in the country would leave or that it not be forced into granting the refugees Lebanese citizenship, wanted to add a subclause in paragraph 2 that would "award special attention to Lebanon's position which rejects Palestinian patriation (*tawteen*) in accordance with its constitution."

The problem with this formulation, everyone tried to explain to the Lebanese, was that it fell under paragraph 2, which dealt with *Israel's* obligations. It imposed a legal burden on Israel that exceeded the requirements of international law by asking it to guarantee that the refugees would not be awarded Lebanese citizenship or would not be allowed to stay in Lebanon even if they chose compensation over return.

Several of us tried, in vain, to explain that this is not an Israeli obligation and that its inclusion would give the impression that Arabs would not accept anything short of the full return of all refugees to Israel— which would make the initiative a total nonstarter for the Israelis and which was, in any case, not the Arab objective. I also told Prince Saud that refugees in Lebanon should not be given any preferential treatment. It would be difficult for any refugee host state, including Jordan, to justify preferential treatment of the refugees in Lebanon.

"We have not accepted compensation, and we never will. We are speaking about the right of return of refugees, and not compensation," declared Ghazi Aridi, Lebanon's minister of information, in a deliberate misinterpretation of Resolution 194.[11]

The Arab summit opened on March 27 with no agreement on a draft. Several Arab leaders, including President Mubarak and King Abdullah II, were unable to attend due to security considerations. Israel obstructed Arafat's participation by vetoing his return to Ramallah. To add insult to injury, the Lebanese would not allow Arafat to address the summit via live satellite on the feeble excuse that the requisite technical co-operation with the Israeli authorities would constitute an act of normalization while the two countries remained officially in a state of war.

Yet we needed to keep the momentum going. In a statement to the press, I argued that Jordan still felt that "the initiative should be kept at a general level to provide a general framework and not a detailed peace plan. The strength of the proposal lies in its simplicity."[12]

Crown Prince Abdullah addressed the summit's opening session with a bold speech in which he acknowledged the right of the Israeli people to live in peace and security, along with all other peoples of the region. He called for normal relations among all countries of the region, a solution to the refugee problem, and the establishment of a Palestinian state with Al-Quds Al-Shareef (East Jerusalem) as its capital. He proposed an initiative to be submitted by the Arab League to the UN Security Council containing all these points. "What I am proposing," he said, "is normal relations and security for Israel in return for a Palestinian state, withdrawal from all Arab lands and a solution to the refugee problem for Arabs." For the first time a Saudi official addressed the Israeli public directly. "I would further say to the Israeli people that if their government abandons the policy of force and oppression, and embraces true peace, we will not hesitate to accept the right of the Israeli people to live in security with the people of the region."[13]

Despite his old age (he is reported to be in his eighties), Crown Prince Abdullah spoke with a vigor of a much younger man. Although he had no formal education, he displays an understanding of world affairs apparently acquired through experience. He speaks in short but pointed sentences. He exudes honesty and wisdom and has all the characteristics of a true Bedouin: simplicity of nature and warmth of heart.

King Abdullah II, in a speech read on his behalf, appealed to the summit to endorse the Saudi initiative, which "constitutes a primary foundation for achieving comprehensive peace in the region."[14]

Assad answered with a speech in which he stated that peace had several components: water, security arrangements, and a region free of weapons of mass destruction. All of these issues should be negotiated, but negotiations over land were unacceptable, he maintained. He was obviously less concerned with visions that might break the stalemate and more focused on the details of any peace agreement that might be struck with Syria. Still, he was essentially endorsing the initiative, although without much enthusiasm.

The Libyans, in a delegation headed by their foreign minister, objected to the idea of the whole Arab world committing to normal relations with Israel, saying that this should be limited to those Arab states having territorial conflicts with the Jewish state, while the Iraqi delegation, headed by Vice President Izzat Al-Douri, made a similar argument but was clearly more interested in Iraq's particular situation. Douri's opposition was uncharacteristically mild, with insinuations that Iraq was ready to go with the Arab consensus.

The opening session ended with the decision to form a committee of Arab ministers to reach agreement on a draft. This consisted of foreign ministers of Arab states neighboring Israel (Jordan, Syria, Lebanon, Egypt, the Palestinian Authority), along with Saudi Arabia, Morocco, and the Arab League secretary-general.

On the day of the opening session, a suicide bomber blew himself up in the dining room of a seaside hotel in Israel, killing twenty people. It was clear that the extremist forces in the Palestinian camp and probably beyond were not happy with events in Beirut. It was also the worst timing possible from the point of view of the moderates who were trying hard to end the Israeli occupation through peaceful means.

THE MEETING WITH JAMIL EL-SAYYED

The draft committee labored over different formulations that would satisfy Lebanon's demands without weakening the initiative, but to no avail. Lengthy discussions with the Lebanese foreign minister to explain why Lebanon's demands about the Palestinian refugees' future status could not be included under Israel's obligations were unproductive. He would not move an inch. Finally, our ambassador in Lebanon approached me. "You are dialing a wrong number," he said. "You need to talk to Jamil El-Sayyed, the director of the public security department, and the strong man in the Lebanese regime." I asked the ambassador to try to arrange for me to sit next to El-Sayyed at a dinner Lahoud was hosting for all the delegations.

He did. I met El-Sayyed for the first time then. He was a few years older than me, very articulate, and mild-mannered, and did not fit the image of a tough security official. El-Sayyed would later be arrested in

2005 together with three other senior Lebanese officials over the killing of Prime Minister Hariri. We got down to business immediately. El-Sayyed had obviously studied the draft: he knew its every detail. He had an acute political intuition, and I immediately knew he was the man with whom business must be done. For two hours, we argued about the sticking point on refugees. I finally had an idea. I asked him if he cared whether the guarantee that Lebanon would not be imposed upon to grant the refugees citizenship was an obligation for Israel, Arabs, or the international community. He said Lebanon was not concerned about whose obligation it was, only that it was acknowledged that Lebanon would not grant refugees citizenship. I then suggested to him that we make that subclause an article in its own right, separate from Israeli and Arab obligations, that distributed this obligation to the international community once detailed arrangements on refugees were addressed as part of any final settlement for the Arab-Israeli conflict. He agreed.

I went to bed feeling relieved that I had been able to avert a catastrophe and produce a forthcoming document that for the first time addressed both publics' needs: Arabs and Israelis. The stage was set for the second and final day of the summit.

I went down from my room at about 9:30 a.m. on Thursday, March 28, full of optimism, but it quickly drained away. I entered the venue to find Lebanese president Lahoud, Lebanese foreign minister Hammoud, and Amr Mousa arguing heatedly. Lahoud was shouting at Hammoud that he had sworn to uphold the constitution and would neither change his mind nor compromise on the refugee issue.

I left the room only to discover El-Sayyed standing outside. When I told him I thought we had had an agreement the day before, he answered casually, "We did." "So how come your president is shouting at your foreign minister?" I fumed. El-Sayyed told me he had had no time to see the president since our conversation the night before and asked me to give him fifteen minutes. He entered the room while I waited outside. A few minutes later, he emerged. "The deal is closed. The president has accepted your formulation," he said matter-of-factly.

The biggest obstacle had been removed. The closing session was delayed for an hour to make sure that the Lebanese had approved the final draft. The final formulation of paragraph 4 read: "Assures the rejection of all forms of Palestinian patriation which conflict with the special circumstances of the Arab host countries." The word "Lebanon" was replaced by "host countries" on Jordan's insistence that refugees in Lebanon should not be given special status.

Libya and Iraq tried to raise reservations in the closing session regarding the whole concept. Crown Prince Abdullah, visibly upset, asked for a vote. If the initiative was not going to be passed unanimously, then let a vote decide it, he argued. This time, no one dared oppose it. At around 1:00 p.m. on Thursday, the Arab Peace Initiative was formally and unanimously passed, and the session came to a successful and historic close. The summit also reached agreement on a nonaggression accord between Iraq and Kuwait.

To this day, I feel that the official English translation of the Arab Peace Initiative did not do it justice (the text of the initiative is reproduced in Appendix 4). For the first time since the beginning of the Arab-Israeli conflict, Arab states came up with a *collective, proactive* effort to solve the conflict by addressing not only their needs but also the needs of Israelis. Specifically, in return for Israel accepting to withdraw fully from Arab lands occupied in 1967, the achievement of a just and agreed solution to the refugee problem, and the establishment of a sovereign, independent Palestinian state on the Palestinian territories occupied since June 4, 1967, in the West Bank and Gaza, with East Jerusalem as its capital, Arab states committed themselves to:

A collective offer to end the conflict with Israel. As a former ambassador to Israel, I witnessed firsthand the importance of this clause to the average Israeli, who remains concerned that Palestinians or Arab states might make further claims on Israel or its territory even after Israel withdraws to its pre-1967 borders and a solution is reached to the refugee problem.

Security guarantees for all states in the region, including Israel. This was a significant offer because for the first time, Israel had been assured that its security would be guaranteed not only by neighboring Arab states but by all Arab states.

A collective peace treaty and normal relations with Israel. This signaled full recognition of Israel and normal relations similar to those between an Arab state and any other state in the world.

An agreed solution to the refugee problem. For the first time, the Arab world committed itself to an agreed solution to the refugee problem, thus addressing Israel's concern that four million refugees would be sent to Israel. The initiative acknowledged that the solution needed to be an agreed one, based on a realistic application of UN Resolution 194.

But in the Middle East, nothing lasts for long. The elation many of us, including myself, felt at such a historic achievement was short-lived, and the plans to start marketing the initiative to the Israeli and Western publics were aborted almost immediately. Israel launched a major offensive into the West Bank on Friday, March 29, a day after the Arab Initiative was passed, invading and laying siege to Arafat's compound in Ramallah and arresting hundreds of Palestinians. One day later, another suicide bomber blew himself up in a Tel Aviv café, killing and wounding twenty-nine Israelis.

King Abdullah II called President Bush and urged him to take immediate action to end Israel's aggression and terminate the siege on Arafat. Saudi Crown Prince Abdullah said that Sharon had lost his mind, but the Arab Initiative would not be derailed. Amr Moussa gave a press statement saying that Arabs could not talk about a peace initiative that calls for normal relations with Israel while Israeli troops bombarded Arafat's headquarters. I summoned the Israeli ambassador to Amman on Sunday and, in an unprecedented move, warned him that Jordan would take "measures" related to its ties with Israel if Israel did not withdraw its troops from the West Bank. The optimism generated by the initiative had suddenly evaporated, and we were back to the drawing board.

CHAPTER FIVE

The Middle East Road Map

A month after the President's speech, King Abdullah of Jordan and his foreign minister, Marwan Muasher, went to Washington to plead with Bush to follow up his words with a plan. Condoleezza Rice, the National Security Adviser, rejected the idea. But in the Oval Office, King Abdullah and Muasher appealed directly to the President. The parties need a guide, Muasher told Bush, to reach the goals laid out in his speech. "Sounds like a good idea to me," Bush replied. Suddenly the road map was born.—James Carney, *Time*, June 9, 2003

THE SITUATION IN THE OCCUPIED territories was deteriorating rapidly. Israel pressed its offensive, occupying more West Bank towns and drawing a wave of international protests. Images of Israeli tanks in Bethlehem, Nablus, Ramallah, and Jenin and the continuing siege on Arafat's headquarters raised emotions in the Arab world to a boiling point.

The king wrote to President Bush on April 3, urging him to work for the withdrawal of Israeli troops from Palestinian cities and the implementation of the Tenet plan as a first step toward resuming negotiations: "We have been instrumental in building consensus for the Saudi initiative, which has been translated into a collective Arab commitment to end the conflict with Israel, guarantee its security and establish normal relations between all Arab states and Israel. Yet the actions of the Israeli government pose a serious threat to all the achievements we have jointly worked towards during the last ten years."

A day later, President Bush, in a White House speech, called for Israel to withdraw and stop its settlement activity. Reiterating U.S. support for a Palestinian state, he also announced that Powell would visit the region. The king had already dispatched me to Washington to meet with

Powell to see if we could reverse the security situation and move the two sides back to negotiations.

During that April 5 meeting, I told him that the Arab street was boiling. I emphasized that a political process, overall parameters, and a time frame to implement all the visions for a solution was needed; the incremental approach had lost credibility, and the time had come for an endgame within a specified timeline. This would be the first of many discussions with the U.S. administration on this issue and the birth of what later became known as the Road Map.

This was my first meeting with Powell as Jordan's foreign minister. Although I had met him when I was ambassador to the United States, this was the first time we sat down for a one-to-one conversation. Honest, personable, and modest, Powell always greeted visitors with warmth, and I immediately felt comfortable with him. He exuded confidence and appeared both knowledgeable and willing to listen. By the time we met that day, however, rumors had already begun to circulate that he was not exactly on the same wavelength as the White House, something his body language, choice of words, and arguments confirmed, though he never would have admitted it. As a consummate diplomat and a loyal soldier he kept his disagreements with others in the Bush administration to himself. I developed an immediate liking for him. He was someone Jordan could do business with, and that meeting started a strong working and personal relationship.

Powell argued that both he and the president had always viewed the Tenet and Mitchell plans as the way to move ahead. I acknowledged this but said that not enough had been done on an endgame within a specific time frame.

He was more interested in what Arab states could do to pressure Arafat, who he felt was saying one thing and doing another. I emphasized that Arab states would not pressure Arafat until they were convinced that the United States was serious about ending the conflict. Powell argued that until Arafat made the right choices regardless of the U.S. commitment the United States could not go further. Deputy National Security Adviser Steve Hadley and Deputy Secretary of Defense Paul Wolfowitz were even less inclined to talk about a political process without Arafat's first addressing the security situation.

Powell understood that the political argument was as important as the security issues. He knew that the Palestinians had to be given hope, and he told me so. But he was fighting a fierce battle inside the administration. To assist in this, he used a newly formed group, the Quartet on Middle East Peace, consisting of UN Secretary-General Kofi Annan, Russian foreign minister Igor Ivanov, High Representative for EU Common Foreign and Security Policy Javier Solana, and himself, to articulate a position that was more balanced than that of the United States but in which the United States would be represented. On April 10, the Quartet met in Madrid, issuing a statement that called for "tangible political progress . . . [including] a defined series of steps leading to permanent peace—involving recognition, normalization and security between the sides, an end to the Israeli occupation, and an end to the conflict." This would be the first in a series of balanced and helpful Quartet positions, even if it was still heavily influenced by the U.S. position and lacked a serious implementation mechanism. Powell would repeatedly use this group to articulate his ideas inside the administration.

The following week Powell visited the region. The king felt that this would be an excellent opportunity to push our ideas through. He presented a memorandum of our thinking to Powell during a meeting in Amman on April 11 and asked me to supply the details. The memorandum suggested the following detailed action plan to end the impasse:

1. An immediate halt of military operations by Israel and an immediate, meaningful cease-fire.
2. An immediate Israeli withdrawal from Palestinian cities, including Ramallah, and specifically including Arafat's headquarters.
3. Immediate agreement on the Tenet security work plan and the implementation of both Tenet and Mitchell plans within a specified time frame.
4. Agreement on international and/or U.S. monitors to help implement the Tenet and Mitchell agreements and observe any violations.
5. A commitment by Israel to comply fully with international humanitarian principles and to allow full and unimpeded access to humanitarian organizations and services, and a commitment to refrain from the excessive use of force and to ensure the protection of all civilians.
6. A commitment by the Palestinian Authority, supported by key Arab states such as Egypt and Jordan, to exercise maximum possible effort

to stop suicidal attacks against innocent Israeli civilians, to take steps to dismantle fanatic organizations' infrastructure, and to stop incitement to violence.

7. After implementation of the Tenet and Mitchell plans, the launching of a political negotiations process on the basis of Resolutions 242, 338, and 1397, the Madrid framework of peace, the land for peace principle, and the Arab Peace Initiative adopted unanimously in Beirut. This negotiations process should have a specified time line and agreed and specific milestones along the way.

Jordan had coordinated this position with Ahmad Maher, Egypt's foreign minister, who had come to Amman the day before. In this meeting, I used the term "Road Map" for the first time with Powell. We proposed a trilateral U.S.-Jordan-Egypt meeting to produce a detailed, time-specific plan that would result in a lasting and comprehensive solution. In a comment that probably reflected his own thinking rather than that of the White House, Powell said that such a plan was consistent with American thinking, and he welcomed the idea of coordinating the effort with Jordan and Egypt. The king also urged Powell to meet with Arafat on this trip.

In a joint press conference with Powell after the meeting, I announced, for the first time, that King Abdullah II had told the secretary of state that the time had come not only to specify security issues but also to also link them to a political process that would satisfactorily address the needs of Palestinians and Israelis. In order for hopes to be restored, I continued, "a specific, detailed, time-lined action plan is needed." The outline of the road map concept was formulated on that day.

I resumed my shuttle visits to promote Jordan's advocacy of a detailed plan with specific timetables to deal with the security and political aspects of the problem. We strongly felt that unless the Palestinians were given hope of a political settlement, they would have no strong incentive to move on issues that addressed only Israeli security concerns. I first visited Saudi Arabia and met with Prince Saud on April 17. He expressed frustration with U.S. pressure on Saudi Arabia to compel Arafat into confronting the violence and its unwillingness to compel Israel to move forward with the peace process. Like me, he sensed that Powell was becoming isolated inside the U.S. administration. Saud also expressed Saudi Arabia's frustration with the Syrian position during the Arab Summit. "We kept agreeing on formulations with them, then they would ask to change the formulations they had agreed to," he told me, in reference to our hair-splitting negotiations with the Syrians and the Lebanese during the formulation of the Arab Peace Initiative.

I briefed him on our meeting with Powell and the memorandum we submitted proposing a plan specifying the obligations of both sides, with timelines. Prince Saud was skeptical. Would the United States commit to such a plan? he wanted to know. His doubts about the Bush administration's commitment were well founded. No sign of such commitment was forthcoming, and President Bush seemed reluctant to get engaged in the Middle East peace process after the failure of the Clinton administration to bring about a settlement between the Palestinians and the Israelis. My view was that even though the White House might not be committed now, we needed to keep urging the Americans in that direction.

From there, I went to Egypt, where I met with Maher and Powell. Powell had just met separately with Sharon and Arafat. He said that he had pressed Sharon hard for a withdrawal and that Sharon had proposed an international conference under the auspices of the United States. Maher and I were both skeptical about convening a conference without a prior withdrawal. Any conference would have to adopt a detailed plan of action with deadlines and milestones for the Palestinians and other Arabs to view it as credible. Powell understood the predicament of the Palestinians, the devastating effects of the occupation and the Israeli incursion into the West Bank, which caused widespread destruction to Palestinian homes and property, including the leveling of the Jenin refugee camp.

MY SECOND VISIT TO ARAFAT

The next day, I traveled to Ramallah to see Arafat, despite obvious Israeli displeasure. Even though we placed the request for this visit before my trip to Egypt, the Israelis, as usual, did not want any foreign dignitary to meet with Arafat. This was part of a campaign to isolate him and make him irrelevant. Nor would Israel officially receive any foreign official on the same trip. Yet along with most in the international community, we felt that the only way to seek Arafat's cooperation in the peace process was to meet with him.

I took with me Dr. Ashraf Kurdi, Arafat's doctor, to check on him, for he had been living under difficult conditions for the past five months. We brought took food, clothing, and mobile phones to ease his impossible living conditions. When the Israelis refused to let those items through the barrier around his compound, I threatened to return and create a diplomatic incident. They finally let us through.

The scene inside the besieged headquarters was not pleasant. The compound was crammed with almost two hundred people, most of them security guards, along with some international peace activists who had insisted on remaining to discourage any sudden Israeli bombardment of the place. Sanitary facilities were sorely lacking, and sufficient sunlight and fresh air had not entered the headquarters for a long while. Whatever one thought of Arafat, it was hard not to feel sympathy for those living in these humiliating conditions.

I briefed Arafat about our meetings with Powell and our discussions about a political process that would begin with security and proceed to a comprehensive settlement. I also conveyed my impression that Powell was understanding but did not have the mandate from the president to make this plan a reality. I relayed what Sharon had told Powell of his intention to withdraw from Jenin and Nablus in the next twenty-four hours. Powell had asked us to help end suicide bombings, and I told Arafat that we agreed in Jordan that this should be part of the detailed plan we envisaged.

Arafat said he was not opposed to a detailed plan, but he also thought that Powell lacked a mandate from the president. He insisted on an Israeli withdrawal from all Palestinian cities occupied since the offensive started before a political process could be launched.

I left for Valencia, Spain, on April 22 to attend the Euro-Mediterranean Conference of Foreign Ministers. By then, Israel had pulled out of Nablus and most of Ramallah, partly because of the international outcry against the excesses of the Israeli army in Jenin, including the massive destruction of homes and other buildings in the Jenin refugee camp. I used the opportunity at the conference to push the idea of a detailed plan with most EU foreign ministers, including Javier Solana, EU External Relations Commissioner Christopher Patten, Joschka Fischer of Germany, Hubert Védrine of France, Josep Piqué of Spain, and Jack Straw of Britain. Solana and Piqué agreed to it, and Solana promised to try to include the idea in the final communiqué. Indeed, the communiqué referred to the need to "start negotiations, and reach, within a well-defined timeline, a political solution based on UN Security Council Resolutions 242, 338 and 1397 . . . and take into account other initiatives, like the Arab Initiative." The communiqué also "welcomed Saudi Crown Prince Abdullah's peace initiative, as endorsed in Beirut by the Summit of the Arab League, as a significant framework towards a comprehensive peace." Other Arab foreign ministers joined me in pushing the EU to endorse the initiative as one of the terms of reference of peace in the Middle East, particularly since we felt that it alone addressed the needs of both sides. But for now we settled for "a significant framework," slowly pushing the envelope.

THE KING'S TRIP TO WASHINGTON

King Abdullah II and I met with President Bush and Colin Powell on May 8. We found that the president had all but given up on Arafat. He was persuaded by the Israeli argument that Arafat was not only unwilling to move against radical Palestinian groups conducting the suicide bombings but that he condoned such operations. The political argument that the Palestinians needed hope and an end to the occupation did not resonate with him while the grave security situation persisted. Powell's position was a bit more nuanced. Though he was frustrated with Arafat for not being more forceful against radical groups, he understood the need to show Palestinians some light at the end of the tunnel. He told the king that he had delivered an ultimatum to Arafat in Ramallah on the need to move forward after the crisis was over or the United States would no longer be able to remain engaged. Ten days earlier, the president had had a difficult meeting with Saudi crown prince Abdullah in Crawford, Texas, where the Saudis proposed an eight-point plan to get out of the crisis, but it was focused more on immediate, interim arrangements and less on the details of an endgame. The president said that he sought to assure the crown prince of his commitment to peace, but it was clear that security considerations dominated the president's thinking and even clearer that he was close to ending any relationship with Arafat. The king again reiterated Jordan's position that political reform within Palestinian society depended on a political solution with a time frame that had a Palestinian state as a result. Bush remained reluctant to commit to an overly detailed plan. To persuade him, the king suggested a rough timeline, telling Bush that he thought a three-year timeline would be reasonable.

When the king asked me to speak, I tried to explain the importance of giving the Palestinians an Arab umbrella to confront the Palestinian extremists while also prodding Arab countries like Syria to comply with the Arab consensus. Providing such an umbrella, through a common Arab position against suicide bombings, would strengthen Arafat both against his radical groups and against hard-line views from countries like Syria. For this to be achieved, I told the president, there must be a credible alternative offering a political solution as defined in the Beirut Arab Summit and with a reasonable timeline. I asked the president for a commitment to such a framework to encourage Palestinians to move forward and to succeed in bringing some results out of the Cairo Arab Initiative meeting that would take place on May 10. Details would be left to the negotiating process. The president said he thought that was a "great idea" and said he was ready to weigh in with the Israelis on certain issues like settlement activity.

After the meeting, Powell approached me and told me the United States was "getting close to the vision you and I had talked about," referring to the need for a detailed action plan with an end game. It was clear Powell was still cajoling the White House to agree on defining what that end game would be. During that meeting, Powell also asked me to "keep pushing your idea of a timeline." Tired as I was, with a marathon trip to Cairo and back awaiting me, I was very encouraged by Powell's words and felt that all the pushing for a detailed plan was slowly changing the White House position.

In a separate meeting with the king, Powell told us that in the next six weeks many ideas would be discussed that would determine the administration's position. This was as close as Powell would come to confirming that there were contending voices within the administration and that no consensus had yet been reached. For the first time, he introduced the idea of a Palestinian "provisional" state (with less than full sovereignty and final borders not defined) as a "way station," an interim measure the administration thought could be useful. Powell also spoke positively about the idea of an international conference to jump-start the political process. I told Powell that the Syrians would not be keen on the idea of a conference before they could see what was in it for them. If an international conference involving all the parties were to be held, the Syrians should attend, I argued. The conference would need to address real issues, including an end to the occupation, for it to be successful, I added. It could not stop at the idea of a provisional state. I also expressed concern that a scheme for a "provisional state" would not be marketable to Palestinians or Arabs because the term implied impermanence.

THE SAUDI MESSAGE IN CAIRO

The Cairo meeting on May 10 was extremely useful in that the different positions of Arab states were crystallizing. Prince Saud elaborated certain "recommendations" for the ministers to reflect on, the result of Crown Prince Abdullah's recent trip to the United States:

- Saudi Arabia believes that the international conference is a means to achieve an end, not an end in itself, and will lay out a timetable for the end game. Saudi Arabia believes that the United States is inclined to go for a comprehensive solution to the conflict.
- If peace is a strategic choice for Arabs, they should behave accordingly. If Arabs believe that the United States is a crucial player in solving the conflict, then they should persuade it of their positions rather than treat it as an enemy.
- The Arab political discourse needs to reflect the spirit of the Arab Initiative. The Arab official media needs to be consistent with the Arab consensus on peace objectives.
- American public opinion cannot understand how those who blow themselves up and kill innocent civilians are glorified by some. Arab states bear a moral responsibility to take a firm stand against such actions.

This was the Saudis' clearest and toughest statement against suicide bombings and countries such as Syria that refused to condemn them. Until this, Jordan had been the only Arab county to have firmly and publicly opposed the bombings on moral and political grounds.

When Amr Moussa asked me to brief the ministers on King Abdullah II's talks in Washington, I reiterated Powell's statement that the administration would articulate a clear position in six weeks, and I emphasized the need to support the moderate faction in the administration (that is, the State Department) against the hawks within the administration who wanted to concentrate exclusively on security and economic issues at the expense of political ones.

I related Bush's reluctance to hold an international conference, recalling President Clinton's failure at Camp David. But I noted that Bush was positive toward a proposal to establish the general framework for a solution and a time frame agreed to at the conference, with details left for negotiations.

I stressed as did Prince Saud, that suicide bombings were a principal obstacle blocking progress in the peace process and that the United States was not going to move an inch so long as the Palestinians were not willing to stop these operations. I called for a collective Arab position to support the Palestinian National Authority against those working against peace. Otherwise, I said, the chances for a settlement were nonexistent. If we did not move, I argued, the United States would not deal with Arafat and would work to replace him.

The Jordanian and Saudi positions prompted a heated discussion. The PLO's foreign minister, Farouq Qaddoumi, who did not support the Oslo process and, ironically, did not represent the PNA's position, took a position directly contradictory to that of the PNA in a fiery exchange with Prince Saud and me over the issue of suicide bombings.[1] The Syrian representative also refused to agree to stop them, stating that what he had heard from us was "very dangerous" talk. The prince then suggested the idea of a truce, or a moratorium (*hudna*), on such operations, agreed to by all Palestinian factions to give the political track a chance. The following points were agreed on:

- The need to set the stage for an international conference, and to demand that it would be comprehensive for all tracks, Palestinian, Syrian, and Lebanese.
- The need for Israel to withdraw to pre–September 28, 2000, lines (before the second intifida was launched).
- The need for the conference to adopt a general framework for a solution with an endgame and a time frame.
- Further study of Prince Saud's suggestion of a moratorium on suicide bombings.
- A meeting of the Arab Initiative ministerial committee, to be held in Beirut on May 17–18.

I was interested in this Saudi position and felt it could help bring about a collective Arab decision on suicide bombings, in the same way that the Saudis had achieved consensus on the Arab Peace Initiative.

The meeting had not been conclusive, but progress had been made. Privately, Prince Saud told me that he had warned Syrian president Bashar Assad on his trip to Damascus that Syria faced a serious problem in the United States and that the consequences of continuing its current policies would be grave. He also said that a summit involving President Mubarak, Crown Prince Abdullah, and President Assad would be held in Sharm El-Sheikh on the next day to convince the Syrians to adopt a more moderate line. Saud asked for my help in drafting a paper containing a summary of Arab, U.S., and Israeli commitments for the next phase to be presented to the trilateral summit in Sharm El-Sheikh, which I did. Arab foreign ministers present approved it after minor modifications. It is instructive to reproduce these commitments, as they summarize what the Arab consensus at this point represented.

Objective
> Implementing the Arab Initiative

Method
> Parallel implementation by all sides of their commitments as outlined below

U.S. Commitments
- Commitment to an overall framework for a final settlement that is consistent with the Arab Initiative, itself based on international legitimacy, the Madrid terms of reference, land for peace, and UN Security Council Resolution 1397
- Commitment to a specified time frame for the above
- Active participation to rebuild the Palestinian infrastructure and refugee camps[2] on a modern basis
- Guaranteeing Israel's honoring of its commitments

Israeli Commitments
- Refraining from reoccupying Palestinian cities
- Ending all forms of violence
- Withdrawing to the September 28, 2000, lines, before the convening of the international conference
- Releasing Palestinian funds and refraining from taking economic measures against Palestinians
- Dealing with the Palestinian National Authority without imposing conditions on it

Arab Commitments

- Adopting a clear Arab and Palestinian stand vis-à-vis suicide bombings and all forms of violence
- Working to rebuild the Palestinian National Authority institutions according to criteria that ensure efficiency and transparency

Position regarding the Peace Conference

Support the convening of an international peace conference based on the following terms of reference:

- Participation by all concerned Arab parties
- Agreement on a general framework for a final settlement as per the terms of reference referred to earlier
- Agreement on a specified time frame to achieve the above

Evaluation

- Political discourse should be unified and consistent with the Arab Summit resolutions regarding the Arab Initiative and on pursuing a strategy of peace
- Developing a plan of action for the Arab Initiative Committee, based on a realistic study of U.S. public opinion and that of U.S. decision makers. Such a plan should be implemented as soon as possible to support the emerging new trend in the U.S. administration toward greater involvement in Middle East issues and to ensure that this trend is in the interest of Arab policies.

The results of these twenty-four hours demonstrated that the Arab position was moving toward the moderate camp and away from the extremist policies of the Syrians. The foreign ministers of Egypt, Morocco, Bahrain, and Yemen, in addition to Amr Moussa, all commended and supported the Saudi and Jordanian efforts. With the exception of the Syrians and the Lebanese, the rest clearly opposed suicide bombings and supported a moderate strategy of peace. I returned to Washington encouraged and upbeat.

Meeting with William Burns on May 13 in Washington, I emphasized that the international conference should not be held without defining an endgame and a timeline. He agreed. He told me that the president was "getting there" and was now thinking of a three-year time frame. He also said the U.S. position was evolving and that the president would spell out terms in reference to settlements, the 1967 borders, refugees (including a limited return to Israel), and a shared Jerusalem.

The U.S. position, however, still lacked the crucial element of commitment to continued engagement in the process. Burns agreed. I suggested commencing a series of meetings to develop a work plan within three or four months. The Israelis must come to the conference accepting its terms of reference and not start arguing over these terms once the conference began. Burns answered that he thought the president could deliver the Israelis.

Prince Saud phoned after the Sharm El-Sheikh summit to tell me it had been a partial success. Although the Saudis and the Egyptians sought a clearer statement from the Syrians on terrorism and suicide bombings, they eventually settled for a more subtle communiqué, "rejecting violence in all its forms." In addition to being noncommittal on the bombings issue, the Syrians also would not confirm their attendance at the international conference, Saud said. We agreed to meet as soon as we arrived in Beirut for the Arab Initiative Committee meeting.

FIGHTING IT OUT WITH THE SYRIANS

At the Beirut meeting on May 17, Prince Saud and I reiterated what we said a week earlier to the smaller group of Arab foreign ministers. This time, Farouq Sharaa of Syria was at the meeting and immediately took a hard-line position, contending that our optimism was unfounded. Arab states had not started the intifada so should not be responsible for stopping it, he argued, adding that the intifada should not be stopped until Arab rights were restored. In typical Sharaa style, he deliberately equated the intifada with suicide bombings and spoke about them as if they were one and the same. In reality, the first intifada was a movement of unarmed civilians; their only weapons were stones and a determination to end the occupation. Suicide bombings were common during the second one, but the purpose of the intifada was to end the occupation, not kill Israeli civilians. Sharaa categorically refused to condemn suicide bombings, which he said would end only when the occupation ended. Referring to the Sharm El-Sheikh summit a few days earlier, he said that the phrase "rejecting violence in all its forms" referred to Israeli violence. Syria, he added, did not think that Palestinian violence existed. Finally, he said, Syria would not accept another international conference on the

Middle East, except as a continuation of the Madrid Peace Conference. Because the Syrians wanted to establish the principle of full withdrawal by Israel from the Golan Heights to the June 4, 1967, border, Syria was anxious not to commit to a conference that might change the Madrid terms of reference. After I explained that we agreed with the Americans that the terms of reference for the conference would be agreed to beforehand, Sharaa announced that Syria would have no further objections.

Sharaa also expressed Syria's disappointment with the Saudis' eight-point plan presented to the Americans, claiming that such a plan would weaken the Arab Initiative. This would be a position the Syrians would adopt repeatedly. Despite repeated assurances that the Arab Initiative defined the overall framework for a solution and that the eight-point plan was a mechanism through which those goals could be achieved, Sharaa insisted that the Arab Initiative was enough and that the international community would show seriousness only if they implemented it without the need for negotiations or an action plan. This was typical Syrian polemics and lack of understanding of how the outside world works. The Syrians would not, or chose not to, understand that framework plans without implementation mechanisms do not work. What we and the Saudis were seeking were means to an end, the means being an action plan that would lead us to the end result: a solution based on the Arab Initiative. Whether the Syrians took this position because they were not directly negotiating with the Americans themselves—a position they always sought—while Saudi Arabia, Egypt, and Jordan were was not clear, although I have always suspected it to be the case.

After two days of heated discussions, the foreign ministers decided in their first official meeting of the Arab Initiative Follow-up Committee to seek a joint meeting with the foreign ministers of the Middle East Quartet in an attempt to push the Arab Initiative forward, possibly by presenting it to the UN Security Council. The committee delegated Prince Saud to contact Powell to arrange such a meeting.

THIRD TRIP TO RAMALLAH

I accompanied Jordanian prime minister Ali Abu Ragheb the next day, May 19, to Ramallah to see Arafat again. Our objective was to convince him to take serious action against suicide bombings. We both explained that our efforts so far had convinced the United States to consider a political framework within a specified time frame. We also briefed him on the king's recent meeting with Bush. We wanted to arrive at an Arab consensus regarding the international conference and secure Syria's agreement to attend. Abu Ragheb emphasized the international community's focus on accountability and transparency within the PNA, a point that did not escape Arafat, but an issue he said he took very seriously.[3] The prime minister also emphasized that the international community would not move without a unified Arab position against violence and suicide bombings. While we were meeting, another suicide bomber killed three Israelis along with himself and injured thirty-five others in Netanya.

The meetings with Arafat were becoming futile. Particularly in an expanded meeting, surrounded by his aides and security staff, Arafat would engage in a long, unfocused monologue and go off on tangents with no apparent link to the discussion at hand. It was very difficult to pin him down to a serious discussion until a meeting had fewer attendees. Still, Arafat's usual response was that he was doing everything being asked of him: he was dealing with corruption, moving against extremist elements, and preparing detailed action plans. As soon as the meeting ended, however, we would be confronted with a different reality. His own people were getting increasingly frustrated. Many Palestinian officials complained to me about Arafat's behavior, but few dared confront him.

I worked closely with several of Arafat's people, particularly with Nabil Shaath, the foreign minister of the PNA, and Sa'eb Ereikat, the chief negotiator. We wanted to make sure that all our efforts were coordinated with the Palestinians and met with their approval. On May 21 Shaath came to Amman, where we both announced agreement on the need to move to final status talks with a timetable set as a way to get the political process moving while addressing the security situation. Russian foreign minister Igor Ivanov, in a telephone call on May 22, announced Russia's agreement on establishing a timetable to end the occupation before convening a peace conference.

The three Arab countries working to advance the peace process were Jordan, Saudi Arabia, and Egypt. The Saudis provided the Islamic credentials, while Egypt was the largest Arab county. Despite its small size, Jordan was intimately knowledgeable about the process, having been directly affected by it for fifty years, and, among Arab states, had a unique understanding of how to market the case to the Western world. Thus the trio formed, for the first time in the Arab world, an effective alliance for peace working to influence policies of the United States and the West instead of merely reacting to them.

A fresh Israeli assault on West Bank cities and Gaza in late May, following a spate of suicide bombings earlier that same week, compromised the security situation. The situation on the ground was becoming a never-ending spiral of violence—precisely what we had warned could happen and had worked so hard to reverse.

In the meantime, U.S. policy had been taking shape. William Burns visited the region in early June to brief Jordan, Syria, Lebanon, Saudi Arabia, and Egypt on the progress of the international conference idea. He outlined a series of steps the United States was planning to take. Powell would first meet with the other members of the Quartet during the G8 meetings to be held June 13–14. That meeting would be followed by a presidential speech later in the month outlining the administration's plan to solve the Arab-Israeli conflict; it was to include an endgame and a three-year time frame. Burns said that discussions were under way about borders, settlements, refugees, and Jerusalem, although he indicated that the president's speech would not tackle these issues in detail. I urged him to adopt the Arab Initiative as one of the terms of reference, but it was obvious the United States was still not ready to do that.

Burns also said that during the three-year period, the United States was still considering, as per Jordan's suggestion, the idea of developing a detailed action plan with "way-stations," or benchmarks, against which progress could be measured. He added that there would be intensive discussions with all parties to prepare for convening the conference at the end of July. The conference would have a plenary session and then split into three groups: the first to discuss the Palestinian-Israeli track, the second to discuss the Syrian-Israeli and Lebanese-Israeli tracks, and a third to discuss a general Arab-Israeli track. I suggested that the third group might help implement the Arab Initiative, and I urged him to exert every effort to entice Syria to attend the conference. Burns said that he would visit Syria to brief its leaders on the administration's ideas but that he would carry a firm message that the Syrian position regarding radical Palestinian organizations with offices in Damascus, like Hamas and Islamic Jihad, would be watched carefully by the United States and would determine the American position in advancing the Syrian-Israeli track.

Burns also said the one other issue President Bush felt very strongly about was Arafat. Although the president had not written him off, Burns said, the United States would demand that Arafat carry out security and economic reforms in the PNA. Burns had already conveyed this message to Arafat during a recent meeting. I reiterated that the terms of reference had to be agreed on before we convened so that the conference would not turn into a debating match, and Burns assured me that prior agreement was indeed the intention.

It was clear from the shift in the U.S. position that the State Department's arguments were making headway. We saw this as an opportunity that should not be missed and were determined to work with Powell and his team.

Sharon visited Washington on June 10 while Israel continued its attacks on West Bank cities and on Arafat's compound in Ramallah. Burns phoned me on June 11 to brief me on the visit. He said that the president had been harsher on Sharon in private than he was in public and talked about the need to give the Palestinians hope. Bush also talked about a timeline and the need to work with Arafat. Sharon, in contrast, had been very tough on Arafat and offered little in terms of a political vision, Burns said. Sharon also had reiterated the Israeli position that there would be no political negotiations with the Palestinians unless the issues of security and reform were tackled. Burns also said that the president did not want to propose endgame parameters as detailed as those of the Clinton administration.

Nabil Shaath called me on June 16 from Washington, where he had relayed to Powell the Palestinian position regarding final status talks. The Palestinians had presented the U.S. administration with a paper outlining their position, closely following where the negotiations had ended at the Taba talks in 2001. The Arab Initiative formed their basic term of reference. The paper included the following points:

- Borders are to be based on the June 4, 1967, armistice line, with minor, reciprocal, and equal boundary rectifications to be agreed on.
- There will be no further claims beyond the June 4, 1967, borders.

- A permanent territorial corridor will be established between the West Bank and the Gaza Strip.
- East Jerusalem will become the capital of Palestine, and West Jerusalem will become the capital of Israel. The city will be open to all. The Palestinians will transfer sovereignty over the Jewish Quarter and the Wailing Wall section of the Western Wall in East Jerusalem to Israel while retaining sovereignty over the remainder of the Old City.
- Security arrangements will be agreed on, with international forces playing a central role in these arrangements. The two sides will strive to establish a regional security regime.
- Neither side will participate in military alliances against each other.
- A just and agreed solution to the refugee problem based on UN General Assembly Resolution 194[4] will be sought, in accordance with the Arab Peace Initiative.
- A comprehensive permanent status agreement will mark the end of the conflict between Palestine and Israel, and its complete implementation will mark the end of claims between them.

This was the first time since Taba that Palestinians had officially declared, in writing, their position on a final status agreement. From Jordan's perspective, it was a fair position that paralleled Jordanian policy. The Palestinians also presented a hundred-day plan for reform, including "condemnation of all acts of violence that threaten the lives of innocent Palestinian and Israeli civilians." Shaath told me that he had informed Powell that the PNA did not favor the idea of a Palestinian provisional state, adding that such an arrangement would be useful only if the provisional state adhered to the 1967 borders.

Prince Saud phoned me the next day to say he was pleased by what he heard from American officials regarding President Bush's speech. We were all now waiting to see the outcome of all the preparatory work of the last few months and how it would be reflected in Bush's speech.

On June 17 I sent William Burns a position paper, indicating our hope that the president's speech would include a commitment to the endgame, based on the 1967 borders with minor and reciprocal adjustments. The paper also stressed the need for a timeline to achieve this, as well as a firm commitment by the United States to help the parties achieve a solution. I was well aware that I was repeating myself, but I also felt that the only way to get the Bush administration to listen was to keep hammering on the issue. The Jordanian position also stressed our commitment to work with the Palestinians and other Arab states to take effective measures against radical organizations opposed to the peace process and to help the Palestinians carry out necessary reforms.

MY LAST VISIT TO SEE ARAFAT AND PRESIDENT BUSH'S SPEECH OF JUNE 24, 2002

Powell called me on June 20. He said that the president was ready to make a statement and wanted to go forward. The recent bombing, he added, had created a foul atmosphere that would postpone the delivery of the speech for a few days.[5] He was highly critical of Arafat, saying that he had not done what he could to stop the bombings and suggesting that Arafat actually might have supported the radical organizations. The president's statement, he said, would call for a final settlement, with "way-stations," but Arafat would have to do more to cut all support and linkages with the radical groups. I reiterated the need for a clear endgame with a timeline. Powell said the statement would include that, but the plan would also be performance-based. I suggested a state "with provisional arrangements rather than a provisional state" that had to be linked to the endgame. He agreed and said that this was what the administration was thinking about.

While the Israeli attacks continued in the West Bank, with Israeli officials vowing "a crushing and decisive offensive" against the Palestinians, the presidency of the European Union on June 22 declared its support for "an end to the occupation and the early establishment of a democratic, viable, peaceful and sovereign State of Palestine, on the basis of the 1967 borders, if necessary with minor adjustments agreed by the parties. The end result should be two States living side by side within secure and recognized borders enjoying normal relations with their neighbors. In this context, a fair solution should be found to the complex issue of Jerusalem, and a just, viable and agreed solution to the problem of Palestinian refugees." The European Union had never before gone so far in articulating its vision of Middle East peace and had never before collectively agreed on what such a peace should look like.

Although the EU statement was a reason for optimism, the U.S. position on Arafat was disconcerting. I had sensed from Powell that the speech would be very tough on Arafat and felt that perhaps something still could be done to preempt such a U.S. position. On June 23, for the fourth time in six months, I traveled to Ramallah to see Arafat. I was extremely blunt with him. I told him what Powell said and added that the suicide bombings had caused not only the Americans but also the Europeans to start pointing fingers at him personally. I urged him to take serious action to cut his ties with the radical groups within the Palestinian Authority before Bush made his speech if he wanted to tone down the American position.

Arafat gave us nothing. Although he was clearly worried about the details of Bush's speech, he had no intention of doing anything to curb the radicals. Abu Mazen told me that day that he had been scheduled to meet Shimon Peres and defense minister Binyamin Ben-Eliezer but scotched the meeting after Arafat gave him nothing to take to the table. I returned to Amman extremely frustrated. We had worked so hard to change the U.S. position, but Arafat was clearly not helping. Although I did not feel that Arafat personally supported suicide bombings, I also concluded that he was either too weak or unwilling to confront his radical groups. This would be our last meeting, although we talked several times later by phone.

Soon after I returned, William Burns phoned me to say that the debate over the Middle East had been extremely heated and said that the president would deliver his speech the next day, June 24. Powell called me the next day to confirm it. He said that the president's message would articulate support for a Palestinian state within three years, with way-stations, but would also be performance-based. He added that the United States still felt that a Palestinian state with provisional borders was useful and said they were working on language that was mindful of what we discussed a few days earlier. The speech would also call on Israel to withdraw to pre–September 28, 2000, lines, stop settlement activity, and "end the occupation that began in 1967."

Then Powell laid the line on Arafat. The speech would call for new leaders among the Palestinians, he said. This was exactly the kind of American policy statement that we had feared and that we felt would complicate efforts to move the process forward. Powell said that an international conference no longer made sense, and although he agreed that ultimately, there must be a comprehensive settlement with Syria and Lebanon, he was noncommittal on their immediate involvement.

President Bush's speech on June 24 was far harsher on Arafat than we expected. He called for Arafat's removal, urging Palestinians to replace him with "leaders not compromised by terror" and to implement financial, political, and security reforms. In return, the United States would support a provisional state of Palestine whose final borders and other aspects of sovereignty would be negotiated between Israel and the Palestinians. The plan envisioned a settlement within three years. The president called on Israel to stop its settlement activity, on Arab states to build closer diplomatic and commercial ties with Israel, and on Syria to close "terrorist camps and expel terrorist organizations" from its territory.

I immediately initiated another round of telephone diplomacy with Prince Saud, Ahmad Maher, and Nabil Shaath. There was consensus that Arab states had to adopt a positive posture regarding President Bush's speech, particularly since it called for a Palestinian state in three years and an end to the occupation. The response should not be "yes, but . . . ," but rather should be a serious, positive "yes, and . . ." policy. This was a very responsible, serious position from all four Arab parties that did not stop at Bush's characterization of Palestinian leadership and politics. Instead of focusing on persons and short-term policies, we all agreed that the higher, more important objective was the end of the occupation and the establishment of a Palestinian state.

Jordan issued an official statement on June 25, welcoming the speech and the U.S. commitment to engage in the process. The statement acknowledged that the speech "was in line with our position that an end game and a timeline should be defined so that the political process could be re-launched on solid grounds." We reminded the international community that the speech was made "possible because of the diplomatic opening created by the Arab Initiative—to which we remain deeply committed," and that a comprehensive settlement, including Syria and Lebanon, remained our objective. Similar statements were made by the Egyptians, Saudis, and the Palestinians. Our strategy of securing gradual support from the United States, even if in small, difficult steps, had prevailed. Next we needed to produce a detailed action plan that recognized the Arab Initiative as one of the terms of reference for peace and that would include Syria and Lebanon. These would be two difficult, but crucial, objectives.

Powell phoned me again on June 26 to review where things stood. He thanked me for Jordan's positive response and reiterated that, although the speech had excoriated Arafat, it also addressed key Arab concerns: a Palestinian state, an end to the occupation that began in 1967, and a call to stop settlement activity. Powell explained that Bush had concluded that he could not work with Arafat and had serious concerns that Arafat had been complicit in some of the suicide bombings. He added that although the Palestinian leadership was a Palestinian problem, the United States felt it could not work with the current leaders.

I told Powell that even though the Jordanian public position had been supportive, Jordan still expected the United States to clarify several issues: What if the Palestinians returned Arafat to power in any new elections? What if they elected Hamas? Who would determine whether each side was meeting its commitments? Who would guarantee movement to the next phase once commitments were fulfilled? What was the administration's position on the Arab Initiative or on a comprehensive solution? What practical steps would be taken to translate the president's speech into an action plan?

I phoned Prince Saud the next day and relayed the details of my conversation. We agreed that the Arab Initiative ministerial committee needed to meet and determine the next steps.

Meanwhile, the Israeli offensive continued. Israel reoccupied the West Bank city of Hebron. It seized on the speech's references to Arafat and disregarded the other issues of substance. The Israelis habitually reduced the whole issue of Palestinian statehood and an end to the occupation to one person: Arafat. The strategy continued even after Arafat died and the moderate Mahmoud Abbas came to power. The Palestinians in turn announced national elections for January 2003, with Arafat running.

MEETING WITH THE QUARTET IN NEW YORK

The Quartet decided to meet on July 15 in New York at the ministerial level and to invite the Saudi, Egyptian, and Jordanian foreign ministers to attend one day later. The invitations were relayed to all three of us on July 6. I phoned both Ahmad Maher and Prince Saud that day and found both of them displeased with the invitations. Saud felt that Syria should have been invited, too. I thought that since the terms of reference were clear to us, and since we all agreed that the Arab Initiative should form the basis for discussions with Israel, the opportunity was there to meet with the Quartet and attempt to influence the process positively. Because Jordan, Egypt, and Saudi Arabia were the three Arab countries with the best relations with the United States in particular and the Quartet in general, I believed that an opportunity to argue the Arab case should not be missed, even if we did not have a comprehensive Arab mandate to do so. At any rate, we agreed to discuss this at the upcoming Arab Initiative Committee meeting in Cairo, which was to take place before the Quartet meeting.

Sa'eb Ereikat came to see me in Amman on July 10 to stress that the Palestinians were taking serious steps on reform but needed Israel to meet its commitments if these steps were to continue. He also said that Arafat had not yet approved the idea of a constitution or of a Palestinian provisional state acceptable to the United Nations and would continue negotiating final status with Israel.[6]

Prince Saud came to Jordan that day to present his idea of developing a new Palestinian constitution that would include all the reforms required of the Palestinian National Authority, including establishing the office of a prime minister. The constitution would give limited authority to the president. Once approved by the Palestinian Legislative Council, elections could be held and the results would be respected by the international community, Saud argued. This process would give international legitimacy to the elections. He reiterated the idea of a moratorium to be respected by all Palestinian factions and added that the new Palestinian government would seek admittance to the United Nations based on UN Partition Resolution 181 (1947), to be followed by final status negotiations between the new Palestinian state and Israel. Though the Americans were not yet backing this proposal, Saud thought we should work on them to do so.

In Cairo, we found the Syrians and Lebanese extremely unhappy about not being invited to the Quartet meeting. Typically combative, Sharaa argued that the three foreign ministers did not have a mandate to speak on behalf of other Arab states. I countered that we were not seeking such a mandate but were only trying to make use of the opportunity to push the Arab case forward. In the end, we all agreed that the Arab Initiative remained our term of reference, having been accepted by all Arab states.

I met separately with Powell on July 16, before the Quartet meeting, and found him in a positive mood. He felt that Sharon was ready to move forward, told me that the Arab Initiative would not be ignored, and stressed the need for security reforms within the Palestinian Authority. I told him that Jordan's principal aim at the meeting would be to translate President Bush's vision of two states within three years into an action plan. "We have the endgame, now we need a plan that would lead us there," I said. I also hoped we could agree with the Quartet on the details of such a plan. On the subject of Arafat, I suggested that we "should agree to disagree." Powell countered that the United States did not care whether Arafat left or stayed. It was only concerned that the Palestinians they dealt with were accountable. Though he disagreed with many of Arafat's policies and tactics, Powell never spoke about him in the derogatory manner of other administration officials. I told him we remained committed to the Arab Initiative and that the 1967 border must be the basis of any solution.[7]

I had made these same points in a meeting with Kofi Annan just before I met Powell. Annan said that there were many points of agreement between the Quartet's thinking and the Arab plan but added that he did not think the Saudi proposal of declaring a Palestinian state that then negotiated with Israel was workable. The UN Security Council would not agree to such a proposal, he said, because of the U.S. veto. He proposed holding elections first in the West Bank and Gaza according to a new constitution and then declaring a Palestinian state once new leadership took office. That state could then be accepted at the United Nations. I informed him that the Palestinians were not interested in declaring a state on less than the 1967 borders. At any rate, Arabs were more concerned that the occupation end after the specified three-year period than with the actions taken to end it.

The Quartet met in New York, first alone, then with myself and Ahmad Maher. (Prince Saud was unable to attend the meeting.) Maher and I reiterated the need for a work plan that would include Palestinian and Israeli commitments. Powell concurred, stating that he thought Israel, too, had commitments and needed eventually to get out of the Palestinian areas. Powell also talked about using a provisional state as an incentive to the Palestinians on the road to full withdrawal and sovereignty in three years. Again, the Arab view was that this was something only the

Palestinians could agree to, but the important objectives for Arab states were an end to the occupation and a fully sovereign Palestinian state in three years. At any rate, we contended that the state should not be provisional, which meant that it could be temporary, but that a Palestinian state could have provisional borders until final borders were determined through negotiations.

The Quartet's final communiqué endorsed the concept of a Palestinian state, but was sharply divided over the issue of Arafat. It called the Arab Initiative "a significant contribution towards a comprehensive peace." Although not enough, we were making progress. The group also endorsed the Jordanian position, for the first time, on the need for "an action plan, with appropriate benchmarks."

On July 17 Saud arrived in Washington, where he, Maher, and I were scheduled to meet with President Bush the next day. Maher and I briefed him on the outcome of the meetings with the Quartet. During that discussion, I repeatedly used the term "road map" to describe the action plan, stressing that we should ask the president for a commitment to it. Saud called Nabil Shaath, who briefed him on the PNA's efforts to arrive at an agreement with all Palestinian factions to stop all violence against civilians in return for Israel's withdrawal to pre–September 28, 2000, lines. He also said that work was proceeding in earnest on a new Palestinian constitution.

During our meeting, Bush told us that he was strongly committed to a Palestinian state and that he thought this goal could be achieved in three years. All parties, including the Israelis, have commitments to fulfill, he stated, but he added that "it is hard to proceed while people are blowing themselves up."[8] He referred to Powell as his "point man" on the Middle East, clearly intending to send a message of support to Powell, who was under attack from other quarters in the administration. That reference gave all three of us hope that the president was becoming more attuned to the moderate view within his administration on the Middle East.

The president made it clear, however, that he did not trust Arafat and that no serious political progress would be made while Arafat remained in office, unless he delegated much of his authority to someone else. It was the most contentious point in our discussions, but there was no doubt that his position on Arafat was final.

I asked the president for a "road map" that would include bench-marks, timelines, obligations, and a monitoring group to measure per-formance. He listened but did not react. Once again, it was clear that the White House was not yet committed to follow up on the vision of a Palestinian state with an implementation mechanism.

Nevertheless, we came out of that meeting energized, feeling that the president was serious about a U.S. commitment to a two-state solu-tion as well as a three-year timetable. I reflected that optimism in a speech at the Brookings Institution on July 19. Few people who attended shared my optimism.

The day of my speech I met with William Burns, who shared with me for the first time the ideas being developed with the Quartet on a de-tailed plan. He said that although the president was aware that such ideas were being developed, he had not yet seen or approved them. Burns said the plan had three tracks—security, humanitarian, and political—and would be divided into three phases:

Phase I: August 2002–Spring 2003
> This phase would deal mainly with security issues. On the
> Palestinian side, these would include political and security
> reform measures, ending violence, putting in place a plan
> for a new constitution, and holding parliamentary elec-
> tions. Israelis would be required to provide humanitarian
> support and withdraw to the September 28, 2000, lines.

Phase II: Spring 2003–End of 2003
> Measures here would center around developing the idea of a
> Palestinian state with provisional borders. The United States
> would only go as far as committing to ending the occupation
> that began in 1967, Burns said, but could not commit to a
> Palestinian state on the exact border of June 4, 1967. During
> this phase, settlement activity would stop completely and the
> Gaza settlements would be evacuated as a first step. An in-
> ternational conference could also be held during this phase,
> to which Syria and Lebanon might be invited.

Phase III: 2004–2005
> Final status negotiations would start at the beginning of
> 2004, to be completed in mid-2005 except for final security

arrangements. During this phase, multilateral negotiations would resume in a new format and in stages.

I had many questions for Burns. I told him that Arab states remained committed to the Arab Initiative as well as to a comprehensive process. The United States was clearly not keen on involving the Syrians and Lebanese at this stage, but we felt there was progress and that we needed to keep pushing the envelope despite this. Further, I told Burns that the plan had no clear monitoring mechanism at every stage to ensure that commitments were met on time by all sides, and I asked him whether he thought Israel would commit to a three-year schedule to end the occupation. He candidly told me that the Israelis were not there yet but that the United States was still committed to it. Burns and I agreed to keep pushing the idea of a road map during King Abdullah II's next visit, due in ten days, and to continue developing these ideas.

I returned to Amman and reported to the king that important progress had been made. Our idea of a detailed action plan with a timeline was clearly picking up steam but still needed a push by the king when he met with President Bush. I suggested that we should show appreciation for the president's support for a Palestinian state in three years, remind him of the Arab Initiative and what it offered Israel, and then ask him for a commitment on a detailed road map to get us to his vision of two states. The plan, I suggested to the king, should include benchmarks, expected obligations on both sides, timelines to meet these obligations, and a monitoring mechanism to ensure compliance.

On July 22, I met Mahmoud Abbas in Amman to brief him on our progress. He agreed with us on the need to stop violence and end suicide bombings, but he was not optimistic that that could be achieved. He was neither sure that Arafat could do it nor certain that the radical groups would accept it. I told him what we believed was the U.S. position: a commitment to establish a Palestinian state in three years, but not until major reforms within the PNA were implemented, and no dealing with Arafat.

Israel was not standing still as the diplomatic initiative rolled forward. Israeli officials emphasized that Bush's plan was conditional on the Palestinians ending all armed operations, including suicide bombings. The Israeli government, however, was not helping create an environment conducive for it, nor did it take all these diplomatic efforts seriously. On July 23, Israel carried out a major raid on Gaza, killing the Hamas military commander Salah Shehade as part of its "targeted assassination" policy, along with fifteen bystanders.

The Arab states' moderate position also was coming under attack from extremist forces in Jordan and elsewhere in the Arab world. Both Islamic and old Arab nationalist parties saw this position as one that compromised Arab rights without explaining how it did so or offering an alternative strategy. Nevertheless, the coordinated work of Egypt, Saudi Arabia, and Jordan was paying off. The work was serious, systematic, realistic, and focused. We were speaking to the West in a language it understood—a pragmatic discourse that emphasized practical steps rather than rhetorical declarations meant to appeal to emotions—and we had made headway. On the eve of the king's next visit to the United States, my hopes had been rekindled that the Israeli occupation could finally be brought to an end and that a two-state solution could be realized.

Stopping first in Paris, the king met with President Jacques Chirac, who agreed with our plan but thought that three years was too long for full implementation. His encouragement was very important as we headed to Washington for our meeting with President Bush.

MY MEETING WITH RICE

I met with National Security Adviser Condoleezza Rice on July 31, a day before the king's meeting with Bush, to test the waters. "You are being tough on Arafat," I told her. "You've basically written him off. You're asking the Palestinians to perform on security, but you are not giving them in return a vision of the next phase. For the Palestinians to cooperate on security, they need to know they will get their state. So, while it is important to stress security, it cannot be an end in itself." I launched into my by now well-rehearsed discourse on the need for a road map. Rice told me the argument was a "nonstarter." The president had given a speech, she continued, and that was enough. "You ask the Palestinians to perform on security, and if they do we will see what happens next," she said. I argued that the Arab side was suggesting ways to end the crisis, including the historic initiative passed in Beirut, but the Israelis were doing nothing and the United States was not helping us.

I returned, demoralized, to King Abdullah II. "We are going to have a very tough time tomorrow," I told him. "I just saw Rice, I presented our idea of a road map, and she simply said, 'No!'" The king was determined. "Let me present the idea to the president tomorrow, and then you will present the details."

THE MEETING THAT LAUNCHED THE ROAD MAP EFFORT

The atmosphere was tense as we prepared ourselves for a showdown. In attendance on the U.S. side were Rice, White House Chief of Staff Andrew Card, special assistant for the Middle East at the National Security Council Flynt Leverett, Assistant Secretary of State William Burns, and other officials. I was extremely nervous.

President Bush started the meeting telling the king that he felt passionately about Iraq and that Saddam Hussein was a thug who should be brought down. One day earlier, King Abdullah II had given an interview to the *Washington Post* warning about the consequences of a war on Iraq. "The meeting is not going well," I thought to myself. Then Bush turned to the subject of the peace process, telling the king that it was hard for him to convince the Israelis to move while they were being attacked by suicide bombers. He said that he planned to push ahead, including on settlements, once the security situation had been addressed.

The king argued the need for a road map, but the president was not moved. He echoed Rice's message of the day before about prioritizing security, building new institutions, and crafting a new constitution, adding that he thought these initial objectives were more important than final agreement on issues such as settlements and Jerusalem. "More than outlining steps, we need progress on the ground first," the president said.[9]

"Why don't you explain our thinking on this," the king said, turning to me. I explained that we needed to assure Palestinians of our seriousness. What we needed, I told the president, was a road map that dealt with security, institutions, and the humanitarian situation in the Palestinian territories but that also outlined the remaining steps till mid-2005 so that Palestinians knew exactly what they were getting and so that Arab states and the international community could win more public support for cracking down on the armed Palestinian groups. "I thought that was clear in my speech," Bush shot back. "What do the Palestinians want from me? I gave them a vision. What more do they want?"

I looked at the king and saw that he did not mind my continuing the discussion. He had given me a once-in-a-lifetime opportunity, and I was not going to waste it. "Frankly, Mr. President, most Palestinians are skeptical that this vision would be realized," I said. "All we are asking for is to take your exact vision and translate it into steps. We are not asking for any commitments you have not already made."

President Bush paused for a moment, looked at me, and said, "I have no problem with that." Then he turned to William Burns. "Why don't the two of you work something out?"

After the meeting, Rice told me that the United States would "work something out" with us to translate the president's speech into practical steps, reversing her earlier position. In the *Guardian* on April 8, 2004, Flynt Leverett told columnist Sydney Blumenthal that Rice had not told the president about her conversation with me. I have no knowledge of U.S. preparations for this meeting, but I do know that during the meeting Rice's face did not betray whatever thoughts she might have had. The Road Map was born.

THE DIFFICULT NEGOTIATIONS

I phoned Burns from London Heathrow Airport the following day, on my way to Amman, to check whether the White House had moved forward. "Your efforts are going to bear some fruit," Burns said. Burns had been U.S. ambassador to Jordan when I was Jordanian ambassador to the United States. He then became assistant secretary of state for Near East Affairs at the State Department, and I worked closely with him in Washington. Burns is the ultimate diplomat: low-key, knowledgeable, a good listener, and a creative thinker. He has a certain reassuring grace about him but is also objective, a man whose thinking and actions are governed by reason. He conveyed even the most difficult messages in a clear and nonthreatening way. He had revised the administration's document after taking into account some of my comments and had forwarded it to Rice. He told me the meeting with the president had been positive and that he would work with me on developing a formal action plan.

Burns called me again on August 6 to tell me that he had showed the ideas to Rice, who was positive and introduced few changes. He told her that he would share them with me and said he wanted my candid opinion. We agreed that these ideas would be presented at the next Quartet meeting on the sidelines of the UN General Assembly session that was to take place in New York in September. Burns informed me that the Quartet had decided to meet with Arab foreign ministers, including the Syrian and Lebanese, at this time.

I next accompanied the king to Saudi Arabia, where he briefed Crown Prince Abdullah and coordinated our positions. We agreed to study the ideas with the Saudis and the Egyptians and then to present them to the Arab Initiative Committee.

I felt confident enough to tell the Agence France-Presse, "In the next few weeks a peace plan will be thrashed out in time to be submitted to the Quartet for discussion." I also announced that "King Abdullah II managed to convince President Bush to translate his political vision for the establishment of a Palestinian state in three years into adequate mechanisms."[10]

We naturally remained concerned about Syria. It was obvious that the Americans were not keen on including Syria at this stage, but it was also crucial for us to strive for a comprehensive settlement and to keep the Syrians engaged and supportive of our moderate position. I thus flew to Aleppo with Prime Minister Abu Ragheb to see President Assad. We found him flexible. The Syrians wanted to make sure that the Arab Initiative was part of the detailed Road Map, something we were dedicated to as well. Assad saw in the road map a positive development, and even Sharaa was upbeat for a change. I thought the ice that was there in Cairo had melted, and I hoped for a productive next meeting of the Arab Initiative in Cairo on September 4 to prepare for our meeting with the Quartet in New York.

Deputy Assistant Secretary of State David Satterfield came to see me on August 27 to review the work done on the Road Map. He stressed that the plan being drafted by the State Department had been shared in full only with Jordan. He said he gave a detailed overview to the Saudis and the Egyptians, but no one had received a written copy of it other than us. He also added that he had discussed the ideas at length with the Palestinians.

I outlined our position and told Satterfield that we requested that a written copy of the plan should be presented to Jordan, Saudi Arabia, and Egypt ahead of the September 4 meeting of the Arab Initiative Committee in Cairo. The three ministers would then meet among themselves before presenting the plan to the Cairo meeting. I stressed that we had to present the meeting with something solid and credible. Our stand should include:

- A commitment by the United States to the three-year framework
- A reference to the 1967 borders
- A commitment to comprehensiveness
- A commitment to the inclusion of the Arab Initiative among the terms of reference
- Clearly defined phases of the action plan, specifically those pertaining to the involvement of Arab states and the commencement of negotiations on the Syrian and Lebanese track
- Clearly defined performance benchmarks for both the Israelis and the Palestinians
- A monitoring mechanism to judge performance and assess progress

I argued that Palestinians' political will to fulfill their commitments in Phase I of the plan (security) was unlikely without clarity and specificity regarding Israeli commitments in Phase III (political). Phase III was too general at this point to be credible, and the language on stopping Israeli settlements was too vague. I also said that the Road Map's phrasing concerning Syria and Lebanon's participation in the proposed international conference was too loose. The United States wanted a clear and unequivocal commitment by all attending parties to renounce violence and its use for political gains. I thought the Syrians would find this too provocative and proposed a compromise, suggesting language that called for "a conference inclusive of all parties and consistent with the Madrid Peace Conference calling for ending the conflict by peaceful means." This would be the first of many negotiations with the Americans to refine the Road Map to make it acceptable to the Arab side. Satterfield agreed to take these points back to Washington.

By the time of the meeting between the Quartet and the Arab foreign ministers, it had become clear that the United States intended to invade Iraq and, as Burns told me in New York, was planning on seriously pushing the peace process forward immediately after declaring victory. The United States was of the view that serious work on the peace process could not start before military action on Iraq ended. We thought that the United States's credibility and image in the region depended heavily on its position vis-à-vis the peace process and that a war on Iraq would destroy what remained of American prestige. If we could not change the American position regarding invading Iraq, only a credible move to push the peace process forward might convince the Arab public that America meant what it said about democracy and freedom. But it was clear the Bush administration thought otherwise. The European Union had also presented detailed ideas about what should be included in the road map, with more details than the Americans were willing to commit to and with positions closer to the Arab position than those of Bush administration. As the United States was preparing for the war, it obviously did not want to jeopardize Israel's cooperation in refraining from any retaliatory military strike on Iraq, should Iraq decide to strike Israel.

The Quartet met first alone on September 17, then with the Arab group. The second meeting was a disaster. The Syrians and the Lebanese, instead of using the meeting to put forward practical ideas, chose to engage in polemics and theatrics. Their performance left such a bad taste in everyone's mouth that the Quartet would not meet with any Arab group for the next three years.

I presented the Jordanian position, stating that the Road Map needed to be specific in all phases, not just the first, and be not only performance-driven but hope-driven as well. I also emphasized the need to include the Arab Initiative as one of the main terms of reference of the peace process to bring all Arab states on board. Finally, I stressed that a comprehensive solution was essential and not a concession to the Arabs, as Israel argued. On the contrary, such a solution, I said, would give Israel a collective peace treaty and collective security guarantees in addition to ending the conflict with all Arab states. Once the Road Map was made public, I concluded, all parties had to commit to and abide by it, with the Quartet acting as the enforcer.

The United Nations, European Union, and Russia were all in favor of finalizing the road map then and there. But the United States strongly objected, apparently out of fear that endorsing the Road Map might compromise Israel's cooperation on Iraq. The Quartet ended up issuing a statement that did not explicitly recognize the Arab Initiative as one of the terms of reference for the process. But it did mention, for the first time, that work was being done on a "three-phase implementation roadmap that could achieve a final settlement within three years." The statement also stressed that this would be a performance-driven plan, with compliance to be monitored and assessed by the Quartet. This was a positive development for us; we thought the only way to reconcile the two objectives of a performance-driven plan and a Palestinian state in three years was to ensure that commitments were being met on time, with monitoring done by a third, neutral party. But there was obviously much work to be done before a detailed, acceptable plan would be published.

From New York, I traveled to Washington, where I met separately with Powell and Rice to review progress. Rice was uncharacteristically upbeat and told me she thought the plan was positive.

By early October, the first draft of the Road Map was virtually completed and was being submitted to the National Security Council for approval. Sharon, clearly sensing that he had irritated Washington with his tactics regarding the Mukataa (as Arafat's headquarters was called in Arabic and where Arafat was under siege and frequent bombardment by the Israeli army), dispatched his trusted adviser, Dov Weisglass, to explain the Israeli position. Until then the Israelis had not taken the Road Map exercise seriously and insisted that political progress was contingent on achieving an end to violence, assuming that it was an attempt by the Americans to pacify the Arabs before an upcoming strike on Iraq.

On October 20 Burns came to Jordan, where he presented the first draft of the Road Map to us. He said that the draft would be shared with all the parties and that it included more of Jordan's suggestions than anyone else's, including the Quartet members. He added that the United States had agreed to about 85 percent of what the rest of the Quartet wanted. The plan, he added, would be finalized after consultation with the parties and announced by the Quartet during their next meeting in December. Burns also informed us that the president had talked to Sharon and urged him to be forthcoming.

The draft we saw in October included important positive shifts toward our positions. For the first time, the Arab Initiative was one of the terms of reference for the process. This was significant for many reasons. It put the endgame on the table: a viable, independent Palestinian state on the basis of the 1967 borders. As an official objective, it gave the process direction and would help address the skepticism many had that the Israeli government's idea of a Palestinian state was on far less than the land occupied by Israel in 1967. It would also maximize the chances that all Arab states would accept the Road Map, having already lent their signatures to the Arab Initiative. The exact reference now read: "The settlement will end the occupation that began in 1967, based on the Madrid Conference terms of reference and the principle of land for peace, UN-SCRs 242, 338 and 1397, agreements previously reached by the parties, and the Arab Initiative proposed by Saudi Crown Prince Abdullah and endorsed by the Arab Summit in Beirut."[11]

Phase I of the Road Map was to be implemented between October 2002 and May 2003 in two stages. Stage 1, between October and December 2002, included the appointment of a new Palestinian cabinet with an empowered prime minister, a commission to draft a new Palestinian constitution, and agreement on an elections law. It also included many security reforms to be carried out by the Palestinian side and gave Israel only a few commitments to fulfill. These commitments included a Palestinian call for an immediate end to the armed intifada and all acts of violence against Israelis everywhere, an end to incitement against Israel, the consolidation of the Palestinian security organizations into three services, and the resumption of security cooperation with Israel. Israel would be asked to end its attacks in civilian areas, stop its demolition of Palestinian homes, transfer all arrears of withheld revenues to the Palestinian ministry of finance, and dismantle settlement posts erected since the establishment of the Sharon government in early 2001.

Stage 2, to be implemented between January and May 2003, would establish a Quartet monitoring mechanism and would commit Israel to withdraw to pre–September 28, 2000, lines before Palestinian elections would be held. The new constitution would be submitted to the new Palestinian legislature after the elections. Israel would freeze all settlement activity, including the building of settlements to accommodate natural population growth, as per the recommendations of the Mitchell report.

Phase II, June 2003–December 2003, would include an international conference, convened by the Quartet, to launch negotiations between the Palestinians and the Israelis on establishing a state with provisional borders and to be concluded by December 2003. Such a conference would include Syria and Lebanon and would revive multilateral talks on water, environment, economic development, refugees, and arms control. There would be further unspecified "action on settlements simultaneous with establishment of a Palestinian state with provisional borders."

Phase III, 2004–2005, would include a second international conference to launch negotiations between Israel and Palestine toward a final settlement and to support progress toward a comprehensive settlement between Israel and both Syria and Lebanon, "to be achieved as soon as possible." Finally, Arab state acceptance of normal relations with Israel and security for all states of the region consistent with the Arab Initiative would be achieved.

Burns spoke in blunt terms. Nothing would move, he said, if the Palestinians did not comply with the first stage of Phase I.

In Jordan, we studied the draft carefully and submitted written comments that I carried to Washington at the end of October. These underscored the importance of the American commitment. "Without the US commitment to implement the plan, it would remain an academic exercise. Armed with this commitment, Jordan believes the details will become less important if the goals and timelines of the plan are adhered to," I argued. We welcomed the reference to the Arab Initiative and stressed that once the plan was finalized, the United States should seek public acceptance by all concerned parties. The plan, we added, must be accepted as a package deal; its provisions could not be cherry-picked. The omission of any mention of Jerusalem—the issue that could make or break Middle East peace—was also a point of criticism. We emphasized the central role of the monitoring and assessment mechanism, arguing that it was the only element that would ensure implementation of the plan within the three-year period specified. Finally, we expressed our view that the "three-year time frame of the road map applies to all tracks, including the Syrian-Israeli and Lebanese-Israeli tracks, and [is] not limited to the Palestinian-Israeli track," as the plan was less than clear about concluding negotiations between Syria and Lebanon on one hand and Israel on the other by the end of the three-year period.

For the second time in less than a month, I met with Rice and Powell in Washington to discuss our comments and review the Iraq question. A military strike against Iraq would put Jordan at a grave risk and would disrupt the flow of oil from Iraq, then our only supplier.

The Americans informed me that Bush was firm with Sharon during Sharon's visit to Washington few days earlier and that the United States would not walk away from the principles it discussed with us, despite Israeli objections.

By that time, the Israeli government had started to sense the seriousness of the Road Map initiative, which was not at all to its liking, particularly its call to end the occupation in three years and its incorporation of the Arab Initiative as one of the terms of reference for a final settlement. Israel had asked the United States to postpone the announcement of the Road Map and the submission of Israel's response until after the Knesset elections on January 28, 2003. Powell informed me that Israel also had reservations about freezing settlement activity and the presence of a monitoring mechanism. To us, a third-party monitoring mechanism was necessary to evaluate whether the Israelis and the Palestinians were meeting their commitments. To Israel, a monitoring mechanism by the Quartet meant the involvement of parties that were seen as less friendly to Israel—Russia, the European Union, and the United Nations—and therefore advocated the position that it would be the judge and the jury when it came to the fulfillment of Palestinian commitments. I urged both Powell and Rice that the president should be the one to announce the Road Map once it was complete, since his declaration would lend it more weight and would make a rejection by any party much more difficult.

SPARRING WITH SHARAA—AGAIN

During the Arab foreign ministers meeting in Cairo on November 10, Sharaa fumed that Syria had not been consulted while the international community hammered out the Road Map and was even more furious that Jordan had been not only fully in the loop but a key driver of the plan. He claimed that there was nothing called "the Road Map," since no official copy had been presented to the Syrian authorities during Burns's last trip to Damascus. This was the beginning of a fiery exchange. The Arabs, I countered, had a choice: either bury their heads in the sand until the Road Map was publicized—at which point they would either have to accept it with all its shortcomings or reject a plan supported by international legitimacy—or get on board now and try to influence its development so that it contained the elements that would make it acceptable to Arabs. I reminded Sharaa that his obstinacy aborted repeated attempts to give Arab foreign ministers a detailed briefing of our efforts in developing the Road Map and that he repeatedly insisted that the Arab Initiative obviated the need for a road map. The Arab Initiative, I explained, was a set of objectives that still needed an action plan. As such, the Road Map was a tool, not an objective. In a typical denial of facts, Sharaa would not budge.

David Satterfield came to the region in mid-November to brief countries on the Road Map's development. He did not share a draft of it in the meeting, saying that the United States needed another ten days or so to finalize the document. Nevertheless, he assured us that the Americans had taken into consideration comments from a number of key stakeholders and had made significant amendments as a result, including expanding the section on the comprehensiveness of the process. Although a de-escalation of settlement activity would take place during Phase I, he said, a complete freeze of all such activities, including natural growth, would not be implemented until Phase II.

I conveyed to Satterfield the Jordanian opposition to postponing the Road Map's scheduled December 20 debut during an upcoming meeting of the Quartet. I expressed our concern that Israel might exploit a delay to derail the whole process, particularly since the Bush administration had started to turn its attention to an invasion of Iraq. Satterfield assured me that the United States had no plan to delay the announcement of the Road Map and stressed that the administration had not and would not accept such a request from the Israelis.

I again underlined the importance of the president's public endorsement as soon as it was revealed, both to signal the Americans' clear commitment and to make it difficult for any party to reject it. It was clear that the White House was not there yet, since Satterfield urged us to continue to make that point. By that time, the gap between the State Department and the White House was clear to all, and it was important for us to have the announcement made by President Bush so that no one could claim that the Road Map had been accepted only by State Department doves, as opposed to the White House and the entire administration.

At a meeting of the Arab Follow-up Committee in Damascus on November 21, I briefed the Arab ministers on our efforts. I made the following points:

- The Road Map was a Jordanian demand to translate U.S. promises of a Palestinian state into reality.
- The Road Map included a foundation for a solution acceptable to the Arabs, including a Palestinian state in three years and the Arab Initiative as one of the terms of reference for the settlement.
- For the first time, the Road Map included an international dimension through the Quartet, breaking the U.S. monopoly on the peace process.
- Jordanian efforts had resulted in major positive improvements to the Road Map, including on adopting the Arab Initiative, emphasizing and elaborating on the comprehensiveness of the process, a monitoring mechanism, a complete freeze on settlements, and adding a clause on Jerusalem.

If any party was to reject the plan, I said looking at Sharaa, let Israel do so, lest the international community ask the Arabs to resolve the conflict without their help. I ended by urging the attendees to adopt a positive attitude. Another round of Syrian grandstanding ensued. Sharaa hit the roof, shouting that Syria had not been consulted. No one, he continued, could ignore Syria's importance. For Syria, it was all a matter of prestige. As far as Syria was concerned, he reiterated, the plan did not exist.

The sparring matches between Sharaa and me had almost become habitual. We came from completely dissimilar backgrounds and represented countries with entirely different worldviews. Other Arab foreign ministers usually appeased the Syrian minister, at least in words. This time, Sharaa had gone too far. Arab League Secretary-General Amr Moussa called Sharaa's denial of the plan "irresponsible." Prince Saud, Ahmad Maher, Nabil Shaath, and Muhammad Ben Issa, the foreign minister of Morocco, all rebuked Sharaa in their speeches and supported Jordan. Syrian theatrics could not overshadow the real issue. Nor could Syria accuse Jordan of working behind its back on an effort in which it had clearly moved the international position much closer to the Arab, largely on its own.

SPARRING WITH THE AMERICANS

Leaks of the amended draft started to appear in the press by mid-November. One of the most negative developments, I thought, was the new language on the Arab Initiative. After I thought we had secured adopting it as one of the terms of reference for a final settlement in the October draft, the new language, which came in a draft document that Satterfield shared with the Palestinian Authority and was passed to us by the Palestinians, read as follows: "The settlements will also take into consideration the continuing importance of the initiative of Saudi Arabia, endorsed at the Arab League Beirut Summit, which is a vital part of the peace on all tracks, including the Syrian-Israeli and Lebanese-Israeli tracks."

This softening on the language on both the Arab Initiative and the comprehensiveness of the process was totally unacceptable. It was my turn to hit the roof. I called the American ambassador in Amman and asked if the media reports were true.

I phoned Burns on November 26, the Thanksgiving holiday. Although he asked me not to believe everything in the press, it was clear to me that softening the language was indeed being seriously considered. Burns also indicated he was no longer sure whether the plan would be announced on December 20.

I was livid and called Flynt Leverett in the White House the same day. I told him I failed to understand how Condoleezza Rice could tell me at the end of October that there would be no delay in announcing the plan, how Satterfield could subsequently reiterate this in mid-November, and how this could all be reversed because of one meeting the administration had with Dov Weisglass, Sharon's senior adviser, who, I had learned, had been dispatched to Washington to convince Rice to postpone the announcement of the Road Map until after the Israeli elections. Uncharacteristically, I could barely maintain my composure. I was the one, I almost shouted, who argued in front of the Arab foreign ministers that the United States was serious about ending the conflict and who took all kinds of abuse, only to find that the United States was leaving the Arab moderates out in the cold. Because the situation was deteriorating so rapidly and Israeli settlement building was proceeding so quickly, we feared that by the time elections were held and a new Israeli government was formed, the atmosphere might not allow for publication of the plan. I added that the language on the Arab Initiative was totally unacceptable. "If we can't accept it, rest assured that no Arab country will," I told him. Leverett was very understanding despite my shouting and promised to relay all this to Rice.

I made the same points in a phone call with Javier Solana, who expressed his complete support for the Jordanian position and promised to do his best to ensure that the original language on the Arab Initiative in the October draft would be restored.

Burns called on December 10 to tell me that the Quartet's December meeting was going ahead but that discussions had been inconclusive on the final language and what would be made public. This was not promising, particularly when I learned from other sources that Rice had indeed overruled Powell on the issue and decided after meeting with Weisglass to postpone the announcement, even if a final draft was near completion, until after the Israeli elections. I reiterated that the only acceptable position for us was one that would keep the Arab Initiative among the terms of reference for a settlement.

THE DIFFICULT BIRTH OF THE ROAD MAP

Burns called on December 19 to inform me that he was able to find language to satisfy our demands. Indeed, the new language did. The Quartet issued the communiqué on December 20, and although it did not include the full text of the Road Map, it did include the language we sought on the Arab Initiative. It read as follows:

> The settlement will resolve the Israeli-Palestinian conflict, and
> end the occupation that began in 1967, based on the Madrid
> Conference, the principle of land for peace, UNSCRs 242, 338
> and 1397, agreements previously reached by the parties, and
> the initiative of the Saudi Crown Prince Abdullah—endorsed
> by the Beirut Arab League Summit—for acceptance of Israel as
> a neighbor living in peace and security, in the context of a com-
> prehensive settlement. This initiative is a vital element of inter-
> national efforts to promote a comprehensive peace on all
> tracks, including the Syrian-Israeli and the Lebanese-Israeli
> tracks.

Burns told me that the Road Map was almost done and that it would include a monitoring mechanism to be assumed by the Quartet, although such a mechanism would also be "U.S. dominated." The plan, however, would not be announced at the December 20 meeting, in deference to the Israelis (see Appendix 5 for the text of the Road Map).

The Bush administration's backtracking on its commitment to announce the plan before the end of the year was frustrating. But I took immense satisfaction from the fact that, despite all the criticism we received from countries like Syria and the Arab media in general, our efforts were largely successful. The battle to have the Arab Initiative included as one of the terms of reference, despite strong Israeli objections, was arduous but ultimately fruitful.

Miguel Moratinos, the EU representative to the peace process (and later Spain's foreign minister), phoned on December 23 to congratulate me. When I expressed my concern that the language might be changed again, Moratinos said Russia was lobbying to bring the Road Map to the Security Council, where it could be endorsed officially by the United Nations.

The year ended with a completed draft of the Road Map, which was unfortunately not published as promised by the Americans. It would not be launched until six months later, in Aqaba.

CHAPTER SIX

Launching the Road Map and the Aqaba Summit

AS FAR AS THE ARAB-ISRAELI CONFLICT is concerned, 2002 will go down in history as the year of Arab diplomacy. The moderate core of the Arab world, represented by Jordan, Egypt, and Saudi Arabia, in a rare display of collective action, adopted proactive, serious, coordinated policies vis-à-vis the conflict that were intended to fill the gap left by those who were unwilling to act. Arab action did not end with the Arab Initiative, which committed the entire Arab world, and most Islamic countries, to a two-state solution arrived at through peaceful means. The three Arab states lobbied the United States and the Middle East Quartet to commit the international community to an action plan that would produce such a solution within three years.

Their dynamism was not matched by other actors. The Bush administration had Iraq on its mind and by the beginning of 2003 was set on invasion. President Bush had made this clear to King Abdullah II on August 1 during the same meeting that Jordan was pitching the Road Map. Bush claimed during that meeting that he was answering a historic calling and that he had a moral obligation not to allow "the crimes against humanity" being committed in Iraq from continuing.[1] The United States maintained that the war on Iraq would dictate its serious engagement on the Arab-Israeli conflict once the war was over. Against this argument, Jordan unsuccessfully contended that a serious engagement on the Arab-Israeli conflict was needed in its own right, and certainly before a war on Iraq was launched if the United States hoped to preserve any credibility in the region. The king repeatedly cautioned that a war executed without serious consideration of postwar realities could open a Pandora's box. But President Bush's mind was clearly set. At the beginning of 2003, the entire international community, including Jordan, was stuck in a holding pattern, having realized that no serious movement on the peace process could be expected until the conclusion of the Iraq war.

The Israelis also made a significant contribution to the state of affairs at the beginning of the year. Prime Minister Sharon was in a combative mood. Israeli incursions into the West Bank that year, under the pretext of stopping suicide bombings, went beyond all limits, violating international law, causing widespread destruction, killing people who bore no responsibility for the bombings, and undermining all attempts to bring back Israelis and Palestinians to the negotiating table. Sharon's sole response to the suicide bombings was a brutal military one, while our argument that the Israelis also needed to look at the core of the problem—an occupation that had been going on for thirty-five years without any hope for a settlement—fell on deaf ears. Israel would not consider any political initiatives before the security situation was not only addressed but fully resolved. Our counter argument was that offering a political horizon for the Palestinians, a ray of hope, through a plan that also addressed the problem of the occupation, in itself would help resolve the security issue.

Israel would have none of that. The Sharon administration was clearly not interested or ready to arrive at a permanent solution to the conflict and certainly acted in a manner that made a solution all the more difficult. Even when the Arabs offered their historical initiative, Israel rejected it on the very grounds where the Arabs gave their biggest concessions. Instead of looking at the major benefits it would draw out of a collective Arab commitment to peace and security for Israel, as well as a permanent end to the conflict as explicitly stated in the initiative, Israel chose to highlight the document's mentioning of UN Resolution 194 while conveniently ignoring the fact that the Arabs made their biggest concession by stating that the solution to the refugee problem should be an agreed one. Despite the repeated efforts in 2002 to move the peace process forward, Israel was obstructionist, even when the efforts addressed its professed and legitimate security concerns. Israel also has since ignored a major point. Despite all the violence by Israel in 2002, and despite the hardening of positions in the Arab world it led to, not one Arab state has asked to withdraw its signature from the Arab Initiative, proving the resilience of this peace proposal to this day. There was a time when Israel accused Arabs of not stepping forward and providing a partner for peace. The year 2002 showed that this was not true, with the core of the Arab world meeting the challenge and being fully engaged.

The Arab record was also not without blemishes. The year 2002 was also the year of the suicide bombings, with more than four hundred Israelis killed, as well as more than a thousand Palestinians killed in Israeli raids that year alone. Believing that such acts would lead to a withdrawal of Israel from the occupied territories when everything else had failed to convince it to do so, radical Palestinians could not understand that their acts of terrorism undermined their just cause in the world as well as the willingness of countries such as the United States to step in. Jordan felt from the beginning that such acts were wrong from both a moral and a political point of view and said so publicly on many occasions. The country's leadership has been chastised in some circles in the Arab world for speaking out, and even by elements within the Jordanian public, including the Islamist opposition in parliament. But the government has stood firm in its opposition to suicide bombings out of convictions that are both moral and political. The killing of civilians is unjustifiable on any grounds, and no matter how just the Palestinian cause may be, suicide bombings quickly eroded the sympathy of the international community, along with our own morality. The continuation of suicide bombings has also allowed the international community to conflate the concepts of resistance and terrorism and to associate the Palestinians with the policies of Al-Qaeda. In reality, the two are quite distinct— although both are immoral for their targeting of civilian populations. Arguably, suicide bombings in the Israeli-Palestinian conflict have been used as a form of unconventional warfare against Israelis because of the severe imbalance of power between Israel and the Palestinians that has allowed Israel to impose a brutal occupation of the Palestinians for nearly forty years. From that aspect, these bombings, clearly wrong from a moral viewpoint, are still different from Al-Qaeda terrorist actions on 9/11.

Among the Arabs, Syria was perhaps the most unhelpful in pushing the Arab Peace Initiative forward. Although Syria had signed on to the Arab Initiative, it would not agree to explicitly condemn suicide bombings, even while all of us in the Arab world condemned the Israeli targeted (and often untargeted) policy of killing Palestinians, often with rockets launched at civilian buildings. After Syria signed the Arab Initiative, it was content to rest on its laurels, believing that it was the international community's turn to demonstrate its seriousness. The Syrians argued that if the international community truly saw merit in the initiative, all it had to do was implement the initiative and thus bring about a solution. Not only did they denounce the idea of an action plan to translate the objectives of the initiative into concrete steps, but they believed that such a plan would compromise the initiative itself, given all the commitments to which the Palestinians were obliged within the plan. Time and again, the Syrians behaved as if Syria was a superpower to which the international community needed to bend. Syria believed that the Arab position was obvious and needed no further articulation or marketing to the wider world. The notion that the size or relative power of regional states alone no longer mattered, that ideas and constant movement had won the day, was lost on the Syrians. Nor did Syria happily accept that Jordan, a small country, was leading the charge with ideas and initiatives, and had the ear of the international community, while Syria was sidelined.

The European Union played a very positive and balanced role in developing the Road Map, and it was much more moderate in its outlook on the region than was the United States. The different views within European ranks—the British, Dutch, and Germans were closer to American policy than they were to that of France, for example—did not prevent the emergence of a European consensus on the Middle East, one that was in general moderate and forthcoming. The European Union also played a constructive role in the Quartet, a role that Secretary of State Colin Powell often used to tame some of the hard-line positions within the Bush administration, particularly on issues related to Israeli commitments under the Road Map. Nevertheless, the United States dominated the peace process, since the European Union was either too weak or unwilling to confront America on this issue. I found working with EU and other European officials extremely useful and developed a strong relationship with Javier Solana, Miguel Moratinos, the French foreign ministers Dominique de Villepin and Michel Barnier, the German foreign minister Joschka Fischer, the Spanish foreign minister Ana Palacio, and others.

New challenges also awaited Jordan in 2003. The American military buildup in the Persian Gulf was under way, and the invasion of Iraq loomed on the horizon. Jordanians were anxious about the political and economic effects a U.S. military campaign against their neighbor would have on Jordan. Chaos in the aftermath seemed almost inevitable, and the prospect of Iraq's fragmentation along sectarian lines was a nightmare for Jordan, as well as for Iraq's other neighbors, since none of them could easily isolate themselves from Iraq's domestic instability. The mere appearance of instability that pointed toward Iraq's fragmentation into Kurdish, Sunni, and Shiite states would invite intervention by neighboring states, with Iran heavily influencing the Shiites in the South, Turkey moving against a Kurdish state at its southern border for fear of radicalizing its own Kurdish minority, and Saudi Arabia wary of a Shiite state on its northern border. More immediately, Jordan was concerned about the effect this would have on the national economy since Jordan also depended exclusively on Iraq for its oil needs, half of which was being given to us free of charge and the other half of which was supplied at discounted rates.[2] Iraq also constituted a major market for Jordanian products, and the loss of that market would have grave consequences for the Jordanian economy.

The British, wary that a war on Iraq would postpone the international community's peacemaking efforts, sought to convene a conference in London. At the conference, the Palestinians were to deal with political reform, discussing a new Palestinian constitution as well as political steps to be taken toward building a viable Palestinian state. The Quartet and some Arab countries attended the conference; the Palestinians participated via satellite since Israel, skeptical that the conference might push the peace process in an unwelcome direction, did not permit them to travel to London. The Israelis were not invited to attend, since the declared objective of the conference was to discuss Palestinian reforms.

Meanwhile, the United States and the European Union were pushing to appoint an empowered Palestinian prime minister and to curb Arafat's authority. But above all, the conference was a public relations exercise ahead of the war on Iraq and produced no tangible progress. Significantly, however, a statement by British foreign minister Jack Straw at the conclusion of the conference, used the still unpublished Road Map's language on a resolution of the Palestinian-Israeli conflict in accordance with terms of reference that included the Arab Initiative.

Assistant Secretary of State for Near East Affairs Burns and I met in Amman on January 22 immediately after he arrived from Damascus, where he had met with President Assad and Foreign Minister Sharaa. Burns gave me a negative impression of the meeting, saying that although he met alone with Assad for an hour, he had seen no change in his position on such issues as Hezbollah or the Palestinian factions in Damascus or Iraq.[3] Burns also told me that the United States would have to be very serious about resolving the Arab-Israeli conflict after Iraq. I emphasized that the text of the Road Map should not be changed, although he could only assure me that he did not expect any "significant" changes. He added that work was being done to convene a Quartet meeting in February to announce the Road Map but that no date had been finalized.

Burns also made it clear that the United States was going to war against Iraq. He confirmed what Bush had already told the king, which was that Iraq was a defining issue for the American president, and he gave me the impression that war would start around the end of February.

The foreign ministers of states neighboring Iraq and Egypt met in Istanbul in January to try to find a way to avert the war on Iraq, but there was little we could do. It was becoming clear that it was only a matter of time before the invasion began.

Elections for the Israeli Knesset on January 28 returned Sharon to the top of the Likud Party list, which won 37 seats (out of 120). It was an overwhelming victory for the Israeli right; Labor could muster only 19 seats. Any hope that a Labor-led Israeli government would accept the Road Map was dashed.

Meanwhile, the Israelis had objected to all the major tenets of the document, amounting to a rejection of the plan. They continued to view an end to violence as a precondition for starting the process and believed that the implementation of the Road Map should proceed according to performance, not a timetable. Israel also demanded that Arafat be replaced before any political progress could be effected. More disturbing, however, was Israel's position vis-à-vis the final objective of the process—a two-state solution. The sole "source of authority" for the plan should be UN Resolutions 242 and 338, Israel maintained, not the Arab Initiative, which Israel did not accept. Yet the main problem with Resolution 242 in this context was that it did not refer to a Palestinian state or to a two-state solution. Israel was also not prepared to accept any monitoring mechanism that was not led by the United States (as opposed to the Quartet or any other international body). And Israel objected to the idea of a Palestinian state with provisional borders, arguing that any Palestinian state should itself be provisional—which implied that a Palestinian state could be temporary and subject to reversal. Israel would also not commit to ending settlement activity, arguing that settlements were an issue to be discussed only in final status negotiations. In reality, this was a stratagem to create enough facts on the ground that would make such a discussion moot when the moment arrived. Nor would Israel commit to the comprehensiveness of the process, a key Arab demand in return for a collective peace agreement with the Jewish state. Most absurdly, Israel wanted negotiations between itself and the Palestinians to encompass all outstanding issues, including an end to the conflict and an end to all claims, territorial and otherwise, but without committing itself to reaching agreement with the other Arab countries with which it had territorial disputes.

The Israeli reservations confirmed Arab suspicions that Israel was not serious about ending the conflict, was not ready to negotiate in good faith, and in fact had rejected the Road Map. It made Jordan even more determined to insist that the Road Map not be changed and that all parties accept or reject it in its entirety rather than pick and choose the articles that suited it.

I met with Dov Weisglass, Sharon's adviser, for the first time in Amman on February 9, 2003. I had requested the meeting in an attempt to understand Israel's true objective from Sharon's closest adviser at the time. I emphasized the need for Israel to accept the Road Map without reservations, highlighting the importance of the Arab Initiative and the consensus Arab countries had reached in addressing Israel's needs once

Arab rights were restored. I also made it clear that Jordan would not accept the Road Map unless the Arab Initiative was one of its terms of reference. Weisglass, known at home and abroad as a smooth talker, contended that the changes to the Road Map Israel was seeking were insignificant and said that Israel was ready to accept "a road map"—as opposed to the Road Map finalized by the Quartet in December 2002. The meeting with Weisglass convinced me that Israel was not serious about a two-state solution that would address both parties' needs, not only its own, and not serious about any final settlement in the short term. My fears were confirmed almost two years later, when Weisglass gave a long interview to the Israeli daily *Ha'aretz* in which he basically stated that Israel did not intend to move to a two-state solution for the foreseeable future.

Arab foreign ministers met in Cairo on February 15, in a last-ditch attempt to avert a war on Iraq and to agree on whether to hold an Arab Summit to discuss the impending war, even if there was little that the Arabs, or indeed the international community, could do. The Arab-Israeli conflict was not discussed. After much debate in the meeting and the days that followed, Arab states agreed to hold the next summit in Sharm El-Sheikh, with Bahrain presiding, on March 1, largely to discuss Iraq—but again with no results.

The summit participants failed to agree on a course of action. A suggestion by the United Arab Emirates that Saddam Hussein resign in order to avert a war sparked an angry exchange between the Iraqi and the Emirati delegations. It was clear that the region was heading for war. Jordan did its best with the Bush administration to avert such a calamity; King Abdullah II's many interviews provoked its ire. In the end, Jordan could do little except scramble to ensure its oil supply and to prepare for the war's consequences, including a possible influx of Iraqi refugees, as best it could. We initiated talks with Saudi Arabia, Kuwait, and the United Arab Emirates to reach an agreement whereby Jordan would be compensated for its loss of Iraqi oil. Saudi Arabia agreed to grant Jordan 50,000 free barrels of oil a day, with an additional 25,000 barrels coming from Kuwait, and another 25,000 barrels from the United Arab Emirates. All in all, that covered our daily needs of 100,000 barrels. Gulf oil assistance has been crucial to Jordan's ability to withstand the economic consequences of the war.

On March 20, 2003, the day the invasion began, Secretary of State Powell called me to say that "the Road Map was on track." I immediately suggested that I travel to Washington to talk about the post-Saddam era and the launching of the Road Map, and Powell invited me to visit Washington on April 25.

William Burns called me on April 1 to tell me that the United States had informed Silvan Shalom, Israel's foreign minister, during his trip to Washington that the Road Map would not be modified and that it would be announced as soon as the Palestinians formed a new government, under the premiership of Mahmoud Abbas.

Arafat had appointed Abbas on March 19 after considerable pressure from the international community, including the United States, European Union, and Russia, but by early April, a new government had not been formed. The delay revealed that Arafat's appointment of Abbas had not been done wholeheartedly. Nor, it seemed, was he enthusiastic about delegating his authority to the prime minister.

Jordan was growing frustrated with the delay because it had a direct bearing on the launch of the Road Map. I phoned Al-Tayyeb Abdel Rahim and Nabil Abu-Rudainah, two senior Arafat advisers, and urged them to announce a new government. Further delay, I argued, would send the wrong signal to the Arab world and the international community. I also told Nabil Shaath, the PA foreign minister, that if a Palestinian government was not in place before my trip to Washington on April 25, it would strip the Arab position of a major argument for launching the Road Map. Shaath acknowledged the point and expressed his frustration that the situation was approaching a standstill. EU representative Miguel Moratinos also called to tell me he had had a stormy meeting with Arafat in which he told him that he did not think he was serious in forming a new government. As I headed to the United States, the United Kingdom, and the United Nations, Arafat finally approved a cabinet list Abbas had presented to him on April 23.

When I arrived in Washington, I sensed that the Bush administration was now more serious about the peace process, no doubt encouraged by its apparent quick victory in Iraq. Condoleezza Rice and I met on April 25 to discuss the peace process. I stressed to her that Mahmoud Abbas must be helped to succeed, adding that the Americans had a special responsibility in this regard. Rice indicated that the Road Map text would not be changed but that the administration was open to "comments" from both sides that would not result in any changes to the text. We also talked about the reconstruction of Iraq.

Three days later, I was assured that Colin Powell was equally determined that the Quartet would announce the Road Map as written. During our April 28 meeting, he said that President Bush had approved the document and that any comments could be taken into consideration during the implementation phase. Powell also expressed his extreme frustration with Syria over the presence of the radical Palestinian factions in Damascus. He said he planned to visit Syria and request that Damascus close their offices, as well as stop supplying Hezbollah with arms and stop providing a safe haven to wanted ex-Iraqi officials.

Indeed, the Quartet finally presented the Road Map, in its December 20, 2002, version, to both the Palestinians and the Israelis on April 30.

The Israelis, keen not to anger the Americans by refusing the document outright, employed a frequently used tactic to abort the Road Map's implementation: Israel publicly accepted the Road Map in principle but then set many conditions for adopting it that essentially amounted to rejecting the plan:

1. Both at the commencement of and during the process, and as a condition to its continuance, calm will be maintained.
2. Full performance will be a condition for progress between phases and for progress within phases.
3. The emergence of a new and different leadership in the Palestinian Authority will be promoted.
4. The monitoring mechanism will be under American management.
5. The character of the provisional state will be determined through negotiations between the Palestinian Authority and Israel.
6. Declared references must be made to Israel's right to exist as a Jewish state and to the waiver of any right of return for Palestinian refugees to the State of Israel.
7. The end of the process will lead to the end of all claims, not just the end of the conflict.
8. The future settlement will be reached through agreement and direct negotiations between the two parties in accordance with the vision outlined by President Bush in his June 24 speech.

9. There will be no involvement with issues pertaining to the final settlement. Among issues not to be discussed are settlement in Judea, Samaria, and Gaza.

10. All references to statements other than UN Resolutions 242 and 338 (1397, the Saudi Initiative, and the Arab Peace Initiative adopted in Beirut) will be removed.

11. The reform process in the Palestinian Authority will be promoted.

12. The deployment of IDF forces along the September 2000 lines will be subject to the stipulation of Article 4 (absolute quiet).

13. Subject to security conditions, Israel will work to restore Palestinian life to normal.

14. Arab states will assist the process through the condemnation of terrorist activity. No link will be established between the Palestinian track and other tracks (Syrian and Lebanese).[4]

These conditions made it clear that if Israel was to cooperate with the international community, its needs, and its needs only, were to be met. Israel's insistence on removing the Arab Initiative as one of the terms of reference despite its offer of a collective peace treaty and security guarantees for Israel, the removal of any commitment to the comprehensiveness of the process, the refusal to commit to the three-year framework, the refusal to stop settlement activity as per the Mitchell report, the refusal to consider any return of refugees to the State of Israel, even a symbolic number, and the insistence on Arafat's removal as a condition before beginning to implement the Road Map were an unambiguous rejection of the plan.

Powell traveled on May 4 to Lebanon and Syria, where he delivered a tough message to Syria and announced that the Syrians had accepted to rein in the radical Palestinian elements in Damascus. Indeed, several Palestinian groups, including Hamas and Islamic Jihad, announced that they would "freeze their operations" in Syria on May 7.

Less than a week later, Powell met with King Abdullah II in Amman. Powell said that he spent a great deal with both Sharon and Abbas and made it clear that he wanted an unambiguous commitment to move forward. He told us that the United States had refused Sharon's request to make changes to the Road Map but also that Sharon had not said he would accept the plan. Powell also acknowledged that the Palestinians had accepted the plan unconditionally and that he had asked them to implement specific measures to address the security situation. I interjected at this point that while this was a fair request, another fair request would be to ask the Israelis to accept the Road Map without conditions.

The tone of this meeting was completely different than the one we had had with Powell during his first visit to the region a year earlier. He was firm, determined to get the Israelis to accept the Road Map, and speaking in the name of the president, something that was lacking during his first visit. Naturally, we saw this as a positive development, even if Israel had not accepted the plan.

Following the meeting I relayed to the Palestinians Powell's message about the need to produce a detailed security plan as a tool to pressure the Israelis to accept the Road Map. Prime Minister Abbas informed me that such a plan was ready to be presented to Sharon during their upcoming meeting on May 18.

That same day I also met with Javier Solana, who was on a trip to the region. Solana expressed his profound disappointment that Israel had not yet accepted the plan, adding that the window of opportunity was short: U.S. elections scheduled for later in the year would divert American attention and energy elsewhere. He was also concerned that Arafat was not doing much to support Abbas and might even be endeavoring to undermine him.

When Abbas and Sharon finally met on May 18, the Israelis made two primary points: first, that accepting the Road Map would create serious political problems for the Sharon government, especially the acceptance of an independent Palestinian state, and could lead to its downfall; second, that the two sides should start implementing points on which there was agreement and postpone the rest. Sharon also told Abbas that he accepted the principle of Bush's June 24, 2002, speech but reiterated Israel's reservations on parts of the Road Map. Specifically, Sharon took issue with the three-year time frame. This specific concern was revealing, for it hinted at Israel's preference for an interim arrangement with the Palestinians for an indefinite period. The Palestinians were justifiably concerned that absent a Palestinian state, facts on the ground were being created through the continuation of settlement activity and the building of the separation wall. In an apparent attempt to limit suicide bombings, Israel had started building a system of walls and other barriers in the West Bank that extended into West Bank territory and expropriated additional Palestinian land.

The Palestinians responded that Israeli predictions that the Road Map would lead to the government's collapse were unconvincing, particularly because Labor was ready to join the government if it fell, and that they could not uphold their commitments until Israel accepted the Road Map. Although Nabil Shaath, who had relayed all this to me in a phone call, was not overly optimistic about the meeting, he said that he still believed the meeting was "not negative" and added that Palestinian security chief Muhammad Dahlan gave a thorough description of the Palestinian security plan.

I was resting in my house on Friday, May 23, when the telephone rang. It was Edward "Skip" Ghnem, the American ambassador. "I need to see you right away," he said. To my great joy, Ghnem told me that the president had called Sharon and asked him for an immediate acceptance of the Road Map. Sharon obliged. The announcement was to be made that day, he added, with plans to convene a meeting with other Arab states in Sharm El-Sheikh and another meeting between the Palestinians and the Israelis in a location to be agreed upon. I immediately suggested Aqaba, and Ghnem said the Americans would work on it.

Powell also called me to tell me the good news. I had one concern in mind. "Did you strike a deal with the Israelis where acceptance of the Road Map by Israel would be on a selective basis? Is there a secret deal with the Israelis?" I asked him. For me, the matter was straightforward. If Israel and the United States had indeed struck a secret deal, then the entire Road Map would effectively be null and void, particularly considering the Israelis' fourteen reservations. Powell assured me that there was no secret deal and that despite the Israeli reservations, the Road Map had been accepted in its entirety.

This was unexpected but welcome news, of course. I felt that all our labor was finally bearing fruit. In the span of a year, we had played a crucial role in convincing the United States to look beyond security issues, then had moved toward offering Palestinians a political horizon, following that up with an action plan to translate that horizon into concrete steps, and finally getting all the parties to accept such a plan. Against great odds, and despite the violence of the previous year, we had made a significant achievement.

In the days leading to the two summits, due to take place on June 3 and 4, we worked closely with the Americans to make the arrangements, particularly since the Americans had decided to hold the second meeting, involving Sharon and Abbas, in Aqaba in acknowledgment of Jordan's peacemaking efforts.

William Burns and Elliott Abrams, the senior NSC official on the Middle East, came to Amman on May 31 for the final preparations. The Arab parties invited to Sharm El-Sheikh were Saudi Arabia, Jordan, Morocco, the Palestinian Authority, Bahrain, and, of course, Egypt. The attendance of King Muhammad VI of Morocco had been derailed by a terrorist attack in Rabat a few days earlier in which scores of civilians died. Mubarak was to speak on behalf of Arab states, while Bush would outline the American position. In Aqaba, the Palestinians and Israel were expected to announce their acceptance of the Road Map and their willingness to put it into action.

Abrams wanted a forthcoming Arab statement in the Sharm El-Sheikh meeting. But I argued that Arab states would need to see how forthcoming the Israeli statement would be, since we could not be seen by Arab public opinion as being more forthcoming than the Israelis. Burns and Abrams stressed that all the statements would be forthcoming and that they had coordinated this with the Israelis and the Palestinians.

Prince Saud phoned me ahead of the summit to express concern over the Americans' insistence that Arab states take confidence-building measures vis-à-vis Israel ahead of a final, comprehensive settlement between all Arab parties and Israel. The Americans had suggested the following text to be part of the communiqué to be issued at Sharm El-Sheikh: "Arab states would adopt forms of interchange with Israel—economic, commercial and diplomatic—as negotiations between Israel and Palestinians continue, as proof of a common intent to see normal relations established with Israel." Saud thought such steps toward normalization were premature. I suggested inserting the word "ultimately" after the phrase "normal relations" to indicate that such measures would not be immediately implemented. Burns and Abrams shared with us the outline of the American, Palestinian, and Israeli statements. The Israeli statement would include "resuming negotiations with the Palestinians in accordance with steps of the Road Map they adopted." I did not think this went far enough toward unconditional acceptance of the terms of the Road Map and said this. I also noted that the American statement had specifically stated what Israel would receive from Arab countries in the context of the Arab Initiative but did not specify what Arab states would receive in return for these commitments, also stated in the Arab Initiative. I was, of course, referring to Israel's full withdrawal from oc- cupied Arab territories. I suggested a text that I thought would be ap- proved by all Arab states. It read as follows: "Consistent with and in the context of the Arab Peace Initiative, we reaffirm the collective offer to Is- rael presented in the Beirut Declaration of March 28, 2002." I thought this text was balanced and fair to all parties.

The Arab foreign ministers taking part in the summit met in Sharm El-Sheikh on June 2. Prince Saud was adamant that Saudi Arabia could make no move toward normalization until all the elements of the Arab Initiative were implemented. Since Jordan and Egypt had already signed peace treaties with Israel, this point was not contentious for either coun- try. Powell attended part of the meeting and grew angry. President Bush would not show up at the summit the next morning, he said, unless the Arab statement included a clause on confidence-building measures. Fine, answered Saud, and Crown Prince Abdullah would not attend ei- ther. We met till 3:00 a.m. but failed to resolve the problem.

President Bush arrived early on June 3, but the summit was delayed while the issue was being resolved. Finally, Bush instructed Powell and Rice to tell Saud that he did not want to embarrass Crown Prince Abdul- lah into doing something that made him uncomfortable. The crown prince subsequently presented himself at the meeting an hour behind schedule, and we all breathed easier.

While we were waiting for the crown prince, Bush approached Ab- bas and had a warm conversation with him. The two developed a very good personal relationship from that day forward. Bush was trying to get Arab leaders to give Abbas their strong support, but he was also aware that control of the security situation was in Arafat's hands.

That day was a rare moment of hope. Everyone was upbeat. "If I did not think we could do this, I would not be here today," Bush told the Arab leaders present at the meeting.[5]

The next day we moved to Aqaba for the official launch of the Road Map. Attending were the Israelis, Palestinians, Americans, and Jordani-

ans. The agreement in Aqaba was clear: the Palestinians would renounce violence and the Israelis would agree to the Road Map and to
commence negotiations that would lead to the end of the occupation and
the establishment of an independent Palestinian state.

The four parties had an introductory meeting before the Palestinians and the Israelis met with the American delegation. President Bush
was unusually stern with the Israelis, admonishing them in front of the
Palestinians for insisting on the "unrealistic" demand of a seven-day
quiet period before the Israelis would agree to sit down with their Palestinian counterparts. He told King Abdullah II that Prime Minister Abbas
needed to be strengthened and that Israel needed to do its part.

President Bush delivered a compelling speech in which he expressed the United States's commitment to the establishment of a "viable, democratic, peaceful, Palestinian state." He also emphasized that
"as the Road Map accepted by the parties makes clear, both must make
tangible immediate steps towards this two-state solution."

Mahmoud Abbas then delivered the most courageous speech of his
life. Despite objections from his own delegation, he called for an end to
the "militarization of the intifada," the disarmament of all Palestinian
groups with the exception of those military and police groups under the
authority of the Palestinian Authority, a complete end to violence, and the
institutionalization of measures to prevent incitement from Palestinian
institutions. He also empathized with the "suffering of Jews throughout
history." It was the speech of a true statesman, in which the occupied, op-
pressed party addressed the suffering of the occupier instead of its own.
The Palestinian delegation was concerned that such a gesture might not
be reciprocated by the Israelis and might therefore backfire with Palestinian public opinion. Abbas would not budge. He wanted to assume the
high moral ground, and he did so with style and courage.

The consideration he displayed unfortunately was not reciprocated
by Ariel Sharon. He showed no empathy for the suffering of Palestinians under the occupation, and he described the end of the occupation in
technical and mechanical terms. While he talked about Israel's understanding of the importance of territorial contiguity in the West Bank for
a viable Palestinian state, he avoided any suggestion of the borders of
this future state or the three-year time frame to which the Road Map referred. Indeed, he did not utter the words "road map" once during his

speech, even though Abbas referred to it as a plan "which we have accepted without any reservation." Sharon also stopped short of promising an immediate and full freeze of all settlement activity, sufficing with a promise to dismantle "unauthorized posts." Sharon might have satisfied the Americans by mentioning issues that were agreed on, but his words did not carry a conciliatory tone. It was a speech strictly for Israeli public consumption; Sharon's Palestinian audience, which almost certainly was as attuned to the Israeli leader as to its own, was not addressed at all.

But that was not all. Raanan Gissin, Sharon's spokesman, met in Aqaba on the day of the summit with the press for an off-the-record briefing on Israel's interpretation of the Road Map. He stressed the point that Israel had no intention of implementing the Road Map beyond Phase II, essentially asserting that Israel could live with a Palestinian state with provisional borders for an indefinite period but was not ready to accept a permanent Palestinian state, let alone end the occupation in three years.

This explicitly contradicted the provisions of the Road Map and U.S. assurances that Israel had accepted the Road Map in its entirety, despite its reservations. I was furious. I gave a long interview to Jordan Television with the purpose of admonishing Israel for its apparent deception. The Israelis, I thought, were not acting in good faith. In another interview I gave to an Israeli publication few weeks later, I stressed, "We are not talking about a provisional state with temporary borders. We are clearly talking about a Palestinian state with permanent borders, based on the Arab proposal. Any suggestion to the contrary is an attempt to play with words and with peoples' future."[6]

Aqaba thus witnessed the difficult birth of what was supposed to be the beginning of a three-year process that would terminate the Israeli occupation of the West Bank, establish an independent and viable Palestinian state, and end Israel's occupation of Syrian and Lebanese lands, resulting in a comprehensive and permanent regional peace. The summit represented the pinnacle of peacemaking efforts in the region and the brightest point along that difficult, long, and painful road. Yet the tone of Sharon's speech and his spokesman's briefing to the Israeli press that day cast an immediate shadow on the seriousness of the Israeli position. Although the summit resulted in pledges by all to end the violence and to restart political negotiations that had been stagnant since

February 2001, we were all hoping for the United States to commit to a sustained effort that would provide traction to a fragile process.

Abbas immediately resumed talks with all Palestinian factions to arrive at a truce, or hudna, to end the armed intifada and stop suicide bombings. However, the radical groups, provoked by Abbas's speech at the summit, were not in the mood to listen. Israel, meanwhile, had begun to dismantle some small "illegal" posts.[7] On June 10, Hamas leader Abdel Aziz Rantisi survived an Israeli assassination attempt, and a suicide bombing the next day resulted in sixteen Israelis dead. Within the span of only a few days, the relatively positive atmosphere created by the spirit of the Aqaba summit had vanished.

The Quartet held its next meeting in Amman on June 22, on the side of a meeting of the World Economic Forum at the Dead Sea. The security situation rather than moving ahead on the political track dominated their discussions.

The Palestinian factions finally agreed to a three-month truce on all armed activity, which was announced on June 29. Mahmoud Abbas, en route to the United States, stopped in Amman to see King Abdullah II on July 22. He reported improvements in the security situation and in coordination with the Israelis. But the Israelis still had not allowed Arafat any freedom of movement, exacerbating the tension that already existed between the two men.

During that meeting, I urged Muhammad Dahlan to submit to the Americans in writing an overview of a three-month security plan the Palestinians intended to implement. I explained that the United States appreciated written plans, not verbal ones, believing that written documents were evidence of a stronger commitment. Abbas agreed to do so once in Washington.

I phoned William Burns to urge him to give Abbas something tangible during his trip to Washington. "You cannot keep talking about supporting Abbas without following this with concrete steps," I argued. Abbas, having been appointed by Arafat under strong international pressure, was a strong supporter of peaceful negotiations to end the conflict and had taken public positions, often unpopular, against suicide bombings and killing civilians. He needed to show Palestinians that his policies were paying off, in terms of improving economic conditions, easing the Israeli siege on the

Palestinian areas, and getting Israel to release Palestinian prisoners. Otherwise, his ability to survive was in doubt. Burns readily agreed.

Abbas came back energized by his U.S. trip. He had made a very favorable impression not only on the Bush administration but also on Congress. He met again with the king on July 30 to brief him on his trip. But the Palestinians did not present the United States with a written security plan, probably out of a fear that it might be leaked. The United States,which had done little to address Israel's failure to help Abbas deliver something tangible to the Palestinians, was starting to blame Abbas instead, feeling that he was either unable or unwilling to firmly act on security issues. Burns informed me in August that Abbas was starting to lose the president's support and added that Palestinian pledges to the Bush administration on curbing violence and implementing a security plan had not been kept.

Meanwhile, the tension between Arafat and Abbas had forced itself onto center stage in domestic Palestinian politics. The Quartet was getting increasingly frustrated with Arafat, who seemed reluctant to address the security situation effectively or to give Abbas authority to do so. Since Israel repeatedly used this as a pretext for not inaction on implementing the Road Map, members of the Quartet in addition to Jordan and Egypt were struggling to find ways to break the impasse. In an attempt to defuse the tension between the two men, I suggested to Abbas and several others, including Javier Solana and Russian foreign minister Ivanov, to agree on a paper that would outline the responsibilities of Arafat and present it to him for approval. After discussing the content of the paper with everyone, I came up with the following draft:

> Commitments of the Palestinian Authority President, Yasser Arafat
> - Proactive support for the Palestinian Authority cabinet in all areas within its mandate and refrain from any acts that aim and/or are perceived as undermining the cabinet's work.
> - Continued and consistent public expression of this support.
> - Consolidation of all security agencies under the command of the ministry of the interior.
> - Abstention from issuing any provocative public statements, which might be construed as inconsistent with the spirit of the peace process.

- Commitment to adhere to all the regulations controlling the financial management of the Palestinian Authority finances as put forward by the Palestinian Authority's ministry of finance. The regulations will guarantee transparency and accountability for the administration of the Palestinian Authority.
- Commitment to guarantee the independence and noninterference in the Palestinian judicial system.

    In return, and only if the above commitments are respected, the international community, including the European Union, the United Nations, Russia, and key Arab states, pledges to:

- Maintain contact with President Arafat, including visits by senior officials.
- Make serious and genuine efforts to secure the movement of President Arafat in and out of the Palestinian territories.

Otherwise, if it becomes evident to members of the international community that President Arafat's support for the Palestinian Authority cabinet is lacking, the international community will take a unified stand against all forms of contact with President Arafat.

This was a tough move, one that presented dilemmas for everyone, including myself. After all, Arafat had been elected; Abbas had not. Arafat's legitimacy was derived from the popular will, yet he was acting in a way that all but prevented any chances of a process that would lead to a two-state solution. It was ironic to reach the conclusion that it was necessary to ignore basic tenets of democratic rule to achieve a bigger and nobler objective: peace and an end to the occupation.

The initiative was designed as an attempt to break the Israeli and American veto against meeting with Arafat, while making it clear to Arafat that he should not put obstacles in the way of the new Palestinian cabinet. I had many discussions with the Quartet members on how best to deliver this to Arafat, but we came to no conclusion. The initiative was never given to Arafat. Abbas, meanwhile, submitted his resignation in early September over what he saw as Arafat's continued undermining of his authority.

The king traveled in September to the United States, where we met with President Bush and his team at Camp David. Bush, feeling that Abbas was not assertive enough with Arafat and did little beyond words to address the suicide bombings issue, told the king that "he bet on Abbas and lost the bet." He added that while he was still committed to the Road Map, he would "never deal with Arafat." That was the strongest position on Arafat we had heard from Bush until then. We found even Powell disappointed with both Abbas and Dahlan for not acting on security. Meanwhile, Israel's excuses for not moving forward were accepted in full, without question. I suggested that we agree on a set of detailed steps that both Arafat and Israel need to take in the short term, but Bush was uninterested. His exact words were: "We are in a war mentality. If we fight terror there (in the occupied territories), I am prepared to gallop."[8] Bush had fully equated the suicide bombings with terror now and had written Arafat off forever.

During a meeting with Nabil Shaath in New York a few days later, I relayed the American position, but it did not seem to penetrate. Shaath had shaken hands with the president at the United Nations and interpreted the niceties that Bush had extended to him as proof that the president was still open to dealing with Arafat. We knew he was dead wrong.

Only three months after its announcement, the Road Map was in serious trouble. Many people had already declared it dead. We thought that to simply abandon the plan was a mistake, since it was a document that had been accepted by all the parties and by the international community. It would be a long time before an alternative plan could muster such international acceptance. Jordan believed that it was important to inject new life into it.

The fact is that both sides failed to live up to their commitments. The Palestinians could and should have done a lot more to deal with the security situation by closing the arms factories, confiscating illegal weapons, freezing funds that were going to illegal organizations, closing the cross-border tunnels through which arms were being smuggled, and implementing a comprehensive security plan. That they did not do so allowed Israel and the United States to do little to place the Road Map into gear and resume political negotiations. Arafat's indecisiveness resulted in obstructing work toward ending the occupation; he refused to lift a finger until he was allowed free movement, and he undermined Abbas every step of the way.

Israel meanwhile squandered a unique opportunity to help Abbas build his authority by allowing him to show Palestinians that they could benefit from his peace policy. In fact, not only did Israel not use the opportunity, but it appeared as if it had made a conscious decision not to do so. Israel made no attempt to make life easier for the Palestinians by easing measures at checkpoints, refusing to release prisoners, withholding money it owed the Palestinian Authority, and pursuing its policy of targeted assassinations. In the end, Abbas had nothing to show his people for his moderation and, especially, his call for an end to the armed intifada. Israel's announcement that it would begin construction on a separation wall signaled to every Palestinian that it had completely abandoned any attempt to reach a two-state solution, delivering a new blow to Abbas's credibility. Israel, it became apparent, was never serious about accepting and implementing the Road Map as written. Instead, Israel created its own understanding of the Road Map whereby it would only accept a provisional Palestinian state comprising about half of the occupied territories only and for an indefinite period.

Arab states also could have done more, namely by expressing their unambiguous, collective condemnation of suicide bombings. Instead of leading public opinion by articulating a moral and a political argument against such operations, most Arab states instead chose to be led by public opinion, which was particularly emotional and emanated from frustration at the continuation of the occupation. This policy of appeasement would soon come back to haunt nearly every Arab country in the form of suicide bombings targeting Arabs in Arab cities in Iraq, Morocco, Egypt, Saudi Arabia, Jordan, and elsewhere.

Last, the United States also could have used its influence with the parties more effectively. There was no serious effort to push Israel into accepting its part of the responsibilities, while the Palestinians were often asked to be in charge of, manage, and monitor things that were well beyond their control. The administration refused to acknowledge the Israeli occupation of the Palestinians as the core of the problem, choosing instead to equate terror à la Al-Qaeda mode with the violence in the West Bank. Bush was not willing to confront obvious Israeli inconsistencies, such as its piecemeal acceptance of the Road Map, postponing the squaring of the circle for some other time that never arrived. Finally, the administration never had the political will to lead a sustained effort and provide daily engagement with the parties necessary to overcome the trust gap between them. By letting issues simmer for a long time, the situation more often than not worsened without a third party such as the United States able to stop such deterioration and make sure the process remained on track.

By September, the peace process was again eclipsed by the situation in Iraq, which by then was deteriorating apace. The Road Map never had a fighting chance. Each side blamed the other, and in the absence of a credible monitoring party able to judge performance, the stronger party, Israel, was able to keep on creating facts on the ground that moved the peace process further from its goal of a negotiated two-state solution and closer to an imposed solution that addressed only Israeli needs.

In November, the United Nations Security Council passed Resolution 1515, adopting the Road Map between Israel and the Palestinians as UN policy and endorsing a two-state solution to the conflict.

A group of Palestinian and Israeli parliamentarians, ex-officials, and academics, led by Yossi Beilin on the Israeli side and Yasser Abed Rabbo on the Palestinian side, produced a document that was signed at the Dead Sea in Jordan in October 2003, which offered a model of a final peace treaty. The Geneva document, named for the Swiss government's official support for it, was based on informal negotiations that resumed where official negotiations at Taba ended in February 2001.[9] Although it was not produced through official negotiations, it remains to this day a testament that a solution between the two parties is possible and can address the needs of both. To critics who claimed Palestinians and Israelis could never arrive at a final settlement between them, the document left no issue unsettled, with detailed solutions for all the thorny issues, including those of refugees, Jerusalem, settlements, borders, and ending the conflict. Should official negotiations start again, issues would of course have to be renegotiated between the two parties. But the power of the Geneva document is in highlighting that it is not beyond the ability of reasonable people on both sides to arrive at a settlement that meets the basic aspirations of both peoples, and therefore one that would last.

At the Madrid Peace Conference, with Foreign Minister Kamel Abu-Jaber, October 1991 (Author's photo)

Presenting my credentials to President Ezer Weizman, Jerusalem, April 10, 1995 (Courtesy Isaac Harari)

My first meeting with Prime Minister Yitzhak Rabin, Jerusalem, April 11, 1995 (Courtesy Israeli Office of the Prime Minister)

Palestinian Authority minister Faisal Husseini and I at Orient House, East Jerusalem, April 25, 1995 (Author's photo)

President Clinton, King Hussein, and I at the Oval Office, June 15, 1998 (Courtesy White House)

The Wye River Agreement signing ceremony at the White House, October 23, 1998 (Courtesy AP, Doug Mills)

King Hussein's funeral, with four U.S. presidents attending, Amman, February 8, 1999 (Courtesy White House)

Trying to convince President Émile Lahoud of Lebanon to support the Arab Peace Initiative, Beirut, March 20, 2002 (Courtesy AFP, Joseph Barrak)

At the Arab Summit Foreign Ministers Meeting, Beirut, March 25, 2002 (Courtesy AFP, Joseph Barrak)

Walking out of the State Department with Secretary of State Colin Powell, Washington, April 5, 2002 (Courtesy AFP, Tim Sloan)

My last meeting with Yasser Arafat in Ramallah, June 23, 2002. The expression on my face said it all (Courtesy AFP, Ahmad Awad)

Foreign Minister Ahmad Maher of Egypt, Foreign Minister Prince Saud Al-Faisal of Saudi Arabia, and I with President George W. Bush and Secretary Powell at the Oval Office, July 18, 2002 (Courtesy AFP, Shawn Thew)

King Abdullah II and President Bush at the meeting that launched the Road Map, Oval Office, August 1, 2002 (Courtesy Yousef Allan)

With EU High Commissioner Javier Solana and Miguel Moratinos in Amman, October 8, 2002 (Courtesy AFP, Leila Gorchev)

Talking to King Abdullah II at the Sharm El-Sheikh summit on the Road Map, June 3, 2003 (Courtesy Yousef Allan)

تصوير : يوسف العلان

President Mahmoud Abbas, President Bush, Prime Minister Ariel Sharon, and King Abdullah II at the Aqaba summit, June 4, 2003 (Courtesy Yousef Allan)

With Foreign Minister Farouq Sharaa of Syria and foreign ministers of states neighboring Iraq, Damascus, November 1, 2003 (Courtesy AFP, Louai Beshara)

King Abdullah II and President Bush at the White House Rose Garden, May 6, 2004 (Courtesy Yousef Allan)

Addressing the United Nations General Assembly on the Israeli separation wall, September 27, 2004 (Courtesy UN, Michelle Poire)

Announcing the capture of an Iraqi terrorist woman in the aftermath of the Amman hotel bombings, Amman, November 13, 2005 (Courtesy AP, Nader Daoud)

Members of the Jordanian National Agenda Committee presenting their work to King Abdullah II, November 23, 2005 (Courtesy Yousef Allan)

CHAPTER SEVEN

Bush's Letters to Prime Minister Sharon and King Abdullah II

IRAQ CONTINUED TO DOMINATE the scene in early 2004. The peace process was going nowhere, and the new Palestinian government of Ahmad Qurei, known as Abu Alaa, having replaced the government of Mahmoud Abbas, did not seem to be willing to do much regarding the security situation. We found the new Palestinian prime minister not enthusiastic about working with the international community or the Americans. He had been among the PLO leadership in exile that had established the back channel with the Israelis that led to the Oslo Accords, and he seemed determined to continue to speak directly to the Israelis, convinced that he could arrive at a settlement on final issues if he did that. But no one on the Israeli side was prepared to talk. Shimon Peres, with whom Abu Alaa enjoyed an excellent relationship, carried little clout in the Sharon government. Nevertheless, the Palestinian prime minister was depending almost exclusively on Peres to help him cut a deal. It never came.

At the start of the year, the United States introduced the Greater Middle East Initiative to its discourse on the Middle East. The GMEI was a blueprint for reform that would cover a geographically redefined Middle East, from Afghanistan to Morocco. The prevalent thinking was that reform was the key to stability and prosperity in the region and, as such, that the priority of reform should supersede all others. Any link between the Arab-Israeli conflict and reform, or the lack of it, was dismissed, ignored, or marginalized.

In an effort to get the United States reengaged in the peace process, the British were working on a detailed security plan with the Palestinians and Israelis, hoping to convince the Americans of its utility. Despite their valiant efforts, however, the plan never got any traction. The Israelis again were not prepared to act, and the Americans' focus at this point had shifted to the issue of reform.

In the Jordanian cabinet, I had taken a strong stand against suicide bombings, believing that time and again they had hurt the Palestinian cause. If the Arab objective was an end to the occupation and the establishment of a Palestinian state, then suicide bombings had certainly not contributed to that goal in any way. On the contrary, facts on the ground demonstrated that suicide bombings were moving us further from that goal. Not everyone shared this view. During one parliamentary session at the end of January in which I was present, a deputy belonging to the Islamic Action Front practically accused me of treason because of this position. I was determined not to be intimidated. My answer was firm. Resisting the occupation is a justifiable right, but killing civilians is not. Jordan would not shy away from taking a principled position on this issue. Many parliamentarians came to praise me after the session for the position I took, and I felt I had made my point. The issue was not raised again in parliament by the Islamic opposition.

We began work on a draft resolution on the Arab-Israeli conflict for the upcoming Arab summit in Tunis, because we believed that the Arab world needed to follow Jordan's lead in publicly condemning suicide bombings. The draft resolution included a clause demanding that Israel announce its unequivocal, unqualified support for the full text of the Road Map, including those provisions requiring the end of the occupation and the establishment of an independent, viable Palestinian state. I met with Ahmad Maher on March 22 in Cairo, where we coordinated our positions regarding this issue ahead of the summit. Maher assured me that Egypt would support the resolution when we submitted it at the summit.

While we were hammering out our plan to move things forward, Israel was also working on a scheme. Prime Minister Sharon raised the idea of a unilateral disengagement from Gaza, against some opposition from his cabinet, and announced that a plan to evacuate Gaza would be ready by midyear. He dispatched Dov Weisglass to Washington to discuss the proposal with the Bush administration, with the aim of securing American support for a plan that clearly deviated from the Road Map, which the United States had publicly endorsed. Sa'eb Ereikat told me that in his meeting with Weisglass on March 14, Weisglass had explicitly stated that Israel considered the Gaza withdrawal as a substitute for, rather than a part of, the Road Map.

I traveled to Washington on March 8 to discuss the reform issue and the peace process but found the administration preoccupied with Iraq and the Greater Middle East Initiative. The United States seemed ready to back Sharon's plan, particularly during an election year when opposing it might have invited domestic pressure. The U.S. position was that the disengagement, under the right conditions, might serve as a useful mechanism to get back to the Road Map. We wanted to make sure that it was part of the Road Map, and not a substitute for it.

On March 22 Israel assassinated the head of Hamas, Sheikh Ahmad Yassin. Not since the assassination in 1988 of Abu Jihad, the PLO's number two in Tunis, had Israel carried out such a high-profile killing. The crippled cleric was killed in his wheelchair by a rocket fired from an Israeli helicopter after he had finished morning prayers at a Gaza mosque. The assassination drew criticism from capitals all over the world, and immediate, widespread protests in the West Bank, fueled the volatile situation. Abdel Aziz Rantisi was immediately named Yassin's successor. He announced that there would be no ceasefire with the Jewish state and that Hamas operations against Israel would continue. Sheikh Yassin had recently been hinting that a long-term ceasefire with Israel might be possible in lieu of peace, which Hamas could not yet commit to. If Yassin was paving the way for the transformation of Hamas into something more palatable to the Israelis, his assassination could not have come at a worse time, particularly since his successor, Rantissi was known to be more hard-line than him on this issue.

While I was in Tunis to prepare for the summit at the end of March, Tunisia announced its wish to postpone the summit. The government took exception to the blueprint on reform in the Arab world due to be submitted at the summit, believing that it did not go far enough in addressing some reform issues, particularly on women's rights.

As a result of Dov Weisglass's recent meetings in Washington, the United States sent three senior officials to the region to discuss the Israeli proposal for "disengagement": Deputy National Security Adviser Stephen Hadley, Elliott Abrams from the NSC, and William Burns from the State Department. We soon found out, however, that what they had come to discuss was far more dangerous than we had surmised.

I met with the group in Amman on March 31. Hadley started the meeting stating that the purpose of their visit was to discuss Sharon's plan and that the delegation would later meet with the Egyptians and the Palestinians. He readily acknowledged that Sharon was talking about an alternative to the Road Map, since there was no longer any Palestinian partner for negotiations, in his opinion. Hadley made it clear that the United States was lining up behind the plan when he stated that the administration was focusing on Gaza once the Israelis withdrew. The Bush administration wanted to catalyze on what the Israelis were doing to push the Palestinians to move forward and ensure a smooth transition with no terrorist acts. If this worked, there would be proof that a Palestinian partner existed, and we could all go back formally to the Road Map, he argued.

I told the group that what was important to Jordan was the larger picture, and that was a two-state solution. Any plan that did not clearly state that as an objective and lead toward it would set off alarms in the region, especially in Jordan. I stressed that the two-state solution should be the yardstick by which any success should be measured. Therefore, I told Hadley, Jordan's support for and cooperation within this plan would depend largely on assurances from the United States and Israel on the two-state solution endgame.

The beginning of construction on the Israeli separation wall, coupled with Sharon's unilateral move to disengage from Gaza, had made clear to Jordan that the Israelis were moving away from a two-state solution—if they had ever been committed to it in the first place. The absence of a two-state solution signaled to Jordan that other much more threatening alternatives—especially, the alternative homeland policy option—had found their way back onto the table, whether by default or by design. A Palestinian state on Palestinian soil had been the core of Jordanian foreign policy for quite some time and had guided all Jordan's recent efforts in Arab-Israeli peacemaking. Any deviation from that objective was thus detrimental not only for the interests of the Palestinians but for those of Jordan.

What we heard from the Americans was unsettling, and Hadley added nothing to allay our fears. On the contrary, he acknowledged that Sharon had appealed to the United States to support the disengagement plan in lieu of the Road Map, which he had described as "dead." According to Hadley, the U.S. objective was to put Sharon's plan in a context to advance the Road Map and President Bush's vision. As such, the administration intended to support Sharon's proposal, even if it differed on what would happen next.

I would not budge, reiterating that Jordanian support depended on the commitment to the endgame of a two-state solution. I also asked Hadley whether the United States intended to give concessions to Israel regarding the Road Map commitments in return for the withdrawal from Gaza, urging him not to do so. William Burns suggested at this point the idea of a Security Council resolution that enforced a two-state solution, an idea I told him was useful.

Burns next turned to an even more troubling issue. Israel had asked the United States for a position on four issues, to be made public during Sharon's visit to the United States in April:

1. The United States will not impose anything on the Israelis or the Palestinians.
2. A commitment by the United States to the security of Israel and that the United States will uphold Israel's right to fight terrorism.
3. New language on territory that read along the lines: "Realism suggests that only through mutually agreed adjustments can there be a solution to the Final Status that takes into account demography and security."
4. Language on the refugee issue that does not refer to the right of return.

I told the Americans that we had no problem with the first point as long as Israel committed itself to the three phases of the Road Map, not a partial commitment with fourteen reservations that voided the plan of any substance. On the second point, I expressed concern that Israel would take this as a carte blanche to enter Gaza at will or to continue its targeted assassination policy.

The real problems for us were, however, the third and fourth points. Israeli could easily manipulate "mutually agreed adjustments . . . that [take] into account demography and security" to annex any portion of the West Bank under the pretext of security, thereby undermining in practice the emergence of a viable Palestinian state. If adjustments were to be made, they had to be minor to be accepted, and the text should reflect that, I argued.

Furthermore, previous negotiations between the Palestinians and the Israelis on the refugee issue had produced practical solutions. Those solutions had made clear that Palestinians would not demand that four to five million Palestinian refugees be permitted to return to Israel. Likewise, polls conducted within the Palestinian diaspora suggested that less than 10 percent of those living in the diaspora aspired to return to pre-1948 Palestine, since they would be moving to a culture with which they were unfamiliar, where their language was not widely spoken, and, in many cases, where their homes no longer existed. Nevertheless, surrendering the right of return altogether was something no Arab was prepared to do. The door could not be closed to *any* number of people to return, a number that can be *agreed to* as per the Arab Initiative provisions.

Hadley thought both suggestions were helpful and promised to look into them and to have another look at the Arab Initiative. I left the meeting feeling extremely uncomfortable, however. The United States was clearly looking for ways to justify Sharon's actions, but more dangerously, it was willing to retreat from its positions on the final status of the occupied territories that had been largely unchanged since 1967. Tampering with this longstanding position and a readiness to abandon the provisions of the Road Map so soon after the parties to the conflict had accepted it did not bode well for the future of conflict resolution.

I expressed my concern about these developments to King Abdullah II right after the meeting. The monarch wrote Bush a letter on April 8, ahead of Sharon's visit to the United States, articulating the Jordanian position and pointing out the dangers inherent in the new American position. The king told Bush that he felt strongly that "the Israeli proposal to withdraw from Gaza should be part of the Road Map leading to the achievement of this vision rather than a substitute for it, which would have dangerous negative repercussions on Jordan." He also cautioned against any "concessions on borders that would suggest any major deviation from the 1967 border arrived at through agreement by the two parties." The king also argued that the door to an agreed solution to the refugee problem should be left open. He sought American assurances on these issues "to protect [the United States's] vision of a two-state solution."[1]

I was attending an April 12 conference in Istanbul on reform in the Islamic world when my mobile phone rang. From the other end came the voice of Colin Powell, saying that he had urged the White House to consider my suggestions but had failed to convince officials to do so. Sharon was scheduled to meet with the president on April 14, and Bush was expected to present the Israeli premier with a public letter specifying all four points that Hadley told us would be included, without modification. I knew that Powell agreed with the Jordanian position, and his frustration was palpable over the phone. I was even more frustrated. I warned him about the dangers of retreating from a long-held U.S. position. Powell accepted my offer to find alternative formulations in a last-ditch attempt to save the situation.

I spoke with William Burns over the phone several times on April 12 and 13, hashing out several formulations that would soften the language. On refugees, I proposed a formulation that would state that Palestinians would go back *predominantly* to a Palestinian state, so as not to close the door. Burns was sympathetic but was unable to modify the final text. The hard-liners in the White House had shot down every moderate position we had proposed.

Bush and Sharon appeared jointly at a press conference following their meeting on April 14. Their exchange of letters was made public, and from an Arab point of view, the content of both letters was disastrous. In his letter to Bush, Sharon stated that "Israel has accepted the Roadmap, as adopted by our government." The statement was nothing new; the fact that it had been included in an official exchange of letters, the text of which had been agreed on ahead of time, was what alarmed everyone. For it signaled that the United States no longer opposed the Israeli interpretation of the Road Map—an interpretation that had stopped short of a full, independent Palestinian state. Sharon's letter claimed that Israel's Gaza disengagement proposal, though not being undertaken under the Road Map, was not inconsistent with it. The letter also indicated Israel's plan to accelerate the construction of the so-called security fence, which Israel maintained is "a security rather than a political barrier, temporary rather than permanent."[2]

Bush's letter to Sharon was even more damaging. On refugees, it stated that "an agreed, just, fair and realistic framework for a solution to the Palestinian refugee issue as part of any final status agreement will need to be found through the establishment of a Palestinian state, and the settling of Palestinian refugees there, rather than in Israel." It was essentially a declaration that no number of Palestinian refugees, not even a symbolic one, would be allowed to return to Israel. On borders, the letter stated made the assertion that "in light of new realities on the ground, including already existing major Israeli population centers, it is unrealistic to expect that the outcome of final status negotiations will be a full and complete return to the armistice lines of 1949. . . . It is realistic to expect that any final status agreement will only be achieved on the basis of mutually agreed changes that reflect these realities."[3]

The king was outraged. Administration spin-doctors spoke about the president's commitment to a two-state solution in order to allay Arab fears, but there was no hiding the fact that Bush's letter—although it had no binding force in international law—had taken the American position another step away from international consensus. It had also undermined the Americans' declared policy that no action should be taken by any party to the peace process that would prejudice the outcome of final status negotiations.

Sharp criticism from the European Union was soon forthcoming. An EU foreign ministers meeting in Tullamore, Ireland, on April 16 declared that the union would not recognize any change to the pre-1967 borders other than those arrived at by agreement between the parties. This was the first time the EU had taken such a strong position on final status. The statement further emphasized that the EU's belief that "the refugee question and the manner in which the right of return may be realized is also a final status issue" that must be negotiated and agreed upon along with all the other issues.

King Abdullah II had been scheduled to visit the White House a few days after Sharon's meeting with Bush, but in the wake of the exchange of letters, he was extremely reluctant to attend before the Americans clarified their position. He dispatched me along with Jordan's intelligence chief, General Saad Khair, and Minister of the Royal Court Samir Rifai to

Washington to meet with Condoleezza Rice and assess the situation. As the three of us headed to Washington, the king flew to San Francisco for a speaking engagement on the West Coast, where he would await the outcome of our meetings.

Adding insult to injury, Israel assassinated Hamas's new head, Abdel Aziz Rantisi, on April 17, while we were on our way to Washington. The king, already in California, declared that Israel was not serious about peace and wished to cancel his meeting with Bush. A meeting at the White House with the president following so closely on the heels of the exchange of letters and, especially, Rantissi's assassination could have been interpreted as indifference to these actions. We three Jordanian officials had a conference call with the king from our hotel in Washington that weekend. I asked for twenty-four hours during which I would see if we could somehow reverse the effect of the letter to Sharon. The king agreed.

We went to the White House on April 19, where Condoleezza Rice and Elliott Abrams were at pains to assure us that the letters did not signal a change in American policy. We countered that the king's visit to Washington would be contingent on a similar exchange of letters between the president and the monarch that stated, in writing, that U.S. policy remained unchanged. We also sought assurances that the two-state solution remained the only acceptable outcome of negotiations in order to protect Jordan's interests lest other solutions were considered. The Americans, eager to receive the king after the uproar that the Bush letter had caused in the Arab world and after Rantisi's assassination, agreed to negotiate a letter from President Bush to the king as a reply to the monarch's letter of April 8. Thus, on Monday, April 19, our small delegation sat down all day with Rice and Abrams to agree on the content of the letter and the public exchanges between the two heads of state.

Meanwhile, the charged atmosphere at home created by the developments of the past few days inclined the king to return to Jordan even while I was negotiating the letter with Abrams. Oddly, a CIA official asked me during a lunch break why, under the circumstances, I was insisting on the king coming to Washington. I had to explain the merits of obtaining a letter from the president that would negate or dilute his letter to Sharon. This incident and the many discussions this official had with General Khair that day made me believe that Khair was convinced of the CIA's argument and was advising the king not to come. Why the CIA and Khair wanted to dissuade the monarch from coming to Washington remains a mystery to me, although I suspected that they believed the visit might invite an open disagreement with Bush. At any rate, I received phone calls repeatedly during the day from the king's entourage on the West Coast to ask me how things were going and suggesting that they were considering returning to Amman. I pressed for more time, until finally, at 4:30 p.m. on Monday, we arrived at a formulation that I thought effectively eliminated the damage caused by what Bush had given to Sharon a few days earlier.

In the end, however, the letters were never exchanged. The king decided to go home. The elation I felt from achieving a new formulation immediately evaporated. To be sure, Elliott Abrams called me shortly afterward to tell me the deal was off. If there was no royal visit, there would be no letter.

For the historical record, I include here the full text of the letter we negotiated to illustrate what could have transpired were the visit to have been completed.

Your Majesty,

Thank you for your letter of April 8th.

I want to respond to your request for certain assurances related to the United States' position on the Israeli plan to withdraw all settlements from Gaza and certain settlements from the West Bank, and to my vision for a two-state solution to the Palestinian-Israeli conflict.

I remain committed to my June 24, 2002 vision of two states living side by side in peace and security, and the road map as the route to get there. As I stated on that date, "Ultimately, Israelis and Palestinians must address the core issues that divide them if there is to be a real peace, resolving all claims and ending the conflict between them. This means that the Israeli occupation that began in 1967 will be ended through a settlement negotiated between the parties, based on UN Resolutions 242 and 338 . . ." The United States views the two-state solution as the only acceptable resolution to the

conflict. We view the Israeli withdrawals from certain settlements and military installations in the occupied territories of
Gaza and the West Bank as steps towards achieving that vision,
and hope that they can have the effect of jump starting
progress on the road map.

As I said last week, the United States supports the establishment of a Palestinian state that is viable, contiguous, sovereign, and independent. *The United States will not prejudice the
outcome of final status negotiations, including on the borders of a
Palestinian state [emphasis added]*; that matter is for the parties. I
reiterate the commitment made in the letter of assurances to
Jordan on the eve of the Madrid Conference in 1991 that "no
party should take unilateral actions that seek to predetermine
issues that can only be resolved through negotiations." A final
settlement on borders and therefore any changes from the
"Green Line" must be mutually agreed by Palestinians and Israelis, and in our view should take into account existing realities on the ground *and the viability of the new Palestinian state,
and should consider all previous efforts to negotiate a two-state solution [emphasis added]*.

The United States will work with all the parties to help
achieve the establishment of a Palestinian state in a timely
manner and in accordance with the roadmap's performance-
based plan. *We view the security, prosperity and integrity of Jordan
as vital, and I am pleased to assure you and the people of Jordan
that the United States will oppose any outcome that might endanger these key interests [emphasis added]*. As part of any U.N. Security Council action related to Palestinian statehood, we are prepared to seek a resolution reaffirming these points.

The United States believes that the barrier being erected by
Israel should be a security rather than a political barrier. It
should be temporary rather than permanent, and therefore not
prejudice any final status issues, including final borders.

As you know, on April 14th I made a statement about the
issue of refugees and its relationship to the establishment of a
Palestinian state. I also said that, like all final status issues, this
issue must be resolved in final status negotiations between the

parties. *Obviously, no issue has been taken off the table [emphasis added]*. The United States remains committed, as the roadmap states, to a "final and comprehensive permanent status agreement that . . . includes an agreed, just, fair, and realistic solution to the refugee issue." The settlement, as the roadmap states, will be "based on the foundations of the Madrid Conference, the principle of land for peace, UNSCRs 242, 338, and 1397, agreements previously agreed by the parties, *and the initiative of Crown Prince Abdullah—endorsed by the Beirut Arab League Summit [emphasis added]*."

The United States will join with others in the international community, including Jordan, to strengthen the capacity and will of the Palestinian Authority to fulfill its obligations under the roadmap and to have all the parties resume the implementation of the roadmap.

Your Majesty, you have been an ardent supporter of the peace process and efforts to resolve the Palestinian-Israeli dispute in a just and fair manner. As a close friend and ally, the United States intends to continue to work closely with you to help achieve that goal.

An examination of the letter shows that the United States acknowledged that it would not prejudice final status negotiations and that any final agreement on borders had to take into account both the viability of a Palestinian state and agreements previously reached by the parties. Such a public assurance from the United States was necessary so that Israel would not feel it had carte blanche to draw borders that were significantly different than the 1967 lines. The United States acknowledged that no issue, including that of refugees, had been taken off the table and that an agreement on the refugee question would be based on the Arab Initiative, where UN Resolution 194 was explicitly mentioned. Again, this negated the previous letter where the United States did not acknowledge the right of any refugees to return to their homes. Finally, the draft of the U.S. letter assured Jordan that it continued to regard a two-state solution as the only acceptable outcome of the peace process and stated that it would oppose any outcome that endangered Jordan's interests.

The king kept me in Washington to discuss the issue of the visit further with the administration. The following day, April 20, Powell told me that the king's postponement of his visit had created tension in the White House and that he needed a few days to talk to the president before further work on the letter and the visit could proceed. He also acknowledged that the letter we had negotiated was excellent. "The State Department would never have obtained such a strong letter," he said candidly, adding that he would have to discuss it with the president now before he could get Bush to agree to sign it.[4] Powell said the administration had hoped people would see the positive points of Bush's letter to Sharon, which reiterated the president's commitment to the Road Map and a two-state solution. While I of course disagreed that the letter was a positive development to the peace process, we both concurred that bilateral relations between Jordan and the United States were important to both states and should not be negatively affected if possible. After I had consulted with the king, the monarch agreed that he would visit in a few weeks, after tempers had cooled down and we could agree on the text of the letter.

Elliott Abrams was less forthcoming in his reaction. He informed me during a telephone conversation that because the visit had been postponed, Condoleezza Rice had ordered a review and a revision of the draft we had agreed to before it was submitted to the president for his consideration. This was hardball politics at its worst. The news of our work on Bush's letter to the king had already been leaked to the Israelis. An Israeli press report quoted "senior Israeli officials" as criticizing Jordan for "working against the disengagement plan." According to the report, "Israel's ire was raised after it was revealed that Jordanian foreign minister Marwan Muasher had held talks with the Americans in an attempt to produce an American declaration that would soften the promises made by President George Bush in his letter to Sharon last week. The Americans refused."[5] The source of the leak apparently had failed to tell the Israeli paper that the Americans were in fact ready to give such a letter, refusing to do so only after the postponement of the visit.

After returning to Jordan, the king gave me clear directions about the necessary conditions for a future visit to Washington. First, he needed an agreement on an exchange of letters, the full text of which would be agreed to before the meeting, and a second letter of similar American assurances to the Palestinians. I worked the phone with Powell, Rice, and Burns.

Rice called me on May 4 to tell me that the president had agreed to sign a watered-down version that would still meet most of our demands and that she planned to meet with Prime Minister Abu Alaa and give him a similar letter. (That meeting took place on May 17 in Geneva, and Bush sent a letter to the Palestinian prime minister on May 11.) The stage was set for the king to visit Washington.

King Abdullah II and President Bush met at the White House on May 6. During that meeting, Bush reaffirmed that the United States would not prejudice final status talks and that in his letter to Sharon, he had been referring only to realities on the ground that had to be taken into account. The two leaders then entered the Rose Garden for a public ceremony and statements to the press that reflected the content of the two letters exchanged between them.

I reproduce here the section of Bush's letter to the king that dealt with the peace process, again for the historical record.[6] Although the revised letter was not as encompassing as the first one, we believed it still contained enough to negate the impression that the United States was unquestioningly backing Israel's disengagement plans and retreating from policy on the conflict established over decades. Israel could not now say that the final word on the issue of borders and refugees had been uttered by the American president, and the exchange of letters between the monarch and Bush expressed a clear preference for negotiations over unilateralism.

> May 6, 2004
> His Majesty
> King Abdullah II
> Of the Hashemite Kingdom of Jordan
> Amman
> . . . . During our visit, I was pleased to be able to discuss the ongoing quest for a just and durable peace in the Middle East. I commend your efforts in the pursuit of peace and justice in the Palestinian-Israeli dispute. I remain committed as ever to my June 24, 2002 vision of two states, Israel and Palestine, living side by side in peace and security, and to the establishment of a Palestinian state that is viable, contiguous, sovereign and independent. I support the plan announced by Prime Minister

Sharon to withdraw settlements from Gaza and parts of the West Bank. This bold plan can make a real contribution toward peace. *The United States will not prejudice the outcome of final status negotiations, and all final status issues must still emerge from negotiations between the parties in accordance with U.N. Security Council Resolutions 242 and 338 [emphasis added].* The Roadmap—the only plan endorsed by the United Nations, the European Union, Russia, the United States, and so many countries around the world as well as by Israel and the Palestinians—represents the best pathway towards realizing that vision, and I am committed to making it a reality.

The text reaffirmed that the United States would not prejudice final status talks on any issue, implicitly including those of refugees and borders. What was strikingly missing, however, was the reference to the Arab Initiative as one of the terms of reference for a settlement.

In the letter Bush was mindful of Jordan's security concerns arising from the disengagement plan and the erection of the separation barrier, and accordingly accommodated our request to include a paragraph attesting to the validity of Jordan's security concerns. "I assure you that my government views Jordan's security, prosperity, and territorial integrity as vital, and we will oppose any developments in the region that might endanger your interests," Bush wrote in the letter. It was the first time Jordan had ever received such written assurances about its security concerns.

The king, in his public response to President Bush, which had been agreed to with the Americans, wanted to ensure that the above issues were apparent to all. In the clearest reaffirmation of Jordan's position regarding a two-state solution, the king said:

I'd like to outline the Jordanian position on the peace process, particularly in the view of recent developments. We feel that any unilateral Israeli withdrawal from Gaza and the West Bank should be part of the road map, and should lead to the achievement of your vision of a two-state solution. Let me stress that a viable, sovereign, independent Palestinian state on the basis of the 1967 borders is also in Jordan's national interest. Failing to achieve such an outcome would invoke other options, all of which will endanger my country's interests and those of the region. This is one of the reasons why Jordan insists on a two-state solution and why it supports the road map as the mechanism to get there.[7]

This was the best articulation of Jordan's efforts and objectives that the king had made since assuming the throne. It explained concisely and clearly why Jordan had been at the forefront of efforts to achieve a two-state solution.

On final status issues, the king was equally candid. "Jordan also believes that all final status issues, including borders, refugees, Jerusalem and settlements, should be a matter for the parties to decide. I am encouraged by what I've heard from you today, sir, that these issues are not to be prejudiced, and should be mutually agreed by the parties."

The Palestinian Authority was extremely pleased with Jordan's efforts to obtain another letter from Bush addressing the Palestinians specifically. Sa'eb Ereikat called me to tell me how proud he was of the king as he watched the Rose Garden ceremony on television, particularly when the king insisted that Arab rights be respected.

Indeed, we had reason to be proud of the effort. Jordan had moved swiftly, when no other Arab country did, to extract such a letter and a public declaration from the Bush administration. I remained somewhat disappointed, knowing that we could have obtained much more, but the result was still extremely satisfying. I took my elation with me to the Arab foreign ministers in Cairo on May 8. This was a preparatory meeting for the upcoming Tunis Arab Summit, but I used the opportunity to brief my Arab counterparts on what had transpired in Washington.

Almost everyone commended Jordan for its effort. Of course, the commendation was not unanimous. One dissenter was the PLO's foreign minister, Farouq Qaddoumi, who was opposed to the whole peace process and was at odds with the Palestinian Authority itself, and the other was Farouq Sharaa. Although I could dismiss Qaddoumi's reaction and attribute it to his general opposition to the peace process and the fact that he was not taken seriously by other Arab foreign ministers or by the PA itself, I was utterly dismayed by Sharaa's reaction. Always suspicious of Jordan's positions and no doubt dismayed that Jordanian diplomacy was far more effective than Syria's, Sharaa would not agree to a statement that I requested be included in the final communiqué acknowledging the letter that Bush sent to the king and reconfirming what it said about not prejudicing final status issues. I did not ask for praise by Arab countries, only for a confirmation of the position we managed to salvage back on final status issues. "Since the United States is saying in a written letter that issues of final status are the responsibility of the two parties alone, let us build on this stance, benefit from it, and use it to move the peace process," I urged my Arab colleagues in a statement I made to the press in Cairo.[8]

Sharaa refused under the absurd pretext that the Arabs did not want the United States not to prejudge the outcome of negotiations but rather were hoping for the Americans' positive interference on the side of Arabs. His logic failed to convince anyone. I insisted on our position, and in a closed meeting that the foreign ministers called for to solve this "crisis," I suggested submitting the issue for a vote, and if Syria wanted to oppose, it could do so on the record. Sharaa backed down, and the statement was included in the communiqué.

This was Arab internal politics at its worst. Here we were, I thought, fighting alone on behalf of all Arabs, using our relationship with Washington to attempt to reverse what would have been an extremely negative development on part of the American position regarding the conflict, and when we succeeded, even in part, we got this reaction from an Arab country for seemingly personal or ego reasons.

In the end, our efforts to put the peace process back on track were unsuccessful. The United States remained adamantly opposed to talking to Arafat, the elected leader of the Palestinians, while the Israelis also outright opposed a return to negotiations before the security situation had been totally addressed. Sharon continued to threaten Arafat, and the new Palestinian government was paralyzed, a condition that had been partly self-inflicted. And the attention of everyone else in the region had been consumed by events in Iraq.

The Arab summit finally convened in Tunis on May 22, and the Jordanian proposal condemning "attacks against civilians without distinction" in an implicit reference to suicide bombings and violence by Israel was adopted. But it was done after a lot of bickering, especially—and predictably—between me on one hand and Sharaa and Qaddoumi on the other. Even though this was the first time all Arab states publicly made such a statement, it came too late to have a profound effect on international public opinion.

The king had one last meeting in 2004 with President Bush, immediately after the G8 summit in Sea Island, Georgia. Bush was totally preoccupied with Iraq at the meeting. When the king finally managed to steer the conversation to the peace process, Bush did not mince words. "I am sick of the Palestinian-Israeli issue," he told the king.[9]

CHAPTER EIGHT

The Israeli Separation Wall

AN END TO THE TWO-STATE SOLUTION?

Good fences make good neighbors.—Robert Frost, "Mending Wall"

Good fences might make good neighbors—when those fences are erected on one's side of the land, NOT on the neighbor's side.—Jordanian position on the Israeli Separation Wall

IN THE YEARS 2002, 2003, AND 2004 Jordan, Egypt, Saudi Arabia, and the international community made a sustained effort to create a process that would lead to a two-state solution, which would resolve, once and for all, the Arab-Israeli conflict and meet the aspirations of the Palestinians and the Israelis alike. Israel had embarked on a parallel project that threatened all prospects for such a solution and with it Jordan's national interests.

Less than a month after Arab states collectively endorsed the Arab Peace Initiative in 2002, the Israeli government announced that it would build a system of walls, fences, ditches, and barriers in the occupied West Bank, extending for fifty miles, in what it described as a response to the Palestinians' suicide bombings and a protection for its citizens. In fact, the real purpose behind the wall was to establish unilaterally the new borders of Israel, as became evident from the public position two years later of Prime Minister Ehud Olmert, and to make living conditions for Palestinians behind the wall so difficult as to drive them out of the West Bank. Two months later, in June 2002, the Israeli cabinet approved the first phase of construction of a continuous barrier in parts of the West Bank and Jerusalem. The barrier for the most part would be built within the occupied territories, thereby consuming Palestinian land and cutting off tens of thousands of Palestinians from access to their property, schools, places of work, and contact with relatives and other Palestinians.

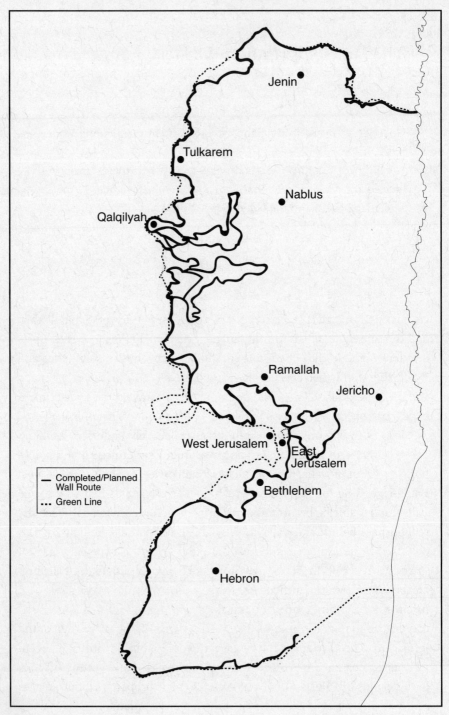

The Israeli separation wall

Israel described this elaborate system of barriers as a "security measure" that was necessary for public safety, not a political border between
it and the Palestinians. But the facts on the ground suggested otherwise.
By the time the Israeli ministry of defense published the planned route
of the wall in October 2003, it was clear that the wall would form a continuous barrier stretching more than four hundred miles through the
West Bank, more than twice as long as the Green Line, the 1967
armistice line between the West Bank and Israel. The barrier would follow a route running almost entirely through land occupied by Israel in
1967. Though sketched to follow the broad contours of the green line,
the barrier would be constructed on the Arab side of the line. At certain
points, it would deviate from the Green Line to penetrate almost fourteen miles into West Bank territory—the width of which ranges from
twelve and a half to thirty-five miles. Overall, the area between the barrier and the Green Line would comprise almost 17 percent of the West
Bank, including all of Jerusalem.

The barrier would affect the livelihoods of more than two hundred
thousand Palestinians, either by placing them into enclaves surrounded
by the wall or by separating them from substantial farmland areas west
of the barrier. It would not only separate Palestinians from their property, extended families, and friends but would severely restrict their
movement in general and reduce the rural population's access to hospitals, schools, and places of work in Tulkarem, Qalqilya, and East
Jerusalem. In Jerusalem, Christian and Muslim Palestinians would be
separated from their places of worship. There is also a strong argument
to be made about cutting off Arab residents of East Jerusalem from the
rest of the West Bank (and vice versa) in an attempt to prevent any possibility of East Jerusalem becoming the capital of a future Palestinian
state.[1] Indeed, a report by the Norwegian Refugee Council published in
September 2006 revealed that thousands of Palestinians have been already forced to leave their homes in the West Bank and East Jerusalem
as a direct result of the wall.[2] More alarmingly, the wall would effectively
cantonize the West Bank, separating not only the West Bank from Israel
but also cutting it into pieces and effectively killing the prospects for the
emergence of a viable, independent Palestinian state with contiguous,
defensible borders.

As the inevitable effects of the barrier became clear, alarm bells sounded in Jordan. The impossibility of a two-state solution introduced three other possibilities for dealing with the Palestinian-Israeli conflict. First, Israel could annex the occupied territories or the Palestinians could ask that their territories be considered part of Israel proper; in either case, the one-state solution required Israel to make the Palestinians full citizens of Israel with equal rights. It is unlikely that either Palestinians or Israelis would contemplate such a solution for long, if at all. It would require the Palestinians to surrender their long-cherished dream of an independent Palestinian state; Israel likewise was unlikely to surrender the idea of a Jewish state. Second, Israel could continue to occupy Palestinian land, at the risk of squandering blood and treasure on low-level conflict for the foreseeable future and of living as a pariah state, shunned by the international community. Or third, it could bring about the immigration of large swathes of the West Bank population, largely to Jordan, by making living conditions in the occupied territories impossible for the Palestinians.

Jordan used all diplomatic channels available to oppose the construction of the separation barrier. We did not accept the Israeli argument that the wall provided a new guarantee of Israel's security, since the course of the wall along much of its length is far removed from any plausible defensive line for the territories on Israel's side of the Green Line. For us, good fences make good neighbors when the fences are erected on your property, not your neighbor's. The two set of fences that Israel constructed around Gaza on its border with Egypt and around its northern border with Lebanon were never contentious for Palestinians precisely because they were constructed along international borders.

THE UNITED NATIONS DEBATE ON THE WALL

By mid-2003, construction of the barrier was of sufficient scale to place the issue on the radar screen of the international community. Secretary of State Powell told me in a telephone conversation in July 2003, one month after the Aqaba summit, that he had spoken to Sharon about the wall and had told him that if Israel wanted to defend itself, it could build a barrier on its side of the Green Line, not on the Palestinian side. Yet, as was usually the case, Powell's principled position was never taken up as policy in the Bush administration, nor did any American effort develop to stop construction of the wall on Palestinian land. In a meeting with King Abdullah II in December 2003, Bush acknowledged that the wall was a problem if it consumed Palestinian land but said that it was diffi- cult for him to assume the high moral ground with Israel while suicide bombings continued.[3]

Consultations with our UN mission in New York as well as the for- eign affairs ministry's legal department persuaded me that Jordan could not stand idly by but had to employ every legal means available to fight this development so detrimental to Jordan's national security. The gov- ernment commenced an international legal and political campaign against the wall.

A Palestinian attempt to pass through a UN Security Council Reso- lution condemning the wall failed to pass in October 2003 because of an American veto. As a result, the Palestinians, backed by Arab states and much of the international community, referred the issue to the United Nations General Assembly, which sought an advisory opinion from the International Court of Justice (ICJ) on the legality of building the wall in- side the occupied territories.[4] Even though such an opinion would be nonbinding in the sense that no power could coerce the parties into im- plementing it, it would still carry weight in the absence of a legally bind- ing Security Council resolution.

The formulation of the question was crucial to achieve objectives that were as much political as legal. The Palestinians' original formula- tion, presented to our UN mission in New York by the Palestinian dele- gation, was the following: "Is Israel under legal obligation to cease its construction of the separation wall, that it is embarked on building in Occupied Palestinian Territory and to dismantle existing parts of the wall under relevant provisions of international law and taking into ac- count relevant Security Council and GA resolutions?" Jordan believed that the essential question to be answered should revolve on the likeli- hood that a resolution requesting such an advisory opinion would be adopted by the General Assembly. Although the overwhelming majority of the UN General Assembly membership legally support the applica- bility of the Fourth Geneva Convention of 1949 on the occupied Pales- tinian territories, with the notable exception of the United States and Is- rael, such requests in the past had almost always run into considerable political opposition from some regional groups such as the European Union. Therefore, ensuring that a vast majority would vote for a resolution to refer the question to the ICJ was crucial. As such, the question had to be formulated in a way that would ensure its adoption by a wide majority in the General Assembly. Jordan's UN mission in New York, which had good legal expertise, worked closely with the Palestinian delegation to modify the advisory opinion.

The General Assembly voted in December 2004, by a margin of ninety votes in favor and eight against, with seventy-four abstentions, for a resolution requesting the ICJ to provide an urgent advisory opinion on the consequences of Israel's construction of the wall in the occupied Palestinian territories, considering Israel's obligations under international law and relevant Security Council and General Assembly resolutions.[5] Most European countries felt that referring the issue to the ICJ would complicate political efforts to move the process forward and hence abstained. Countries that voted against referring the issue to the ICJ were Australia, Micronesia, Israel, Marshall Islands, Nauru, Palau, and the United States.

The final formulation of the question posed by the General Assembly resolution, worked closely with our mission in New York, read as follows: "What are the legal consequences arising from the construction of the wall being built by Israel, the occupying Power, in the Occupied Palestinian Territory, including in and around Jerusalem, as described in the report of the Secretary-General, considering the rules and principles of international law, including the Fourth Geneva Convention of 1949, and relevant Security Council and General Assembly resolutions?" The adopted resolution was better than the original one in many ways. It avoided casting the question in an affirmative manner that requested an answer regarding Israel's obligation to stop the wall and dismantle it. Instead, it sought to determine the legal consequences arising from the construction of the wall, requiring the court to answer in a way that would comment on issues other than the wall itself, such as settlement activity and the occupation itself.

The court ended up addressing, among other things, the legal consequences for states and international organizations vis-à-vis the wall and any facts created by it to ensure that no legitimization is extended to it. The original formulation would have confined the ICJ's answer only to Israel without touching on important consequences for other states and international organizations.

Once the issue was referred to the ICJ, Jordan had to decide whether to submit a written statement to the court or to make an oral representation. Both options were available to any country should it wish to exercise it. We were aware that Israel was exerting tremendous pressure, partly through the United States, to ensure that the petition for an opinion not reach the ICJ. Israel also approached Jordan directly. In the many meetings held between Israeli and Jordanian security officials, the issue was brought up. Why would Jordan want to get involved in a purely Israeli-Palestinian affair, asked the Israelis repeatedly?

Israel's foreign minister Silvan Shalom regularly raised the issue with me in our meetings in New York and at the EU-Mediterranean dialogue sessions. A man of Tunisian descent, Shalom has a temper and disposition that is most unusual for a foreign minister and consequently, within a few minutes of meeting almost anyone, manages to antagonize his interlocutor. Our chemistry was no better. If there is one thing I cannot abide, it is Israeli officials who profess to be more intimately familiar with Jordan's national interests than I am. I made it clear to Shalom that Israel could campaign against Jordan all it wanted, but on this issue, we would stand firm. If Israel wished to defend itself, it could erect the barrier on its side of the border, I said. I was also at pains to remind Shalom that Jordan was the first Arab country to take a categorical and principled position against suicide bombings targeting Israelis, often inviting criticism from several Arab governments or parts of the Arab public, who saw such operations as a legitimate form of resistance to an occupation that itself targeted civilians in more ways than one. We would not be doing that if we were looking for popular decisions, I said, in response to his insinuations that we were taking such a position for public relations reasons. Our dialogue went nowhere, and my relationship with Shalom remained prickly ever after. I understand that I am not the only foreign minister to have had such an experience.

THE HAGUE PRESENTATIONS

We were well aware of the pressures that Israel might exert on us, including possibly through the Bush administration, with which Jordan had very strong relations. In the end, my argument to the Jordanian government prevailed that this was a matter of national interest and that Jordan was waging a campaign not to win over popular opinion but rather to preserve its interests and to try to prevent a development that had direct negative implications on these interests. We decided therefore, that the approach would be legal and highly professional. As such, we solicited the help of Sir Arthur Watts, an elderly, world-renowned, and highly experienced and respected British lawyer who had worked with us on several peace process–related issues, including the important issue of refugees. Watts is a no-nonsense, low-key man who exudes confidence. I had met him in December 2003 in London and had been immediately struck by his grace, his humility, and his knowledge of the issues. I knew he would be the right man for the job.

Jordan also had to determine the content of its presentation. The case before the ICJ was somewhat complicated by the fact that it involved Jordanian territory captured by Israel during the 1967 War. However, Jordan's administrative and legal disengagement from the West Bank in 1988 (see Chapter 1) brought to the fore questions about Jordan's sovereignty over the territory from an international legal perspective. Jordan feared that Israel might raise the West Bank's legal status as an occupied territory. (It should be stated that Israel had heretofore never acknowledged the West Bank as an occupied territory but considered the West Bank as "disputed" territory, arguing that Jordan's presence in the West Bank on unification had been "belligerent" and not internationally recognized. Ultimately, Israel has claimed that no state has ever exercised sovereignty legitimately over the West Bank.) The court could respond to the Israeli argument in two ways: it could either state that the West Bank was now recognized by all members of the international community—except Israel—as occupied, or it could tackle the issue of Jordanian sovereignty over the West Bank, which would be time-consuming and would not address the direct question posed to it by the General Assembly.

All of these issues had to be addressed before the court. We thus decided to submit both oral and written proposals, and we formed a team from our legal department, our mission in New York, and Sir Arthur Watts to prepare both arguments, due to be submitted in January at the

ICJ in The Hague. The oral presentation, a high-profile affair covered by the international press, demonstrated the seriousness of our position; the written proposal was not available to many.

Prince Zaid Bin Raad, our youthful and able ambassador to the United Nations, and Watts both gave highly impressive presentations before the court. Prince Zaid explained, "Jordan has repeatedly condemned the attacks mounted against civilians in Israel, particularly where they have resulted in the loss of innocent life. Those suicide bombings have indeed been nothing less than horrific. But those events do not stand by themselves. Israel's argument, centered as it is on the specific suicide bombings of the last three years in particular, must be weighed against almost four decades of Israel dominating, and, by virtue of its occupation, degrading an entire civilian population." The prince articulated Jordan's opposition to the construction of the barrier within occupied Palestinian territory. "If Israel has a security problem, then in principle Israel can protect itself by taking suitable measures *within its own territory*. If the wall had been constructed wholly within Israel's sovereign territory, these proceedings would not have come about," he contended.

Watts elaborated: "If the wall defends anything, it is the position of Israeli settlements in the Occupied Territories: but no exceptional right of self-defense can be invoked, Mr. President, to defend that which is itself unlawful."

THE ICJ'S DECISION

The court took several months to study the case after all the presentations were submitted. I admit that I felt nervous during these months, and so did the team at the ministry. After all, even though an advisory opinion could not be enforced, it carried considerable political and moral weight, coming from the highest international court in the world. Its opinion would not only reflect the legal status of the wall but, by considering the consequences of building the wall, would also constitute a ruling on the legality of the Israeli occupation itself.

When the ICJ announced its decision on July 9, 2004, it surpassed Jordan's most optimistic expectations. The decision touched on several aspects of the Palestinian-Israeli conflict, not just the barrier.

The court declared that the territories seized as a result of the 1967 war between Israel and Jordan were occupied territories, that Israel remained an occupying power, and therefore that it bore the responsibilities of an occupying power specified under international law. The court further stated that The Hague Regulations of 1907, which outline the laws and customs of war for an occupied power, are Customary International Law, and thus binding on Israel even though it is not a party to these regulations.[6] By so stating, the court implied that Israel did not occupy a land without an owner in 1967. It rejected Israel's argument that The Hague Regulations do not apply because Jordan was not a sovereign power over the territories occupied in 1967.

The court also ruled that Israeli settlements in the occupied territories, including those in East Jerusalem, breached international law, and that the construction of the wall would create a fait accompli tantamount to annexation. It also rejected the Israeli argument that the wall was a necessary self-defense mechanism, stating that, under Article 51 of the UN Charter, this self-defense was a right exercised against another state and not in a territory under the control of an occupying power.

The court further ruled that the route of the wall through the territories, combined with the configuration of settlements, would severely impede the Palestinians' right to exercise self-determination—a clear acknowledgment of the Palestinians' right to self-determination. The ICJ opined that Israel had an obligation to cease the construction of the wall, including in East Jerusalem, and to dismantle those parts of it constructed in the occupied territories.

EVENTS SINCE THE DECISION

Particularly heartening was the fact that all the court's decisions on the matter were taken by a vote of at least thirteen to two, most by fourteen to one, with the American judge the lone dissenter. Jordan had scored a major victory that not only settled once and for all the legal argument about the wall but that blunted many of the arguments Israel had used to justify its occupation of Arab territory.

Unfortunately, facts on the ground did not reflect the legal victory at The Hague. Although the court's opinion required the UN secretary-general to submit regular reports on the construction of the wall and to suggest ways of forcing Israel to cease its construction, nothing of substance was done. At the time this book was being written some three years following the ICJ's monumental opinion, Israel had accelerated the pace of its construction and had declared its intent to impose a unilateral solution to the conflict, where the wall would be the basic foundation of a political border between Israel and the Palestinians, the very political outcome Jordan had sought to avert.

THE BIG FREEZE

My direct involvement with Jordan's quest for a two-state solution came to a halt at the end of October 2004 when King Abdullah II asked me to become deputy prime minister in charge of reform. By then, it was clear that the Road Map was going nowhere and that both the Palestinians and the Israelis were to blame, even if not equally. The one international player capable of influencing the course of events, the United States, was bogged down in its own issues—both immersed in Iraq and simply not serious about pushing the peace process forward or implementing a credible monitoring mechanism to ensure that the two parties met their commitments under the Road Map.

Meanwhile, the status quo was not static. Israel went forward with the construction of the wall, despite clear international opposition and condemnation, and settlement construction proceeded apace, particularly in those areas that would facilitate the creation of irreversible borders. Public opinion in the Arab world became increasingly disillusioned about the chances for peace. More worryingly, the Arab street was becoming progressively anti-American.

But that October brought with it another big "surprise." Dov Weisglass, Sharon's trusted adviser, gave a long interview to an Israeli newspaper in which he stated that Israel was not ready for a final settlement with the Palestinians and planned instead to withdraw unilaterally from Gaza and to "park conveniently" in the West Bank for a long time to come. When asked if he thought his major achievement was to have frozen the political process legitimately, Weisglass ventured the following response: "This is exactly what happened. You know, the term 'political process' is a bundle of concepts and commitments. The political process is the establishment of a Palestinian state with all the security risks that entails. The political process is the evacuation of settlements, it's the return of refugees, it's the partition of Jerusalem. And all that has now been frozen." He went on to point out that "until the Palestinians turn into Finns," the "nightmare" of having to evacuate Israeli settlers from the West Bank and permit the establishment of a Palestinian state would be indefinitely postponed. "Effectively, this whole package that is called the Palestinian state, with all that it entails, has been removed from our agenda indefinitely. And all this with authority and permission. All with a presidential blessing and the ratification of both houses of Congress. What more could have been anticipated? What more could have been given to the settlers?"[7]

Such statements did not endear the Israelis, or certainly the Americans, to Arab public opinion. Although Weisglass later claimed that he had been misquoted, it is hard to see how this could have been the case, given such extensive elaborations in the interview. His statements buttressed the argument of all those in the Arab world who believed that Israel had never been serious about establishing a Palestinian state and that it was only buying time until it established facts on the ground that suited its own version of a solution—a long-term interim arrangement that would avoid Palestinian independence for the time being and one that would not ultimately result in a viable, contiguous, and sustainable Palestinian state. Meanwhile, the absence of any criticism, let alone condemnation, of Weisglass's comments by the United States was not lost on Arabs, who viewed Washington's silence as yet more proof of Western hypocrisy in its dealings with the Arabs. One can only imagine the outcry that would have ensued if an Arab politician had made similar proclamations in an interview.

Is a two-state solution dead? I certainly hope not. Hope cannot be killed for millions of people living under occupation and yearning to live freely and govern themselves. But a discussion of the realities can no longer be taboo. The construction of the wall and the confiscation of Palestinian land to feed continued settlement building must be reversed if a viable Palestinian state is to emerge.

Israel might be able to solve its problems in the short term by building a wall around itself and effectively creating a Palestinian ghetto in the process. But history has shown us that no people can live in isolation of others, whether they are as powerful as the Israelis or as weak as the Palestinians. No wall can squelch the basic human desire to live in freedom and dignity. The fortress mentality should have been relegated to the past with the falling of the Berlin Wall. Certainly, no one can enjoy tremendous prosperity while their neighbors are in poverty; it is a recipe for disaster.

A unilateral solution, therefore, is not in the Palestinian interest and certainly not in the Israeli interest either. It also definitely runs directly against the Jordanian national interest. The two-state solution must not be allowed to die.

CHAPTER NINE

Arab Reform

In 2002, the United Nations Development Programme published its first report about human development in the Arab world. Its chairperson for the Arab world, the able Dr. Rima Khalaf Huneidi, a Jordanian who became the Arab world's first woman deputy prime minister, assembled a group of Arab intellectuals and activists to identify the major challenges facing the Arab world. The result was a bold, highly articulate document that criticized the region's slow movement toward reform. The document identified three major challenges facing the region: the lack of wide political freedoms, the limited role of women, and a widening knowledge gap between the Arab region and the rest of the world.

The report generated a lot of waves, particularly among Arab governments, which immediately disagreed with its findings. Until then, political reform was not on the radar screen of most Arab governments, which preferred to continue to ignore it as a central component of human development in the region. At one meeting of Arab foreign ministers in Cairo that I attended, the subject came up. Most foreign ministers were highly critical of the report, dismissing it as too simplistic or general. One foreign minister confidently proclaimed, "Who says that Arab women are discriminated against in the Arab world? Has anyone asked them? They are living a very good life, respected by society, which has awarded them all their rights."

THE STATEMENTS OF THIS FOREIGN MINISTER represented a general state of denial that had persisted for years but was about to collapse. Arab governments, both conservative and "progressive," equally have largely ignored or resisted political reform in their societies. Though ad hoc programs to expand certain political freedoms had been undertaken here

and there, no Arab country could claim a systematic process of political reform that would encourage the kind of political and civil development necessary to the infrastructure of a democratic society complete with an
evolved system of checks and balances, allowing for true accountability and
transparency of the political process. The lack of such an infrastructure was
poignantly clear after the American war on Iraq began in 2003. The destruction of the old, brutal system—especially the Iraqi army, which was for
all intents and purposes the only functioning institution in that country—
left a power vacuum because of the lack of functioning political parties and
a robust civil society. The void was immediately filled either by political parties that had largely operated from outside the country or by the religious
parties. The postwar disintegration of public order allowed organizations
such as Al-Qaeda to find a foothold in Iraq, which they happily exploited to
plan and commit terrorist acts and fuel strife, contributing to the country's
disastrous slide toward civil war.

Arab governments offered three arguments for not making political
development a priority—a policy deficiency that placed the Arab region
near the bottom of all the regions in the globe on the democracy scale.[1]
Foremost among the reasons was the Arab-Israeli conflict, which, they
contended, rendered all other challenges secondary, which is like claiming you can't walk and chew gum at the same time. "No voice can be
higher than that of the battle [for liberation]" (La sawt ya'loo fawqa sawt
al-ma'araka) was the slogan raised by President Nasser in Egypt. Democracy could and should wait thus until a resolution of the Arab-Israeli
conflict brought about fuller stomachs and happier days, the argument
went. Even then opposition parties did not raise political reform or
democratization as a major issue, instead basing their opposition on the
governments' position regarding the Arab-Israeli conflict. There was no
healthy debate in the public sphere, thus, making it easier on governments to dismiss the issue of democracy altogether.

Later, and particularly after the Iranian revolution and the rise of political Islam, a new argument materialized: political party development
in the Arab world threatened to strengthen Islamist parties, most of
which were alleged to be radical and armed. This development, leaders
contended, would invite regional instability, an argument buttressed by
the experience of Algeria, where the Islamist party won a majority of parliament seats in 1992 but was prevented from taking power by the army.

A violent civil war ensued, resulting in the deaths of tens of thousands of Algerians.

A third reason had to do with the sequencing of reform. Lacking a moderate middle class that could form the nucleus of a healthy political reform process, Arab governments argued that economic reforms had to precede political reforms. This argument, however, ignored the fact that economic reform was unlikely to be successful without institutions that consolidated good governance, a solid system of checks and balances, an independent judiciary, and a free press. In fact, where economic reform has occurred it has often proceeded with little transparency and has led to corruption that has discouraged domestic or foreign investors, thereby failing, in most instances, to improve peoples' economic well-being or create a substantial middle class. In the words of the 2004 UN Arab Human Development Report, the argument of "bread before freedom" has practically meant that "most Arabs have risked losing out on both."[2]

Nevertheless Arab regimes took an almost collective, if unstated, decision actively to discourage, if not prevent, political party development in Arab countries. Civil society became, and remains, a bad word in many parts of the Arab region. The patriarchal ruling elite continued to claim a monopoly on knowing what was best for Arab people when it came to steering Arab countries out of imperialist rule, leading the economic growth process, and solving the Arab-Israeli conflict without compromising Arab rights. Everything else, including democracy, had to wait, and did.

The Arab regimes' opposition to political pluralism met the acceptance of the international community concerned with preserving regional stability to ensure a steady oil supply and was equally agreeable to many Arab citizens throughout the region. Consequently, democracy was blocked not exclusively for internal reasons. The external environment was also not conducive to reform. It was only after September 11, 2001, that the West began to believe that Arab political stagnation had been detrimental to its own interests and started actively to champion reform. By then, however, American prestige in the region had fallen so far, mostly thanks to the United States's apparent double standards toward Israel and the Arabs, that after September 11, 2001, many believed that American enthusiasm for reform was cynical, inspired by its own security interests rather than a genuine concern for the Arab condition or a fundamental ethical desire to advance democratic principles. If U.S.

security concerns were at the heart of the matter, many Arabs reasoned, why had the United States neglected to address another threat to American and regional security that to them was so evident: the Israeli occupation and the unspoken American support for it? At worst, many Arabs regarded this omission as another example of American duplicity.

The lack of a gradual, serious political reform process in the Arab states has had three almost predictable results: increasing corruption among the ruling elite; the suppression of any attempt to develop national, democratic, nonreligious parties; and the intimidation and depoliticization of the Arab street.

Unchecked by any competing interests and power groups, ruling elites have grown increasingly nontransparent. The Transparency International "Corruptions Perceptions Index" of 2005 lists twelve Arab countries (together with the Palestinian Authority) with a score of seventy or more (one being the best) out of 158 countries included. Without a free press, opposition parties, or a vibrant civil society, the privileges of the elite expanded, and their interest in protecting them grew in tandem. Self-aggrandizement superseded loyalty to the state and merit as a virtue.

The absence of real national democratic and nonreligious parties that might have served as alternatives to religious parties and organizations allowed religious groups—sometimes with the encouragement of the ruling regimes—to fill the political and social void. The religious parties dominated the public sphere alongside Arab governments. More important, over decades they developed a vast network of social services, augmenting the services the state was able—or unable—to provide. Unimpeded by countervailing voices, religious groups delivered a resonant message about the efficacy of religion as state policy and through their philanthropy and social services constructed a broad and deep support base. By the time some Arab regimes were ready to contemplate political reforms in the mid-1980s and early 1990s, religious groups—especially the Islamists—had had a decades-long head start over other groups, which in any case, had difficulty emerging.

This is largely due to the intimidation and depoliticization of the Arab street, which is the third consequence of Arab regimes' policies. A study conducted by the Center for Strategic Studies at the University in Jordan showed that a full 74.6 percent of Jordanians are reluctant to criticize their government for fear of retribution. Further, 94.8 percent said that they did not belong to any political party, and a further 94.2 percent stated that they had no intention of joining a political party.[3] This confirms a trend that similar studies conducted over the past few years have pointed to. Taking into account the fact that Jordan enjoys a relatively more open system than most Arab countries, these results do not bode well for the state of affairs in the rest of the Arab world. The failure of such policies may have reinforced the strength of religious groups—at the least, it has allowed them to flourish—and left Arab societies with few alternatives for nonsectarian political representation and organization: an unaccountable ruling elite or religious groups. Radicalized and sometimes violent, these groups have continued to gain strength to this day.

The Arab regimes' policy of maintaining the status quo to preserve their interests and prevent groups such as the Islamists from gaining in power resulted in exactly the opposite result: a ruling elite increasingly viewed by Arab publics not as moderate but as nontransparent, and the ascendancy of religious groups that use Islam for political purposes. Thus, they grew wary of an elite that ruled without accountability but were also skeptical of religious groups, some of which promised good governance but also seemed to threaten political and cultural diversity.

One must differentiate here among the different political Islamist movements in the Arab Muslim world. The West tends to look at such movements as monolithic. They are not. They can be generally classified into three main groups:

1. *The violent, extremist, exclusionist movement.* These groups resort to terror and refuse to work from within current systems. They reject participation in elections, or any domestic political process. They adopt a *Takfiri* ideology, rejecting any individual or group that does not agree with their view, whether they are Muslims, Arabs, or foreigners, and believe that killing them is legitimate. These groups regard themselves as the "true" representatives of Islam and claim a monopoly on understanding (and enforcing) Islamic law. They see themselves as being engaged in a global struggle against any society that does not subscribe to their values. Their theater of battle is the entire world, including Muslim societies that they consider un-Islamic for a variety of reasons. Al-Qaeda falls in this category.

2. *The militant resistance movement.* These groups see violence, including violence against civilians, as a means to national liberation. Their
   activities are usually confined to national territories under occupation
   and to the territory of the occupier. Hamas in the West Bank and
   Gaza and Hezbollah in Lebanon are among the representatives of
   this group. Although they started as groups outside the system, they
   are increasingly participants in the political process through elections, even as they continue to carry arms. The latter fact is a point of
   much debate in Palestinian and Lebanese societies—and indeed the
   international community—today.
3. *The peaceful movement.* These groups have decided to seek and participate in power through elections and have advocated peaceful means
   to push through their ideology. The Muslim Brotherhood in Jordan
   and the Islamists in Morocco are examples of the peaceful movement.

These distinctions play an important role in the evolution of these
movements as they have responded both to Arab and Western policies.
They also have important implications for the development of policies
necessary to encourage the continued moderation of the third group, ensure that the second group transitions to peaceful participation in the
political process, and isolate the first group, with which no compromise
is possible. The policy of inclusion that King Hussein followed in Jordan, for example, by allowing the Islamists to operate openly from the
beginning, has encouraged their moderation, in contrast to many other
Islamist movements in the Arab world that have resorted to violence as a
result of state repression.

Such was the case in the Arab world when the nineteen hijackers
struck the United States on September 11. The tragedy not only took pre-
cious lives but also shook the regional status quo by raising questions
both in the West and in the Middle East of what happened and why.
What brings people to murder others in such a hideous manner in the
belief that such an act is worthy of their entry into heaven? Who was to
blame for this? Were Islamic cultural values to blame? Was it the lack of
democracy in the Arab world? Was it frustration with U.S. policies in the
region? Was it an extension of the Arab-Israeli conflict? Did it represent
a clash of civilizations? Was it all of the above reasons, or none of them?

The answer varied depending on who was asked. Regardless, one almost immediate result was to push the issue of political reform in the region on to the West's radar screen. The lack of democracy in the region was now seen by some in the United States and elsewhere as the only reason leading to September 11, to the exclusion of all other reasons. The neoconservative school in the United States began pushing the idea that the advent of democracy in the region should be a principal U.S. objective, without any links to any other issue, including the peace process and Iraq. Democracy should stand on its own merit, this school argued, and should be applied to a geographical area defined by the West with little regard to each country's social, political, and economic particularities. Other issues such as Israel's occupation of Arab land (something undemocratic by definition) or, later, the multiple undemocratic aspects of the American war on Iraq, such as human rights abuses in Abu Ghurayb, for example, were conveniently ignored by this school, without understanding that American credibility would be affected by these issues.

THE GREATER MIDDLE EAST INITIATIVE AND THE TUNIS DECLARATION OF PRINCIPLES

In December 2002 the United States launched the Middle East Partnership Initiative (MEPI), a program designed to support political and economic reform in the Middle East, as well as education and women's empowerment. The program would provide additional funds to countries of the region who meet a certain set of performance indicators related to the areas above.

As the United States was hosting the G8 summit in 2004, it sought to broaden support for its political reform initiative for the region by soliciting the support of the other G8 countries. In advance of the meeting, the United States had started working on the Greater Middle East Initiative, intended to promote political reform and trade liberalization in the region. An initial draft of the document, produced without consultation with any country in the region, was leaked to the press and appeared in the prominent Arabic daily newspaper *Al-Hayat* in February. It met immediate criticism. To Arabs, the initiative was a plan written by others to which they were expected to submit. It defined a "broader" Middle East, one that extended from Morocco to Afghanistan, countries that shared few features except Islam as the dominant religion. The document made no mention of the Arab-Israeli conflict and seemed to suggest that the advent of democracy in the region was a prerequisite for peace and an end to Israeli occupation of Arab lands. This touched a raw nerve among all Arabs and Muslims, who saw this policy as at best ill-defined and at worst intended to prolong the Israeli occupation indefinitely. This elephant in the living room—whether real or imagined—prompted suspicions that the GMEI was designed as a conspiracy against Islam, not as a genuine plan for political reform.

Such was the atmosphere when Arab foreign ministers met in Cairo on March 3, 2004, to prepare for the Arab Summit due to take place at the end of the month in Tunis. We went there mindful of the backlash that an externally imposed reform program might invite. This pointed to the need for the Arab world to advance its own declaration of principles on reform if it wanted to address the issue seriously and to dissuade the United States from going ahead with its initiative.

In Jordan, we had been thinking of the need for political reform even before the GMEI made its appearance. After September 11, it became clear that reform needed immediate attention. King Abdullah II started consulting with a group of individuals, of whom I was one, about the next steps. The king asked for a blueprint of what needed to be done. I was instructed to prepare a paper on political reform to include the major areas that the kingdom needed to address. I argued that the country needed an independent and free media, equal rights and legal protections for women, the development of political parties, an independent judiciary, and enhanced attention to human rights. I also emphasized that good governance could not be attained without proper attention to meritocracy. Nepotism, widely practiced in Jordan by the government, parliament, and the bureaucracy, has resulted in a widely held perception among Jordanians that not all Jordanians are equal, I argued, emphasizing the need to develop a system Jordanians would perceive as fair. The political system in Jordan allowed for a diversity of opinion within it and tolerated voices such as mine calling for reform within that system.

The group was very encouraged by the monarch's attitude to the process, initiating it and encouraging us to be open and creative. "What I need is thinking outside the box," he often told us. The result of these discussions led to a change of government whose principal mandate was to advance political reform in the country. One of my last functions before the government resigned was to represent the Jordanian government at the release of the second UN Arab Human Development Report. Jordan had agreed to host the launch, a gesture that signaled Jordan's commitment to its objectives. The new government, in which I served again as foreign minister, prepared a blueprint of the major areas to be considered, as outlined above.

I had thus prepared a draft declaration of principles on reform to submit to the Arab foreign ministers meeting in Tunis, based on the government's work, but was reluctant to present it as a Jordanian initiative, given some Arab countries' antipathy to Jordan.

To my astonishment, the word being spoken everywhere, reform, was not even an item on the agenda of the meeting, and attempts to include it met strong resistance at first. Syria, again, was the principal spoiler. Just as predictably, Syria took the head-in-the-sand approach to the entire issue, arguing that Arab countries should not feel compelled to respond to a mere article in a newspaper. As far as Syrian foreign minister Farouq Sharaa was concerned, reform, like terrorism and the Road Map, was a nonissue and therefore merited no discussion. Although other countries were less adamant, they were nevertheless reluctant to add the issue to the agenda, suggesting that it was not of immediate concern.

Jordan argued that Arabs' failure to act would invite external intervention in Arab affairs and therefore that Arabs needed homegrown political reform processes. Developing these, I said, was the only way to fend off outside pressure. Collective action did not mean that every Arab country had to—or could even be expected to—move at the same pace, given their different conditions and systems. But we could no longer afford to discuss reform in abstract terms. Rather, I argued, we had to reach an Arab consensus on its elements. If we believed that the Arab-Israeli conflict resolution was somehow linked to the reform process and should be included in any reform plan, then we should explicitly state it in a plan of our own, or else the Western argument that the two issues were not linked would prevail. In any case, the Arab-Israeli conflict could not always be invoked as justification for the denial of rights and freedoms. Regional conflict could not explain, for example, the persistent denial of women's rights. Neither could the lack of political development be ignored as a principal factor feeding social frustrations and subsequently encouraging Arab publics to abandon moderation in favor of extremism. The two processes—peace and reform—had to move together. Finally, we had to make clear to the world that if a dialogue on reform was to be successful, any external support for it should not be perceived as a conspiracy against Islam. For all these reasons, we felt that the upcoming summit in Tunis would be the perfect opportunity for the Arab world to agree on a homegrown document rather than be confronted with a plan drawn up by others from outside the region.

It was interesting to note that, in general, the smaller Arab states were most supportive of the reform idea, with the exception of Morocco (which was relatively large and initiated important reform initiatives). Thus, countries such as Bahrain, Kuwait, Yemen, Qatar, and Jordan, which had already initiated some reforms, supported the idea of developing a homegrown plan more readily than did the larger Arab states such as Egypt, Saudi Arabia, and Syria. Perhaps the former countries felt their small size allowed them more maneuverability than big states in moving their political systems, either because they had smaller bureaucracies to contend with or because embarking on a reform process required fewer financial resources than it would in larger states.

Sharaa relegated reform to a peripheral issue, a mere preoccupation of the media. The comparison between the proactive approach of Jordan and the reactive one adopted by Syria could not have been clearer. On the second day of the meeting, the Egyptians presented a compromise in the form of a one-page paper that was largely rhetorical, general, and noncommittal. Although it mentioned reform, it did not map out the areas to be addressed. Thus, even though momentum was building to include the issue on the summit's agenda, the paper lacked the specifics necessary to convince either Arab publics or the outside world of our seriousness.

The Jordanian delegation decided to submit its own paper, knowing fully that doing so might invoke the criticism, if not outright hostility, of many Arab states.

The three-page paper defined the areas of reform that the Arab world needed to address:

- Reinforcing and widening the base for public participation in the decision-making process;

- Expanding the scope of political freedoms, including freedom of the press and freedom of opinion;
- Upgrading the judiciary;
- Liberalizing the economy to meet the needs of the global free economic systems;
- Upgrading and expanding the scope of vocational training and education, and developing local knowledge bases to interact with the world; and
- Allowing all segments of society, without discrimination, to participate equally in all walks of life.

The paper also emphasized the need for a homegrown process because comprehensive reform was, in the twenty-first century, a necessity and a prerequisite for attaining sustainable development for each country in the Arab world. It also highlighted the need for an international commitment to resolve the Arab-Israeli conflict, and reconfirmed the Arab world's "undisputed, total condemnation of terrorism in all forms and regardless of motives and causes." Last, the paper stressed the need to develop a set of mechanisms and work plans to implement reform programs, and it welcomed dialogue with and support from the international community.

A heated debate ensued, and reform quickly, if inadvertently, became one of the main issues discussed during the foreign ministers' meeting. The Saudis were weary of one blueprint being applied to all without considering the level of political, economic, and social development in each country. They were obviously worried about such issues as civil society and the status of women in their country. The Omanis took a generally very conservative attitude, arguing that the West was exaggerating concerns about reform in Arab countries, while the Libyans dismissed the entire concept as a Western plot. On the other hand, countries like Yemen argued for giving attention to human rights issues, having just held a regional conference on the issue in January. Tunis also argued for more socially progressive policies, especially in terms of women's issues. In the end, the Egyptian foreign minister, Ahmad Maher, approached me to say that Egypt was willing to work with Jordan to produce a joint paper that could be submitted for discussion at a later date. Jordan's approach had succeeded.

The meeting had given us enough ammunition to urge the United States to abandon its initial version of the GMEI. On March 8 I traveled to Washington to convince the Bush administration that producing a document would backfire in the Arab world by confirming the Arabs' worst suspicions about American intentions vis-à-vis the region and Islam.

In Washington, I met separately with all the administration principals: Colin Powell, Condoleezza Rice, and Paul Wolfowitz, to whom I reiterated our concerns: that it was important for Arabs themselves to own the process and for the United States to be forthcoming on the Arab-Israeli conflict. I presented the Jordanian draft resolution to the Arab League and specifically asked whether the document was persuasive enough to discourage the administration from announcing an American blueprint for the region during the G8 summit. I told both Powell and Rice that I needed an answer before the Arab foreign ministers' next meeting on March 25 to prepare for the summit.

More nuanced than Rice, Powell acknowledged that no reform plan made in America would work in the region. Any such plan needed to reflect the will of the Arab countries, although the United States could provide assets and partnership to the process. He thought that Jordan's initiative was sound and that if Arabs could create such a reform plan, "it would have an electrifying effect in the entire Arab region."[4] In a hearing of the Foreign Operations Subcommittee of the House Appropriations Committee a day later, Powell clearly expressed his interest in Jordan's initiative, telling the committee that he had had "a very good discussion with the Jordanian foreign minister, . . . who is interested in developing a set of principles with respect to reform that the Arab nations would consider to take a look at."

Rice was also forthcoming, if less enthusiastic. She hinted that she wanted the credit for any reform effort in the region to go to President Bush, but she could not ignore the fact that an Arab state, Jordan, had presented a credible initiative of its own. Her only reservation, she said, was that women's empowerment should be more explicitly mentioned. Jordan had no quarrel with this, but it had couched language on women's empowerment in diplomatic terms in order to win the acceptance of all Arab countries.

By the time the visit ended, Jordan's argument had already scored major points. It echoed the efforts already under way in the region to push the reform process forward such as the UN Arab Human Development Reports and other efforts by civil society in the Arab world,[5] and it supported the European allies' argument favoring a homegrown process. In response to our question whether our effort would be sufficient for the United States not to proceed with its own blueprint for reform in the region, Rice confirmed that this would indeed be the case if the issue of women's empowerment was mentioned more explicitly.

An important hurdle had been crossed. Jordan had been able to use its good offices with the United States to move the argument to a level that both the Arab world and the United States could accept. Otherwise, U.S. efforts to impose a plan not only would have backfired but also would have hurt the cause of reformers in the region. After all, American credibility had been seriously diminished because of its role in the peace process and the war in Iraq, which had rendered the American conspiracy against Islam the handiest argument that status quo forces could deploy against reform. Indeed, this argument is used even today in the region. Instead of criticizing the message, the traditionalists have always found it to be more convenient to flay the messenger and cast doubt on the whole effort.

By the time I arrived in Tunis at the end of March to brief Arab foreign ministers on our Washington trip, the attitude of Arab officials had been transformed. Outright resistance had given way to willingness not only to place the issue on the agenda of the summit but also to discuss what the content of a declaration of principles on reform would entail.

When the Arab summit convened at the end of May 2004, serious discussions by Arab foreign ministers produced a detailed document on reform in the Arab world.[6] It was accepted by all Arab countries except Libya, which was adamant that it would not yield to external pressure. Though it was, from a comprehensive Arab perspective, a response to the threat of external intervention in Arab affairs, the document still represented a serious attempt finally to give reform the necessary attention. The result was the "Statement on the Process of Development and Modernization in the Arab World." We were no longer talking about reform in the abstract but had succeeded in defining its specific elements. These included:

- Expanding participation and decision making in the political and public spheres;
- Upholding justice and equality among all citizens;
- Respecting human rights and the freedom of expression;
- Ensuring the independence of the judiciary;
- Promoting the role of all elements of society and strengthening the participation of all, both men and women, in public life;
- Pursuing the advancement of women in Arab society and buttressing their rights and social position to foster their contribution to development through their active participation in the different political, economic, social, and cultural spheres;
- Acknowledging the role of civil society in overall development;
- Forging a comprehensive Arab strategy for economic, social, and human development to strengthen the concept of good governance;
- Modernizing and upgrading the education system;
- Cooperating with the international community in the context of partnership based on mutual interests;
- Intensifying efforts with the international community to achieve a just, durable, and comprehensive settlement to the Arab-Israeli conflict on the basis of the Arab Peace Initiative and relevant United Nations resolutions.
- Continuing partnership among Arab states and between the Arab world and the international community to combat and uproot terrorism in all its forms; and
- Adhering to the values of tolerance and moderation to strengthen the culture of dialogue among religions and cultures, and spreading the values of solidarity and peaceful coexistence among peoples, thus promoting understanding and friendship within the framework of common respect.

The document was surprisingly thorough. It contained all the necessary elements for reform and emphasized the importance of the two principles: ownership of the process and the need for serious work to resolve the Arab-Israeli conflict. The clear position on the importance of moderation and tolerance was a stand against extremism and terrorism. The Arab Center had won the day, and the goalpost had been moved. This was yet another example of how a country as small as

Jordan could promulgate ideas that would move the Arab consensus forward.

The U.S. position also shifted because of the Tunis document. Arab efforts had clearly been recognized and acknowledged by the time the G8 summit was held in Georgia in June. King Abdullah II, having been invited to attend the summit together with several Arab leaders, reflected his optimism about the prospects of reform in the region. "The Tunis statement, the Sana'a declaration[7] and other efforts by Arab civil society, including the Alexandria Declaration have created an atmosphere where Arab states are looking at themselves in the mirror," the king said. He emphasized that as Arab states pursued reforms, international support to affect a comprehensive solution to the Arab-Israeli conflict was necessary. Without that, he said, "our ambitions will not be truly fulfilled."[8] The king also called for a Marshall Plan for the Middle East based on performance of each country in the area of reform as a way to encourage the process and send a clear message to those who were not taking reform seriously. The final draft of the G8 summit on reform in the region changed dramatically from the first U.S. draft, leaked in February. It emphasized that "change should not and cannot be imposed from outside" and highlighted the importance of "resolving the Israeli-Palestinian conflict as an element of progress in the region." Beyond that, the content of the statement mirrored that of the Arab summit declaration.

The picture was not entirely rosy, however. The Tunis discussions had not stipulated the attachment of an implementation mechanism. Most Arab countries strongly objected to this, arguing that a uniform blueprint was impractical because each country had reached a different stage of political, social, and cultural development and therefore should determine for itself how to implement the principles contained in the declaration and report its progress to the Arab League.

Although this argument had some justification, there was no question that many countries had used and would continue to use this as an excuse to do little more than pay lip service to these principles. The discussions also revealed serious deficiencies in how Arab governments viewed certain issues like women's empowerment and civil society. Many of the ministers in attendance would not even acknowledge that problems in these areas existed. The Arab world cannot keep fooling itself, or the world for that matter, by proclaiming that women are not discriminated against in Arab society. Although this issue is not unique to this region and is as much a societal as a legal issue, we need to acknowledge the problem if serious efforts to address it are to be undertaken. Sadly, such acknowledgment is still lacking in many Arab countries.

Civil society is another case in point. Political party development is still at a nascent stage. Nongovernment organizations are not regarded as advocacy groups that can contribute to the development of a system of checks and balances, professional societies, or cultural clubs that make society more vibrant. Rather, the definition has been narrowed to charitable organizations concerned mainly with social work with no role in political or public affairs. Without the enhancement of civil society, corruption, nepotism, and stagnation will continue to plague Arab societies. Discussions on the mere inclusion of the phrase "civil society," as opposed to "nongovernment organizations," consumed hours at the summit. The Tunis document may have defined the key elements of Arab reform, but we were still at the beginning of the road. The argument now needed to shift from defining reform to starting a serious process of implementing it.

OTHER REFORM EFFORTS IN THE ARAB WORLD

Reform efforts in the Arab world were certainly not confined to the Tunis Declaration or to Arab governments for that matter. Civil society in parts of the Arab world has been active in pushing for change. Although many of these efforts continue to be ad hoc and sporadic, some are worth mentioning. The Alexandria Declaration of March 2004 was an attempt by a group of civil society organizations from several Arab countries to establish the principles of political and economic reform that preceded the Tunis Declaration, although the group did little to follow up on their efforts. More recently, Kuwaiti women were granted full political rights, including the right to vote and stand for office, after an extremely heated debate in parliament. Although the Kuwaiti government supported that effort, Kuwaiti women played an active role in lobbying both government and parliament to effect this change. Municipal elections in Saudi Arabia represented another positive step in giving the population wider participation in the decision-making process.

Perhaps one of the most hopeful developments occurred in Morocco with the enactment of the 2003 Family Law, which went a long
way toward ensuring equality between men and women. Pressure from
civil society, supported by King Muhammad VI, resulted in parliament
finally passing the law. According to the new law, women are their own
guardians after they reach eighteen, they have the right to divorce, and
they have custody rights over their children. In a bold and probably
unprecedented move, Morocco also established a Justice and Reconciliation Committee, which conducted hearings to expose the system's past
abuses of dissidents and come to terms with such practices.

THE CHALLENGE OF REFORM: THE CASE OF THE JORDANIAN NATIONAL AGENDA

Five months after the Tunis Arab Summit, King Abdullah II asked me to
become deputy prime minister in charge of reform. The government
had just concluded a one-year study on how to overhaul the public sector, and one of the study's major recommendations was the development
of a national agenda, a framework that would define Jordan's priorities
in the political, economic, and social spheres and their relationship to
one another. These objectives would then be translated by successive
governments into specific goals for public sector institutions and define
what each had to achieve and focus on. The areas of focus included such
themes as widening the decision-making process, political party development, women's empowerment, freedom of the press, judicial independence, fiscal reform, investment promotion, employment support
and vocational training, social welfare, and education and infrastructure
upgrade. The final document included timelines to achieve such
objectives—all legal discrimination against women in Jordanian laws is
to be abolished by the year 2015, and a balanced budget should be
reached by 2016, for example. In order to accurately monitor implementation, performance indicators were set in the document. Thus, Jordan's
measure of economic freedom by the Heritage Foundation, for example,
would be improved from its current rank of fifty-one to a rank of twenty
by 2017. The percentage of small and medium enterprises' contribution
to employment would rise from their current rate of 33 percent to 45 percent by the year 2017, and so on.

Because governments in Jordan are formed not out of political parties with programs that have won the electorate's approval but rather from a collection of individuals, such an agenda had to offer a long-term vision for the country's major policy objectives until a political party system is developed. Its credibility rested on its development through an inclusive process that drew on the insight of a compendium of political, economic, and social actors. The framework would exceed the parameters of the Tunis Declaration by providing not only a set of objectives but also a measurable action plan with a set of macro- and micro-performance indicators to demonstrate the state's seriousness in implementing the stated objectives. It also called for capacity building within public sector institutions so that they would be able to implement such an ambitious plan. As such, public sector reform leading to the institutionalization of a merit-based public sector was to be a crucial component in ensuring that set objectives had a chance of being realized.

There is little room in this book to write in detail about what may be uniquely a Jordanian experience. But the opposition that the effort faced, and the lessons learned from it, extends well beyond Jordan to the whole region.

The king appointed an inclusive Royal Committee, headed by myself, which comprised people across the spectrum of political, social. and economic forces in the country, including government, parliament, media, women's activists, political parties, and the private sector, and entrusted it with developing this framework. He did not interfere in the work of the committee and asked only that its recommendations be submitted to him at the end of the process. This process, though, came under attack as soon as the committee was formed to begin working on the agenda. Criticism came from two different circles. One group, referred to as the "old guard," began to cast doubt on the agenda before the document was even written. The old guard is mainly a collection of individuals associated with the public sector—government officials, ex-officials, and long-serving bureaucrats who understood too well that reform ultimately would entail a complete revision of Jordanian political culture, one that would become merit-based, rather than one that often gave privileges such as jobs and education to an elite few. That circle of opposition also included personalities who had dominated Jordanian politics for so long that they fundamentally believed that politics was too serious an affair to be administered by the public. They regarded themselves as the true "guardians of the state" and opposed any widening of the decision-making process. The old guard was joined by a handful of businessmen who have accrued both wealth and power thanks to their close alliance with the state.

In short, the old guard believed that widening the scope of public participation in the decision making-process would come at their expense. They, of course, could not come out directly against a reform effort. Who could rationally oppose reforms intended to better the lives of millions of Jordanians? It was also difficult for them to attack the effort too directly because that would constitute an attack on the king, who had initiated it. Instead, they sought to discredit the reformers. The old guard found its own label for those steering the reform effort, decrying them as "neoliberals" who were implementing an American agenda against the Jordanian state. They depicted a merit-based system as something that would lead to the state's disintegration rather than its reinforcement, as something that would supplant the constitution rather than one that would uphold it.

One of my most vivid memories is of a meeting convened by King Abdullah II with a group of senators who were vocally opposed to the reform agenda. What transpired exemplifies the profound challenge to reform not just in Jordan but in the region. King Abdullah II explained that he supported the process in the belief that it would deliver a qualitative jump in the country's overall development. He said that the expansion of the middle class was essential and that this, in turn, meant that the cake would get bigger, with enough slices for all. The senators resolutely opposed this. One hard-liner answered that he could not support this "group of people [advisers of the king] who consider merit more important than allegiance to the state," as if the two were mutually exclusive.

The group was able to mobilize part of the media to their side. A well-organized campaign against the effort was waged in some newspapers (because of the liberalization of the press in Jordan, there were dozens of weekly tabloids in addition to the four daily Arabic newspapers). The campaign was extremely vicious and personal, stopping just short of declaring that certain members of the committee were traitors. And worse still, it was successful: the public cast doubt on an effort meant to improve the quality of life across the board even before the ink on the National Agenda was dry.

It was an illuminating experience. For although there was no true political party in Jordan with the exception of the Islamic Action Front (the political arm of Jordan's Muslim Brotherhood), the traditional ruling elite was well entrenched, held together by shared interests, possessed disproportionate access to important resources such as the media, and could mobilize effectively. The old guard was a political party in everything but name.

No countervailing force existed to match the influence of the traditional elite. Prominent liberal individuals, though outspoken, were neither united nor organized and could not effectively argue their case collectively to the public. The forces favoring the status quo recognized this and used it to their advantage, putting words in the reformists' mouths and interpreting, or rather misinterpreting, all that the reformist camp stood for in order to discredit them. It became apparent to many later on, once the National Agenda was publicized, that the claims and accusations leveled against its efforts and members were unfounded. In meetings with several prominent lawmakers (including the speakers of the lower and upper houses of parliament) and journalists to explain the outcomes of the National Agenda once they were finalized, I was told time and again that the work was serious and commendable and did not correspond to the image that had been conveyed by the press or the political elite.

In any case, the squabbling among the pro- and antireform elites was of little or no interest to the public, which had come to doubt the state's political will to follow through on reform. Over the years, programs for reform had been adopted and abandoned enough times to create doubt and apathy toward new promises. Jordan's first experiment with political pluralism in the 1950s was abruptly halted after free elections returned to parliament secular nationalist parties closely aligned with the radical Arab camp in Egypt and Syria. They ultimately threatened the dissolution of the state, and the state in turn imposed martial law, which for three decades circumscribed most political activity in the country. Jordan's economy fell into an economic slump in the mid-1980s, culminating in the collapse of the Jordanian dinar. The imposition of economic reforms led by the International Monetary Fund, including the lifting of subsidies on commodities, provoked violent protests in some areas of the kingdom in the spring of 1989. The accusations of state corruption and the fact that economic reforms meant that Jordanian citizens would bear an increasingly bigger share of the country's economic burden clarified the need for reform. King Hussein thus called for elections, and a process of political liberalization began. Then, an inclusive committee was also asked by the king to write a "National Charter," a new contract between the state and its citizens that defined the rules of the political game and allowed the political system to open up somewhat. Many reforms were introduced, including lifting the ban on political parties, easing restrictions on the media, which allowed privately owned newspapers to proliferate, and restoring electoral politics, which permitted the emergence of a more assertive parliament. As a result, the Islamic opposition won close to one fourth of the parliament seats in the 1989 elections. That process experienced difficulties, however, after the signing of the peace treaty with Israel in 1994. Concern about opposition to the treaty slowed down the process of political reform; many recommendations by the National Charter committee were put on indefinite hold; and by the mid-1990s, the reform process had stalled for all intents and purposes. Thus, by the time work started on the National Agenda at the beginning of 2005, a significant portion of the public, though supportive of reform, was disenchanted by years of disappointment and had come to doubt the state's sincerity. They saw the National Agenda as another act of political theater and did not engage in any significant way in a national debate about the parameters and pace of reform—if they had heard of the National Agenda at all. In fact, a poll conducted in June 2005, four months after the National Agenda was launched, found that a full 85 percent of Jordanians had not even heard of it, let alone formed an opinion about it. The statistic speaks to the extent of Jordanian society's depoliticization. It pointed to the almost complete absence of civil society.

Such was the scene when the National Agenda Steering Committee commenced its work. To its members' credit, they labored through, withstanding biting accusations from the forces that opposed them.

All hell broke loose, however, when the committee began discussion of Jordan's electoral law, which had been a matter of considerable controversy since 1989. The existing law is totally district-based and discriminates between rural and urban areas in favor of rural districts. In practice this means that tribal or family candidates have better chances of electoral success than party candidates running on a political or social platform. Thus, instead of parliament being formed of several political parties, each with a clear program, the legislature is largely, with the exception of the Islamists, composed of individuals with no clear platform beyond personal aggrandizement and benefiting their friends and family.

The committee debated whether and how the electoral law should be changed to encourage the formation of political parties with national appeal. Conservatives opposed the introduction of party lists to the electoral law, fearing that any such changes would bring to power the Islamists, which was the only organized political party and enjoyed support particularly in urban areas. Liberals countered that without electoral reform, a system of checks and balances could not develop, nor could any party emerge to balance the power of the Islamists. Nor would citizens be able to choose among competing programs for political, economic, and social advancement. Further, there was concern that changing the electoral law might increase the representation of Jordanians of Palestinian origin in parliament. The National Agenda Steering Committee arrived at an undeclared consensus not to debate this highly controversial issue at length for fear that it might undermine the other changes it was trying to introduce to the electoral law. Over time, a consensus emerged: first, the status quo was not a sustainable option, and second, the system must be opened gradually as long as political parties were absent from the scene in order that the Islamists would not enjoy an unfair advantage over everyone else. After numerous heated debates, the committee adopted a compromise: it would propose an electoral law that would assign one portion of the seats to district candidates and another to party lists, with the mix being decided by the government according to the evolution of the political process.

The committee finally succeeded in producing a very progressive document on reform in Jordan, which addressed all aspects of the Tunis Declaration and more and incorporated measurable targets for each objective. As such, it was unique in the Arab world.

In addition to mapping a plan to adjust the electoral process equitably, the National Agenda included a plan to eliminate legislation discriminating against women within ten years. The National Agenda, in its final form, also proposed legislation that would allow civil society organizations to pursue their activities free of state interference. Several

laws were suggested to ensure freedom of the press and allow the unimpeded operation of private television and radio stations in the country. In
addition, the agenda suggested numerous initiatives to address the
country's biggest economic and social challenges during the coming
decade, including the budget deficit, the country's rising energy bill, reforming and improving the pension system, per capita income, social
security, and health care and insurance.

But the agenda was more than a set of proposals. Perhaps the most
important element was its call for a new relationship between the state
and its citizens, one that promised the implementation of a merit-based
system and that aspired to improve not only the overall quality of life for
all Jordanians but also the quality of public services.If implemented, it
would bring about a qualitative improvement in Jordanians' lives and
would institutionalize a new work ethic based on merit, productivity,
and results.

The old guard relentlessly campaigned against the reformers, citing
the electoral success of Islamist parties in Egypt (in 2005), Iraq (in
2005), and later the Palestinian territories (in 2006) as proof of the dangers of opening up the system. "See, we told you so. You open up the system, and this is what happens. The Islamists come in," was their argument.

In fact, their argument is disingenuous. The Islamists enjoy success
in large part where governments fail. The shortcomings are manifold:
lack of good governance, shoddy social service provision, bureaucratic
indifference to citizens' rights and needs. The list is long. Islamist parties promise cleaner government, at the very least, and their promises
ring true because they have delivered—especially critical social services
at the grass roots—when governments have not. Those who are sin-
cerely concerned about checking the influence of the Islamists would ad-
vocate widening the political sphere so that a credible alternative to both
the Islamists and the ruling elite would emerge. Indeed, such a credible
alternative is what many reformers in the region are aspiring to. "See,
we told you so. You DON'T open up the system, and this is what happens.
The Islamists come in," is their counterargument.

Many believe that the Islamists' ascension has influenced the U.S.
attitude toward reform in the region. Although American officials deny
it, many in the region believe that the Bush administration has con-

cluded that pushing for elections without the presence of a strong, secular civil society may lead to undesirable results. If the United States fears the electoral success of the Islamists, it is worth noting that their popularity has grown as a result of the collective failure of the international community, including the Arab states and Israel, to resolve the Arab-Israeli conflict. Almost without exception, politicized Islamist movements in the region have made the restoration of Arab rights within the context of the Arab-Israeli conflict a central feature in their platforms. The popular appeal of the Islamists because of this issue alone cannot be underestimated.

The National Agenda experiment with reform points to a fact that is little understood by the West, one that applies not only to Jordan but to the region as a whole. Reform does not happen because the leadership of a country wishes it. Complex factors, including an entrenched establishment and bureaucracy whose interests make it highly resistant to any reform process, are involved. The expectation that democracy can spring up overnight in a country just because the leadership wants it or a dictator has been overthrown or free elections have been mandated is wishful thinking. Unless the many factors affecting that process are understood and addressed in a systematic and sustained manner, democracy and reform in the region will remain elusive.

WHY HAS A SYSTEMATIC REFORM PROCESS EVADED THE ARAB WORLD?

There is no question today that the Arab region has lagged behind all others in its political reform process, and there has been no shortage of scholarly inquiry into why this is so. Several reasons have been cited, although none offers a satisfactory explanation. Many analyses have pointed to various aspects of religion. One argument is that Islam is a religion that discourages opposition to the ruler and other democratic norms. This neatly overlooks Islamic scholarship throughout centuries that asserts Islam's emphasis on individual reason and freedom and on the importance of social consensus. One of the earliest examples in Islamic history is an anecdote told about the second caliph, Omar Bin Al-Khattab, urging his followers to straighten any deviation they see in him. More recently, the Egyptian Islamic scholar Muhammad Abdo opined at the turn of the twentieth century: "States that have built their power on the basis of consultation, entrust the nation to elect trustworthy people who will establish the public laws of the kingdom and monitor their implementation by the government. Such elections cannot be legitimate unless the nation has the full freedom to choose, without any pressure from the government or from others, with no temptation and no intimidation."[9] Such works are outside the scope of this book, though the interested reader can be referred to the works of Ibn Khaldun, Ibn Rushd (Averroes), or leading nineteenth- and twentieth-century Muslim scholars such as Abdo, Jamal El-Din Al-Afghani, and Rifa'a Al-Tahtawi to mention but a few examples.

Many Western scholars assert Islam's emphasis on patriarchy but without explaining why Muslim societies should be more trapped by patriarchal rule than Western Christian societies. In any case, arguments that cite religion as the cause for retarded political development overlook entirely the contemporary evidence: millions of Muslims today live in democratic societies. Indonesia, the largest Islamic country, Turkey, and Malaysia are all examples of Islamic countries with clearly established democratic norms and vibrant political societies.

To state it succinctly, cultural determinism has barely shed light on the state of affairs in the Arab world. Although a more conservative, less tolerant interpretation of Islam began to seep through Arab societies beginning in the mid-twentieth century, a more pragmatic investigation might concentrate on the failures of the educational system in the Arab world in the past century. It is a system that has been put together by the postindependence, nonreligious ruling parties in the Arab world, specifically designed to yield generations that are reluctant to criticize political or social axioms as curricula continued to encourage submission, obedience, subordination, and compliance rather than free critical thinking in the minds of Arab students.[10]

The continuation of the Arab-Israeli conflict has undeniably been a major impediment to overall development, including political development. The security imperative has channeled vast resources into military expenditures that could have been deployed elsewhere. At the same time, leaders have used it as an excuse—in some instances more legitimately than others—not to reform. In some instances, Arab governments argued that the combination of democracy and conflict would bring to the fore radical elements that would exploit public emotions to radicalize the whole region and, ultimately, widen the conflict. In fact, it is precisely the failure to resolve the Arab-Israeli conflict that has allowed radical movements to flourish by exploiting the emotions of those who have been aggrieved by the conflict. Their growth has made peace harder to achieve than it might have been even ten years ago. At the same time, although some states may have been more justified than others in deploying the security argument as a reason for postponing some reforms, this hardly accounts for the appalling state of women's rights, for example, or the inattention to good, transparent governance.

Oil has also been a major factor. In both the countries that possess it and the countries that export their labor to oil-producing states, oil has meant the easy accumulation of wealth. Economic prosperity has diluted the need and the demand for political reform for a long time in the region, and because of oil, the West has regarded stability, not reform, in the Middle East as its chief priority.

All of these factors have converged to impede the process of reform in the Arab world. But these are not the only ones. Most important is that the postcolonial nationalist political parties have not been democratic. The argument of these parties after independence was that nation-building superseded democracy, deftly ignoring the fact that democracy is a main pillar of nation-building. Thus, the Nasserites in Egypt, the Baathists in Syria and Iraq, and the nationalists in Tunisia and Algeria all used nation-building or the Arab-Israeli conflict (the security argument) as pretexts for suppressing freedoms and opposing the development of political parties that could threaten their standing. The argument at first was convincing to many, particularly when these postindependence parties delivered on certain economic and social programs such as land reform and equality for women. Opposition to such policies was branded as disloyalty—to Arab causes, to the state, or to the party. The culture of allegiance—in monarchies and republics—meant that "diversity" was a bad word. Both were equally guilty of focusing their attention not on systems but on leaders; the emergence of ideologies or systems outside the cults of personality were discouraged when possible, repressed when necessary. Although nationalist parties in particular paid lip service to democracy and freedom, they were in fact the worst abusers of both.

Consequently, modern Arab states lack a key foundation of modern statehood: an institutionalized system of checks and balances that can ensure healthy social, economic, and political development of society and that limits the power of any one group. At the same time, these systems failed to deliver on either economic development or solving the Arab-Israeli conflict. The result was the emergence of Islamic parties, in some instances increasingly radical, who held out promise of good governance and their own strategy for regional conflict resolution.

The Arab world is a mosaic of ethnic and religious communities, all sharing the same language, history, and civilizations. There are Muslims: Sunnis, Shiites, and other schools of jurisprudence; Christians of all denominations; and Jews. There are Arabs, Kurds, Armenians, Circassians, Chechens, and Berbers. Instead of regarding diversity as a source of strength, the public was taught that differences must be suppressed in service of the larger common goals of all Arabs. Arabs grew to think monolithically, one-dimensionally. Critical thinking was neither valued nor taught, and truths were always absolute rather than relative. A whole generation was raised on the notion that allegiance to the country meant allegiance to the party, system, or leader and that diversity, critical thinking, and individual differences were treasonous.

HOW CAN WE MOVE FORWARD?

This indeed is also a dilemma facing Arab countries. It would be hard to argue against holding elections or for postponing them indefinitely. The argument of a gradual but serious opening up of the political system while continuing to hold elections seems to be the best available option. To accomplish this, two principal rules should be agreed to and adhered to by all those who want to engage in political activity:

1. *Commitment to political and cultural diversity.* Both governments and political parties are concerned with any model where democracy could be used once for a party to gain power and then, having gained power, the ruling party might deny the right for other political groups to organize. It is the famous "one man, one vote, one time" argument. Many secular groups are also weary of Islamic groups coming to power and then imposing their cultural values on the rest of society. To prevent such an outcome, each Arab society must arrive at a national consensus in which all parties commit to political and cultural diversity under all circumstances and would legally prevent any

group from denying other groups the right to organize. That also means that we would be talking about not just majority rule but also minority rights. That is a key part of democratic societies, or else majority rule would turn into an autocratic regime. Such a principle was explicitly stated in the Jordanian National Agenda, for example.

2. *Commitment to peaceful means.* All political parties or individuals should commit to pursuing political objectives through peaceful means. This means that parties participating in the system cannot also bear arms (Hezbollah in Lebanon is a case in point); nor can one support those who do carry arms and target civilians. That clearly would fall under incitement, not freedom of speech. Incitement would be specifically and narrowly defined by legislation so that the state cannot use such legislation for repressive purposes. That commitment was also explicitly stated in the Jordanian National Agenda.

If these two principles are adhered to, in deeds as well as in words, and become part of the national culture and national constitutions, true political development can become possible while assuring society that the principle of a peaceful rotation of power is respected. In this context, the argument for a gradual, evolutionary process becomes even more relevant. The need for a built-in system to resist the tendency of parties to commit to pluralism on paper, only to abandon this commitment the minute they come to power, cannot be overstated. Developing such a system, and knowing the steps involved and to which end they lead, can assure all political groups and therefore encourage them to commit to the new rules of the game. It would also deprive governments of any excuse not to open up the system and would pave the way for the development of a political culture inclusive of all forces in society.

If it is true that political party development will need time to mature in the Arab world, it is also true that the other components of good governance must be given immediate attention and time to emerge. Corruption, human rights abuses, and circumscribed freedoms must be addressed first by amending the legal environment but then by ensuring that respect for human rights and freedoms and fighting corruption become values that are part of the national political culture.

Perhaps there is no issue more pressing than education here to deal with the long-term aspects of the problem. Although the Arab world has made critical strides in eradicating illiteracy and educating its citizens, the focus has been increasingly toward quantity, not quality education, or toward science, technology, and computers at the expense of civics and other liberal disciplines. It is no longer important only to ensure that the educational system is free of incitement or intolerance; the curricula must teach values of tolerance, diversity, and respect for the other as sources of strength, not weakness, for society. Although the educational systems in the Arab world have concentrated on establishing more universities and in making computers more available to students, attention to the content of the educational system and the retraining of teachers has lagged behind. Educational reform is crucial to the nurturing of a democratic culture, without which all other legal reforms would be meaningless.

Jordan hosted the launching of the Third UN Arab Human Development Third Report 2004, *Towards Freedom in the Arab World,* in Amman on March 24, 2005. Dr. Khalaf Huneidi and I, then deputy prime minister in charge of reform, jointly presided over the launching ceremony. By then, the momentum in the Arab world that culminated in Tunis was fading. In my speech, I thanked the Arab intellectuals who worked on the report, expressing the hope that "the day would come when Arab authors would be able to publish their views freely in the Arab world without the need for an umbrella of an international organization." I went on to express my view that although we might differ about how to achieve personal and public freedoms in the Arab world, "we should never disagree on the ultimate objective of guaranteeing and protecting freedoms to arrive at an Arab society that sees in cultural diversity and in the diversity of thought, elements of strength rather than elements of weakness." It is a hope I still cherish, and it is one worth working for.

CHAPTER TEN

Is There Hope for the Arab Center?

YEARS FROM NOW, WHEN THE HISTORY of the modern Middle East will be written, what will it be titled, "The Center Could Not Hold" or "A New Beginning"? Will the Middle East still be plagued by separation walls, suicide bombers, radical ideologies, authoritarian regimes, and a never-ending occupation, or will moderation, democracy, peace, and diversity prevail?

That the Arab Center exists is something I have attempted to show beyond doubt in this book. It is a center that has been proactive in recent years in searching for a satisfactory solution to the Arab-Israeli conflict. Indeed, most political initiatives of the past five years—notably the Arab Peace Initiative and the Road Map—have been initiated by the Arab Center to break the deadlock and push the peace process forward.

Yet today, a number of factors, beginning with the nature of the center itself, have put its moderation and dynamism at risk.

The Arab public must be convinced that a proactive, pragmatic Arab discourse is not limited to the peace process but extends to other concerns: good governance, economic well-being, and inclusive decision-making. The erratic approach of Arab regimes to reform has compromised the credibility of both their domestic and foreign policies, especially in regard to the peace process. Certainly, the three Arab countries collaborating on peace efforts have yet to work together on these other issues, and in fact they sometimes hold opposing views on them. Loss of credibility on daily issues has extended to a loss of credibility of the moderate Arab Center on the Arab-Israeli conflict. Many Arabs have come to view the pragmatism of the Arab Center as compromising with the Western powers rather than as an attempt at ending the Israeli occupation, establishing a viable Palestinian state, and bringing stability and prosperity to the region.

Although the Arab Center has made an honorable effort to resolve the Arab-Israeli conflict through moderation, its major shortcoming is that it remains focused entirely on the peace process, with no attention to the creation of the public awareness necessary to ensure the success of their efforts. For the Arab Center to recapture public confidence it must start seriously and systematically to address citizens' problems through a system of checks and balances.

Coexistence, diversity, and moderation are values that cannot apply to the peace process alone but must be practiced internally in Arab societies. Arab governments cannot demand that Arabs accept relations with Israel, an enemy state for decades, while refusing to accept opposition parties in their own countries, and still be seen as credible by their publics.

This anomaly requires the urgent attention of the Arab Center. Radical ideologies in the Arab world are on the rise, fueled by deprivation, a lack of opportunity, a sense of powerlessness, and an overwhelming sense that ordinary people's concerns are irrelevant to Arab regimes. Without proper redress, the diverse composition of this region will be in jeopardy. The forces of the status quo must be made to understand that by resisting change, they risk not only their privileges but the systems they are trying to protect. If the Arab Center wants to keep power, it must also share it. Unchecked, absolute power is no longer a sustainable option—if it ever was. Thus the center must confront not only the causes of growing radicalism but also its own entrenched old guard who, in order to protect their short-term interests, are risking a stable and prosperous future for their countries. An Arab Center that is willing to address all these issues need not be the same Arab Center dealing with the peace process: Jordan, Egypt, and Saudi Arabia. The Arab Center needs to be viewed as a force committed to a holistic way of life that addresses issues of peace, reform, and diversity rather than a static set of countries or groups.

If the Arab Center makes an earnest effort to do this, I have little doubt that it will convince its citizens, quickly, of its good intentions to develop systems of accountability and balanced power. Nor do I doubt that the Arab Center can be more forceful in pushing forward Islam's message of tolerance, which rejects indiscriminate violence and which embraces the vibrant diversity that exists both within Islam and within all predominantly Muslim countries. A study conducted by the Center for Strategic Studies at the University of Jordan in five Arab countries (Egypt, Jordan, Lebanon, Syria, and Palestine) showed that 60 percent of respondents believed that religious fanaticism is a problem in their society. More than two-thirds of the respondents thought that interpretation in religion should not be closed. (In the Sunni stream of Islam, the door to interpretation and reasoning, *ijtihad,* has been closed since at least the thirteenth century.)

In addition, Arab civil society has not been an effective agent of change. Discouraged in some instances, coopted in others, it has more often simply been openly opposed by governments. Consequently, the forces for change in the Arab world, other than the Islamists, have remained largely secular and elitist, unmobilized or disorganized, and out of touch with the grass roots. Preaching democracy from university and think-tank pulpits is insufficient. As long as the message of civil society does not resonate among the average man or woman on the street and thereby fails to mobilize people and win seats at the polls, the value of civil society will not constitute a true alternative to the unchecked ruling elite and religious parties.

Civil society must muster the courage to answer religious parties, which have claimed a monopoly on truth, and argue that opposition to their policies is a challenge to religion itself. Progressive forces have yet to argue convincingly otherwise. Nor have progressives effectively distinguished between secularism and atheism. As long as they are reluctant to confront such issues head-on, status quo governments and religious parties will continue to enjoy a functional alliance that steers the Middle East away from moderation and into more violence, exclusivism, and intolerance.

But the Arab Center cannot succeed alone. It requires a dramatic change of policies by Israel. Israel cannot continue to rule by the sword. The Israeli occupation of the West Bank and Gaza is the longest of the twentieth century in the world. As long as it persists, Israel will be viewed as a usurper of Arab land. Israel also cannot continue to behave as if American political and military support alone will deliver the peace and security Israelis need. Two major developments are changing the status quo in a manner that will prolong its security dilemma. The first is the rise of radical Islamic parties such as Hamas and Hezbollah, which do not believe in peaceful solutions and are turning a political conflict into a religious one. Israel's military superiority has not shielded its citizens from the violence of these organizations, nor has it neutralized them. The Israeli war in Lebanon against Hezbollah in the summer of 2006 is a stark example of the limits of military power. Hamas and Hezbollah have found much support within all Arab communities, not just among Palestinians. Increasingly, people believe that the moderation of the Arab Center has not delivered and that only violence can do so.

The second factor is routinely referred to as the demographic time bomb, a simple but powerful factor in the conflict that Israeli politicians have ignored for too long. Within the area comprising historical Palestine—today's Israel, West Bank, and Gaza—the number of Arabs will exceed the number of Israeli Jews within few years. Jewish immigration into Israel has slowed, but not reversed, this trend. Israel faces a tremendous choice about its identity and the nature of the state: Does it want to continue to rule over other people by force, threatening its Jewish and democratic nature? Or does it wish to preserve by ending the occupation?

The Labor Party was the first major Israeli party to realize these challenges to the Jewish and democratic identity of Israel. The Oslo Accords, signed between Israel and the PLO in September 1993, were the first sign not only that the two sides were at last ready to recognize each other but also that Israel had begun to face the reality of the occupation and address it. Although it was then still taboo to talk about a Palestinian state—Yitzhak Rabin spoke of a Palestinian entity, not a state—the road to a two-state solution had begun. In his last major speech to the Knesset, on October 5, 1995, one month before he was assassinated, Rabin justified Israel's signing of what is known as Oslo B—the Palestinian-Israeli agreement that specified Israel's withdrawal from major tracts of Palestinian land and the handover of authority to the Palestinians in many areas. I quote him here at some length to demonstrate the significant transformation in the Labor Party's thinking since the 1970s. Rabin said that the Jews were privileged to return to the land of Zion and establish a state there, but he added:

> We did not return to an empty land. There were Palestinians here who struggled against us for a hundred wild and bloody years. Many thousands, on both sides, were killed in the battle over the same land, over the same strip of territory, and were joined by the armies of the Arab states. Today, after innumerable wars and bloody incidents, we rule more than two million Palestinians through the IDF [Israel Defense Forces], and run their lives by a Civil Administration. This is not a peaceful solution. We can continue to fight. We can continue to kill—and continue to be killed. But we can also try to put a stop to this never-ending cycle of blood. We can also give peace a chance. . . . We preferred a Jewish state, even if not on every part of the Land of Israel, to a bi-national state, which would emerge with the annexation of 2.2 million Palestinian residents of the Gaza Strip and the West Bank. We had to choose between the whole of the land of Israel, which meant a bi-national state, and whose population, as of today, would comprise four and a half million Jews, and more than three million Palestinians, who are a separate entity—religiously, politically, and nationally—and a state with less territory, but which would be a Jewish state. We chose to be a Jewish state. We chose a Jewish state because we are convinced that a bi-national state with millions of Palestinian Arabs will not be able to fulfill the Jewish role of the State of Israel, which is the state of the Jews.

After Rabin's death, the Labor Party officially endorsed a Palestinian state. It has taken Likud longer to internalize the demographic issue, but many of its members have arrived at the same conclusion. Prime Minister Ariel Sharon, a fervent believer in Eretz Israel and the architect of Israel's settlement policy, made the transformation publicly for the first time during a meeting with President George W. Bush on February 7, 2002. At a White House press conference, Sharon stated that through negotiations "and at the end of the process, I believe that the Palestinian state, of course, will be—we'll see a Palestinian state." Sharon's successor, Ehud Olmert, said at a conference in Israel that he supported the creation of a Palestinian state and acknowledged that Israel would have to withdraw from parts of the West Bank to maintain its Jewish majority. However, the proposed unilateral withdrawal from parts of the West Bank which Olmert advocated, and which secured his victory in the 2006 Israeli elections, was a nonsolution to circumvent a political settlement with the Palestinians. The war on Lebanon of 2006 rendered it invalid in all events, and consequently unilateral withdrawal—or convergence, as it was called in Israel—no longer enjoys consensus either within Olmert's newly formed Kadima Party or in Israeli society in general.

For the first time in the conflict, the Arab world has proposed a political settlement that would guarantee Israel's security. And in 2002 every Arab state endorsed this proposal—including the hardest of the hard-liners. Moderates on both sides of this conflict must unite and endorse such a settlement before it is too late and the region is plunged into darkness for the foreseeable future. Today the fight is no longer between moderate Israelis against radical Arabs or moderate Arabs against radical Israelis. The real fight is within each society, between the moderate and radical forces in their midst. For peace to prevail, the Arab and Israeli centers must join forces and agree on a solution that addresses the needs of both sides against extremists on either side who are advocating solutions mutually exclusive of the needs of the other side. So far, extremist ideologies on both sides have managed to radicalize the moderates, rather than the other way around. Because of such tactics by Arab radicals as suicide bombings, the Israeli public has turned to the right and has lost hope for a peaceful settlement with Arabs. Likewise, Israel's renewed focus on military solutions to political problems—exemplified in the incursion into the West Bank of 2002, the war on Lebanon in 2006, and the government's policy of targeted assassinations and collective punishment—has exhausted popular Arab good will and helped turn Arab societies to the right.

The Palestinian parliamentary elections of early 2006 constitute a case in point. Palestinians voted into office Hamas, also known as the Islamic Resistance Movement, which violently opposed peace with Israel and has been responsible for some of the most atrocious terrorist attacks on Israeli civilians. Hamas supplanted the Fateh leadership, which had de facto ruled Palestinian affairs since the emergence of the PLO in the mid-1960s, and negotiated, through Yasser Arafat, the Oslo Accords of 1993. Fateh effectively became the ruling party upon the creation of the Palestinian National Authority. Presidential and parliamentary elections legitimated its authority, and the Fateh leadership subsequently negotiated all agreements reached with Israel throughout the 1990s. To the outside world, the election of Hamas seemed to reflect incorrigible Arab hatred of Israel and thus a vote against a restoration of the peace process, which by January 2006 had been moribund for five and a half years.

The interpretation should be more circumspect. Only one year earlier, the Palestinian electorate voted to power as head of the Palestinian National Authority Mahmoud Abbas, a moderate and a champion of the peace process. Moreover, a poll conducted weeks *after* the elections showed that a full 76 percent of Palestinians wanted the new government, a Hamas government, to negotiate a political settlement with Israel. It also showed that people were fed up with corruption, which was widespread among the Palestinian Authority. This was not an antipeace vote, then, but an anticorruption one. People were ready to sacrifice a government pursuing the issue they most cared about, an end to the occupation and the hope for independence, for a party that promised them a clean government.

The historical record shows that active American involvement in the conflict has benefited the peace process and that in its absence the situation has deteriorated into death and destruction. September 11 has proved wrong the logic of the American claim that the United States cannot want peace more than the parties itself. It not only can; it must. The absence of peace now threatens America's national interests. Letting the parties simmer in their own juices has only allowed extremists to capitalize on popular frustrations to reap more chaos and violence. Al-Qaeda is waging a war not against the United States or Israel but against the entire world—including Muslims and Arabs—and it can and does exploit the anger and misery of those in the region to further its twisted agenda.

To be sure, the Arab-Israeli conflict is not the only grievance in the region, as I have tried to show. Economic stagnation and poor governance are others. But to realize how these frustrations become assets to radical organizations, one has to only consider that within a decade and a half, Hezbollah and Hamas have transformed themselves from marginal organizations to prominent political actors in Lebanon and Palestine and today can count on a support base far wider than the locales in which they were born. Although its objectives differ, the same can be said for "international" radical groups such as Al-Qaeda.

American engagement in the region must be comprehensive in that it sees the relationship among peace, reform, and radicalism. So far, the United States has tried to compartmentalize them, advocating reform without putting it into the context of the Arab-Israeli conflict, and urging democracy without a strategy to cope with elected governments whose policies it finds repugnant. The U.S. insistence on compartmentalization of these issues has ultimately compromised its credibility even while it believed it was doing the region some good by, for example, ridding it of a thug like Saddam Hussein.

The United States can play a more constructive role and in fact still has leeway to do so; all the criticism and controversy surrounding its engagement in the Middle East demonstrates how strongly Arabs and Israelis believe the United States alone possesses the power and authority to be a force for peace and justice in the Middle East. Therefore, the United States must demonstrate a genuine desire to work with the region's moderate core as a partner rather than as a patron. Partnership means collaboration on issues of concern to both parties, not to one party alone. If the United States wants to have credibility dealing with the issue of reform in the region, an issue that has become of vital interest to U.S. security interests, it must show the region that it is serious about a direct and sustained engagement in the Arab-Israeli conflict—with a resolve to end it, including a willingness to censure and encourage both parties, rather than simply support a never-ending peace process. The U.S. regional involvement today is preoccupied with Iraq and Iran, but the continuation of the Israeli occupation of Arab land remains at the center of the Arab world's radar screen. No other issue has managed to dislodge that concern. To the contrary, containing the challenges that Iraq and Iran pose will be much harder without a just, comprehensive solution to the Arab-Israeli conflict. The United States must, for its own sake, acknowledge this, and once again engage in peacemaking.

Partnership also means the willingness to listen to all partners. The Arab-Israeli conflict is not a zero-sum game, and its solution does not mean a loss for Israel. To the contrary, everyone wins with a just, comprehensive solution. Though the Arab Center has proved its ability to take courageous action to end the conflict peacefully, without the active support of the United States—in deeds, not just words—the center will soon be overwhelmed by radicalism. Sadly, the Arab Peace Initiative, the center's crowning achievement in dealing with the Arab-Israeli conflict, was largely ignored by the United States. Consequently, the three Arab states that championed it—Egypt, Saudi Arabia, and Jordan—are today on the defensive in the Arab world. Mahmoud Abbas, the most moderate Palestinian leader in the history of the conflict, has nothing to show his people for his moderation, despite repeated calls to the United States for tangible support. It has become easy and routine for the radicals to point to the Arab Center's policies of the past years and ask: What have they accomplished for the Palestinians? Have they achieved an end to the occupation? Have they delivered a two-state solution? Today, the Arab Center has no counterargument. The Arab Center cannot survive on lip service alone. If its advice continues to be largely ignored and if the United States continues to behave as if it did not exist, it may well soon vanish. The Arab Center must be able to show results or no one will listen to it. And it will either collapse from exhaustion or be outpaced by extremism.

The European Union has better appreciated the need to partner with the Arab world. Although the Europeans are no less concerned than the United States about their security or economic interests, they have approached the challenges of the region differently. In recent years, they have demonstrated greater sensitivity to the peace process, a willingness to listen, and a more sustained direct engagement. They have acknowledged the complex interlinkages among crucial issues. On reform, they have entered with many countries of the region into "partnership agreements" and "joint" action plans that dealt with all the issues that the United States is concerned with—political reform, the empowerment of women, freedom of the press, to name a few—but through joint plans commonly agreed to with the countries of the region, and have avoided rhetoric or actions that suggest the European Union is trying to impose its values on the region by force. It is no coincidence, therefore, that the Arab public views such attempts as far more benign than those of the United States.

Where do we go from here? Is the Middle East doomed to perpetual violence and instability? After so much bloodshed, and so many attempts to solve the conflict, one reality stands out: there is no military solution to this conflict. Both sides have tried it, and failed. All that remains is a negotiated political settlement to share both the land and fulfill the dreams of both communities. Fortunately, there is no need to start from square one. If anyone has doubts, one need only look at such documents as the Clinton parameters, the Geneva Initiative, or the Arab Peace Initiative to have a clear idea of what such a solution entail, and what both sides are prepared to accept.

However, the possibilities of the Oslo Accords have been exhausted and its shortcomings revealed. A gradual process of confidence building has not worked, mainly because it gave the detractors of the peace process too much time to operate. They were able to destroy peace as quickly as it was built. At the same time, the light at the end of the Oslo tunnel was dim, or nonexistent. For it did not specify what a final settlement should look like, and the two parties therefore found themselves engaged in endless negotiations and negotiations over negotiations. The trust between the two parties is today at an all-time low, and where the parameters of a final settlement are today known to all, the tunnel to it has been destroyed by the extremists on both sides.

This is why any return to a gradual political process is, in my opinion, futile. Many forces against peace stand ready to derail the process if given the chance. Time has revealed their determination and capabilities. I also do not see how the two parties can present any new solution radically different from the ones they have already agreed to. The drawing board must be abandoned and a solution implemented relatively quickly so that the forces against peace do not have time to stop it.

How can this be done? The United States, in collaboration with the Quartet, can present the outlines of a final settlement to the two parties, based on all the initiatives above. The two parties can then be given a short time to work out the details of such a solution, with the active help of the United States and the international community. Then a plebiscite should be conducted to endorse that solution. Despite all the mistrust and spilled blood, all polls suggest that a solid majority on both sides want a political solution and are ready for a settlement. This settlement needs to be presented as not one between Israel and the Palestinians or between Israel and Syria but one between Israel and the whole Arab world that would bring a permanent end to the conflict. As such, I believe it would be endorsed by the Israeli public as well as by the Arab world.

The Middle East is a region accustomed to exclusionist policies and mutually exclusive dreams. Both Arabs and Israelis have been guilty of this. Whether on issues of peace, reform, or tolerance, both parties have not been successful at reaching out either to the other side or to their own societies. This book need not be an account of missed or lost opportunities but rather a reminder of roads built but not traveled, of a needed resolve to end this long journey of bloodshed.

This book is also a call for Arabs and Israelis to embrace diversity in the region rather than demonize it as a destructive force, and to adopt policies of inclusion. If Israel wants finally to abandon its iron wall policy and be accepted in the region, it needs to accept, indeed work for, the right of Palestinians to live on their land free of occupation. And if the Arab Center is to triumph, ridding itself of the image its opponents paint of an apologist for the West or a compromiser of Arab rights, it must plant the seeds for a time when the peace process will end and the challenge of a robust, diverse, tolerant, democratic, and prosperous Arab society remains.

KING HUSSEIN'S LETTER TO PRIME MINISTER RABIN REGARDING THE JERUSALEM LAND EXPROPRIATION ISSUE

Amman,

21st May 1995

I have just returned home and felt it my duty to write to you over the issue of your government's decision to confiscate additional Arab land in the City of Jerusalem. I had followed over the recent days developments pertaining to this explosive issue with a concerned and heavy heart. I was in no doubt that there would be an American veto at the Security Council over any proposed solution on the subject. Some may deem that a victory for your Government but honesty, responsibility and friendship compel me to suggest that there is no victor in this instance rather there are many losers. I am, my friend, deeply concerned, for pre 1967 East Jerusalem has a very special place in my heart and conscience as it does all Jordanians.

Holy Jerusalem further, is not only a Palestinian issue but one that is of equal concern to all the followers of the three great monotheistic religions.

I wish you could contemplate the following:—

A—Jordanian sovereignty over Eastern Jerusalem which is a sovereignty under International law, having been acquired on authority of the peoples' referendum, makes it impossible for Jordan to waive.

B—Against this solid reality and foundation however, and since the Palestinian dimension of Palestinian National rights on Palestinian soil, has been recognized with the Madrid Peace Conference, as it did in the partition plan of 1947 and consolidated in the Oslo Accords and the Washington D.O.P. negotiated between your Government and the Palestine Liberation Organization, (the sole legitimate representative of the people of Palestine), Jordan has in a positive and constructive attitude redefined its position to continue to insist that the Holy City, hallowed by the three major world religions, shall be, and remain, of international religious (ecumenical) status, belonging to the whole world, under the authority of the very act which legitimized the birth of the State of Israel, namely the General Assembly Resolution number 181 of 1947.

Further to that and since the Madrid Peace Conference and the Oslo Accord were founded on Security Council Resolution 242 the preamble of which specifies the inadminissibility of the acquisition of territories by war, and since Western Jerusalem was and is the de facto Capital of Israel it is, and will continue to be, our position that in the context of peace East Jerusalem should become the Capital of the Palestinian Entity. The symbol of peace shall thus be Holy Jerusalem between the Children of Abraham and their descendants for all times to come as is God's will. Jerusalem would also become the Capital of both Israel and Palestine a living symbol and essence representing the reality of peace between the Israelis and the Palestinians for all times.

All these worthy objectives can only crystallize with sincere, dedicated and genuine efforts by all concerned. Only when this process is complete and is authenticated by free popular support on the Palestinian side can Jordan totally withdraw from the political scene regarding Jerusalem.

The Oslo Accords and the Washington D.O.P.'s philosophy which we lauded, envisioned the breaking of a new dawn of peace and security, for all Palestinians and all Israelis. The issue of Jerusalem, charged as it is to all concerned was left to be addressed through negotiations at the end of the transitional period. The crimes committed since the Washington D.O.P. against the innocent in Hebron and Israel have seriously undermined the essence of confidence building between the two peoples. I am thus completely at a loss to understand why now should the Government of Israel contribute to its further serious deterioration by unilateral action in Jerusalem and the confiscation of even an inch of Arab land. With all due respect my friend, this should not stand and we seek your wisdom, courage and farsightedness to reconsider urgently and fully the action and repercussions and to act accordingly, recent events at the Security Council notwithstanding.

Your Government and the Palestinians, as per your earlier agreed schedule, can then negotiate a mutually satisfactory, balanced and just solution to the issues of respective territorial rights in Jerusalem, rather than dealing with some of them now in a unilateral way and thus further damaging the credibility of both sides and seriously threatening the Peace Process.

Dear Prime Minister, the peace camp to which both of us belong, deserves no less than your considered and immediate action to restore faith to its adherents and to retrieve the advantages which have been given to the skeptics and the enemies of peace by recent developments.

I have written frankly and candidly my friend, because you have grown to expect I believe, no less from a fellow builder of peace dedicated to it and deeply concerned and committed to realizing it for all our future generations.

APPENDIX 2
NOTE VERBALE TO THE ISRAELI FOREIGN
MINISTRY ON ABSENTEE PROPERTY

August 31, 1995

The Embassy of the Hashemite Kingdom of Jordan to the State of Israel presents its best compliments to the Ministry of Foreign Affairs of the State of Israel and has the honor to refer to the Israeli law on the implementation of the Treaty of Peace between the Hashemite Kingdom of Jordan and the State of Israel.

In this regard, the Embassy is instructed to communicate the following:

It is the opinion of the Government of the Hashemite Kingdom of Jordan that Section 6 of the said legislation to the non-applicability of the Properties of the Absentees Law to Jordanians appears to be inconsistent with the Treaty of Peace between the two states.

The legislation in question applies as of the date of ratification of the Treaty (November 10, 1994). Its only effect therefore is to prevent further Jordanian property from being regarded as absentee property by reason of events occurring after 10 November 1994. In the overwhelming majority of cases the properties of Jordanians will continue to be vested in a State Official of Israel.

This, in the considered opinion of the Government of Jordan, is inconsistent with the status of peace and the provisions of the Treaty, in particular the following provisions thereof: (article 7(2)(a)) in which the parties agreed *inter alia* to remove all discriminatory barriers to normal economic relations; (article 8) in which they agreed to alleviate problems of refugees and displaced persons arising on a bilateral level; (article (11)(1)(b)) in which they undertook within three months "to repeal all adverse or discriminatory references in their respective legislation and subparagraph (d) of the same article in which they undertook "to ensure mutual enjoyment by each others' citizens of due process within their respective legal systems and before their courts."

The Government of Jordan therefore feels compelled to register its objection to the said legislation and to officially request the Government of Israel to consider amending it so that this clear inconsistency with the Treaty of peace is removed.

The Embassy has the honor to renew to the esteemed Ministry the assurances of its highest consideration.

THE CLINTON PARAMETERS

TERRITORY

Based on what I heard, I believe that the solution should be in the mid-90%'s, between 94–96% of the West Bank territory of the Palestinian State.

The land annexed by Israel should be compensated by a land swap of 1-3% in addition to territorial arrangement such as a permanent safe passage.

The parties should also consider the swap of leased land to meet their respective needs. There are creative ways for doing this that should address Palestinian and Israeli needs and concerns.

The Parties should develop a map consistent with the following criteria:

- 80% of the settlers in blocks
- Contiguity
- Minimize annexed areas
- Minimize the number of Palestinians affected

SECURITY

The key to security lies in an international presence that can only be withdrawn by mutual consent. This presence will also monitor the implementation of the agreement between both sides.

My best judgment is that the Israeli withdrawal should be carried out over 36 months while international force is gradually introduced in the area. At the end of this period, a small Israeli presence would remain in fixed locations in the Jordan Valley under the authority of the international force for another 36 months. This period could be reduced in the event of favorable regional developments that diminish the threats to Israel.

On early warning situations, Israel should maintain three facilities in the West Bank with a Palestinian liaison presence. The stations will be subject to review after 10 years with any changes in status to be mutually agreed.

Regarding emergency developments, I understand that you still have to develop a map of relevant areas and routes. But in defining what is an emergency, I propose the following definition:

Imminent and demonstrable threat to Israel's national security of a military nature requires the activation of a national state of emergency.

Of course, the international forces will need to be notified of any such determination.

On airspace, I suggest that the state of Palestine will have sovereignty over its airspace but that the two sides should work out special arrangements for Israeli training and operational needs.

I understand that the Israeli position is that Palestine should be defined as a "demilitarized state" while the Palestinian side proposes "a state with limited arms." As a compromise, I suggest calling it a "non-militarized state." This will be consistent with the fact that in addition to a strong Palestinian security force, Palestine will have an international force for border security and deterrence purposes.

JERUSALEM AND REFUGEES

I have a sense that the remaining gaps have more to do with formulations than practical realities.

Jerusalem

The general principle is that Arab areas are Palestinian and Jewish ones are Israeli. This would apply to the Old City as well. I urge the two sides to work on maps to create maximum contiguity for both sides.

Regarding the Haram/Temple Mount, I believe that the gaps are not related to practical administration but to the symbolic issues of sovereignty and to finding a way to accord respect to the religious beliefs of both sides.

I know you have been discussing a number of formulations, and you can agree on any of these. I add to these two additional formulations guaranteeing Palestinian effective control over Haram while respecting the conviction of the Jewish people. Regarding either one of these two formulations will be international monitoring to provide mutual confidence.

1. Palestinian sovereignty over the Haram and Israeli sovereignty over [the Western Wall and the space sacred to Judaism of which it is a part][the Western Wall and the Holy of Holies of which it is a part].

There will be a firm commitment by both not to excavate beneath the Haram or behind the Wall.

2. Palestinian shared sovereignty over the Haram and Israeli sovereignty over the Western Wall and shared functional sovereignty over the issue of excavation under the Haram and behind the Wall as mutual consent would be requested before any excavation can take place.

Refugees

I sense that the differences are more relating to formulations and less to what will happen on a practical level.

I believe that Israel is prepared to acknowledge the moral and material suffering caused to the Palestinian people as a result of the 1948 war and the need to assist the international community in addressing the problem.

An international commission should be established to implement all the aspects that flow from your agreement: compensation, resettlement, rehabilitation, etc.

The U.S. is prepared to lead an international effort to help the refugees.

The fundamental gap is on how to handle the concept of the right of return. I know the history of the issue and how hard it will be for the Palestinian leadership to appear to be abandoning this principle.

The Israeli side could simply not accept any reference to right of return that would imply a right to immigrate to Israel in defiance of Israel's sovereign policies on admission or that would threaten the Jewish character of the state.

Any solution must address both needs.

The solution will have to be consistent with the two-state approach that both sides have accepted as the end to the Palestinian-Israeli conflict: the state of Palestine as the homeland of the Palestinian people and the state of Israel as the homeland of the Jewish people.

Under the two-state solution, the guiding principle should be that the Palestinian state will be the focal point for Palestinians who choose to return to the area without ruling out that Israel will accept some of these refugees.

I believe that we need to adopt a formulation on the right of return to Israel itself but that does not negate the aspiration of the Palestinian people to return to the area.

In light of the above, I propose two alternatives:

1. Both sides recognize the right of Palestinian refugees to return to Historic Palestine. Or,

2. Both sides recognize the right of the Palestinian refuges to return to their homeland.

The agreement will define the implementation of this general right in a way that is consistent with the two-state solution. It would list five possible final homes for the refugees:

1. The state of Palestine

2. Areas in Israel being transferred to Palestine in the land swap

3. Rehabilitation in a host country

4. Resettlement in a third country

5. Admission to Israel

In listing these options, the agreement will make clear that the return to the West Bank, Gaza Strip, and the areas acquired in the land swap would be a right to all Palestinian refugees.

While rehabilitation in host countries, resettlement in third world countries and absorption into Israel will depend upon the policies of those countries.

Israel could indicate in the agreement that it intends to establish a policy so that some of the refugees would be absorbed into Israel consistent with Israel's sovereign decision.

I believe that priority should be given to the refugee population in Lebanon.

The parties would agree that this implements Resolution 194.

I propose that the agreement clearly mark the end of the conflict and its implementation put an end to all its claims. This could be implemented through a UN Security Council Resolution that notes that Resolutions 242 and 338 have been implemented through the release of Palestinian prisoners.

I believe that this is an outline of a fair and lasting agreement.

It gives the Palestinian people the ability to determine the future on their own land, a sovereign and viable state recognized by the international community, Al-Qods as its capital, sovereignty over the Haram, and new lives for the refugees.

It gives the people of Israel a genuine end to the conflict, real security, the preservation of sacred religious ties, the incorporation of 80% of the settlers into Israel, and the largest Jewish Jerusalem in history recognized by all as its capital.

This is the best I can do. Brief your leaders and tell me if they are prepared to come for discussions based on these ideas. If so, I would meet the next week separately. If not, I have taken this as far as I can.

These are my ideas. If they are not accepted, they are not just off the table, they also go with me when I leave the office.

THE ARAB PEACE INITIATIVE ADOPTED AT THE BEIRUT ARAB SUMMIT, MARCH 2002

The Council of the League of Arab States at the Summit Level, at its 14th Ordinary Session,

- Reaffirming the resolution taken in June 1996 at the Cairo extra-Ordinary Arab Summit that a just and comprehensive peace in the Middle East is the strategic option of the Arab Countries, to be achieved in accordance with International Legality, and which would require a comparable commitment on the part of the Israeli Government;
- Having listened to the statement made by His Royal Highness Prince Abdullah Bin Abdul Aziz, the Crown Prince of the Kingdom of Saudi Arabia in which his Highness presented his Initiative, calling for full Israeli withdrawal from all the Arab territories occupied since June 1967, in implementation of Security Council Resolutions 242 and 338, reaffirmed by the Madrid Conference of 1991 and the land for peace principle, and Israel's acceptance of an independent Palestinian State, with East Jerusalem as its capital, in return for the establishment of normal relations in the context of a comprehensive peace with Israel;
- Emanating from the conviction of the Arab countries that a military solution to the conflict will not achieve peace or provide security for the parties, the council:

1. Requests Israel to reconsider its policies and declare that a just peace is its strategic option as well.
2. Further calls upon Israel to affirm:
    i. Full Israeli withdrawal from all the territories occupied since 1967, including the Syrian Golan Heights to the lines of June 4, 1967 as well as the remaining occupied Lebanese territories in the south of Lebanon.
    ii. Achievement of a just solution to the Palestinian Refugee problem to be agreed upon in accordance with UN General Assembly Resolution 194.
    iii. The acceptance of the establishment of a Sovereign Independent Palestinian State on the Palestinian territories occupied since the 4th of June 1967 in the West Bank and Gaza strip, with East Jerusalem as its capital.
3. Consequently, the Arab countries affirm the following:
    i. Consider the Arab-Israeli conflict ended, and enter into a peace agreement with Israel, and provide security for all states of the region.
    ii. Establish normal relations with Israel in the context of this comprehensive peace.
4. Assures the rejection of all forms of Palestinian patriation which conflicts with the special circumstances of the Arab host countries.
5. Calls upon the Government of Israel and all Israelis to accept this initiative in order to safeguard the prospects for peace and stop further shedding of blood, enabling the Arab countries and Israel to live in peace and good neighborliness and provide future generations with security, stability, and prosperity.
6. Invites the International Community and all countries and organizations to support this initiative.
7. Requests the Chairman of the Summit to form a special committee composed of some of its concerned member states and the Secretary General of the League of Arab States to pursue the necessary contacts to gain support for this initiative at all levels, particularly from the United Nations, the Security Council, the United States of American, the Russian Federation, the Muslim States and the European Union.

APPENDIX 5
A PERFORMANCE-BASED ROADMAP TO A PERMANENT TWO-STATE SOLUTION TO THE ISRAELI-PALESTINIAN CONFLICT

The following is a performance-based and goal-driven roadmap, with clear phases, timelines, target dates, and benchmarks aiming at progress through reciprocal steps by the two parties in the political, security, economic, humanitarian, and institution-building fields, under the auspices of the Quartet [the United States, European Union, United Nations, and Russia]. The destination is a final and comprehensive settlement of the Israel-Palestinian conflict by 2005, as presented in President Bush's speech of 24 June, and welcomed by the EU, Russia and the UN in the 16 July and 17 September Quartet Ministerial statements.

A two-state solution to the Israeli-Palestinian conflict will only be achieved through an end to violence and terrorism, when the Palestinian people have a leadership acting decisively against terror and willing and able to build a practicing democracy based on tolerance and liberty, and through Israel's readiness to do what is necessary for a democratic Palestinian state to be established, and a clear, unambiguous acceptance by both parties of the goal of a negotiated settlement as described below. The Quartet will assist and facilitate implementation of the plan, starting in Phase I, including direct discussions between the parties as required. The plan establishes a realistic timeline for implementation. However, as a performance-based plan, progress will require and depend upon the good faith efforts of the parties, and their compliance with each of the obligations outlined below. Should the parties perform their obligations rapidly, progress within and through the phases may come sooner than indicated in the plan. Non-compliance with obligations will impede progress.

A settlement, negotiated between the parties, will result in the emergence of an independent, democratic, and viable Palestinian state living side by side in peace and security with Israel and its other neighbors. The settlement will resolve the Israel-Palestinian conflict, and end the occupation that began in 1967, based on the foundations of the Madrid Conference, the principle of land for peace, UNSCRs 242, 338 and 1397, agreements previously reached by the parties, and the initiative of Saudi Crown Prince Abdullah—endorsed by the Beirut Arab League Summit—calling for acceptance of Israel as a neighbor living in peace and security, in the context of a comprehensive settlement. This initiative is a vital element of international efforts to promote a comprehensive peace on all tracks, including the Syrian-Israeli and Lebanese-Israeli tracks.

The Quartet will meet regularly at senior levels to evaluate the parties' performance on implementation of the plan. In each phase, the parties are expected to perform their obligations in parallel, unless otherwise indicated.

PHASE I

Ending Terror And Violence, Normalizing Palestinian Life, and Building Palestinian Institutions—Present to May 2003

In Phase I, the Palestinians immediately undertake an unconditional cessation of violence according to the steps outlined below; such action should be accompanied by supportive measures undertaken by Israel. Palestinians and Israelis resume security cooperation based on the Tenet work plan to end violence, terrorism, and incitement through restructured and effective Palestinian security services. Palestinians undertake comprehensive political reform in preparation for statehood, including drafting a Palestinian constitution, and free, fair and open elections upon the basis of those measures. Israel takes all necessary steps to help normalize Palestinian life. Israel withdraws from Palestinian areas occupied from September 28, 2000 and the two sides restore the status quo that existed at that time, as security performance and cooperation progress. Israel also freezes all settlement activity, consistent with the Mitchell report.

At the outset of Phase I:

- Palestinian leadership issues unequivocal statement reiterating Israel's right to exist in peace and security and calling for an immediate and unconditional ceasefire to end armed activity and all acts of violence against Israelis anywhere. All official Palestinian institutions end incitement against Israel.
- Israeli leadership issues unequivocal statement affirming its commitment to the two-state vision of an independent, viable, sovereign Palestinian state living in peace and security alongside Israel, as expressed by President Bush, and calling for an immediate end to violence against Palestinians everywhere. All official Israeli institutions end incitement against Palestinians.

Security

- Palestinians declare an unequivocal end to violence and terrorism and undertake visible efforts on the ground to arrest, disrupt, and restrain individuals and groups conducting and planning violent attacks on Israelis anywhere.
- Rebuilt and refocused Palestinian Authority security apparatus begins sustained, targeted, and effective operations aimed at confronting all those engaged in terror and dismantlement of terrorist capabilities and infrastructure. This includes commencing confiscation of illegal weapons and consolidation of security authority, free of association with terror and corruption.
- GOI takes no actions undermining trust, including deportations, attacks on civilians; confiscation and/or demolition of Palestinian homes and property, as a punitive measure or to facilitate Israeli construction; destruction of Palestinian institutions and infrastructure; and other measures specified in the Tenet work plan.
- Relying on existing mechanisms and on-the-ground resources, Quartet representatives begin informal monitoring and consult with the parties on establishment of a formal monitoring mechanism and its implementation.

- Implementation, as previously agreed, of U.S. rebuilding, training and resumed security cooperation plan in collaboration with outside oversight board (U.S.–Egypt–Jordan). Quartet support for efforts to achieve a lasting, comprehensive cease-fire.
- All Palestinian security organizations are consolidated into three services reporting to an empowered Interior Minister.
- Restructured/retrained Palestinian security forces and IDF counterparts progressively resume security cooperation and other undertakings in implementation of the Tenet work plan, including regular senior-level meetings, with the participation of U.S. security officials.
- Arab states cut off public and private funding and all other forms of support for groups supporting and engaging in violence and terror.
- All donors providing budgetary support for the Palestinians channel these funds through the Palestinian Ministry of Finance's Single Treasury Account.
- As comprehensive security performance moves forward, IDF withdraws progressively from areas occupied since September 28, 2000 and the two sides restore the status quo that existed prior to September 28, 2000. Palestinian security forces redeploy to areas vacated by IDF.

Palestinian Institution-Building

- Immediate action on credible process to produce draft constitution for Palestinian statehood. As rapidly as possible, constitutional committee circulates draft Palestinian constitution, based on strong parliamentary democracy and cabinet with empowered prime minister, for public comment/debate. Constitutional committee proposes draft document for submission after elections for approval by appropriate Palestinian institutions.
- Appointment of interim prime minister or cabinet with empowered executive authority/decision-making body.
- GOI fully facilitates travel of Palestinian officials for PLC and Cabinet sessions, internationally supervised security retraining, electoral and other reform activity, and other supportive measures related to the reform efforts.
- Continued appointment of Palestinian ministers empowered to undertake fundamental reform. Completion of further steps to achieve

genuine separation of powers, including any necessary Palestinian legal reforms for this purpose.

- Establishment of independent Palestinian election commission. PLC reviews and revises election law.
- Palestinian performance on judicial, administrative, and economic benchmarks, as established by the International Task Force on Palestinian Reform.
- As early as possible, and based upon the above measures and in the context of open debate and transparent candidate selection/electoral campaign based on a free, multi-party process, Palestinians hold free, open, and fair elections.
- GOI facilitates Task Force election assistance, registration of voters, movement of candidates and voting officials. Support for NGOs involved in the election process.
- GOI reopens Palestinian Chamber of Commerce and other closed Palestinian institutions in East Jerusalem based on a commitment that these institutions operate strictly in accordance with prior agreements between the parties.

Humanitarian Response

- Israel takes measures to improve the humanitarian situation. Israel and Palestinians implement in full all recommendations of the Bertini report to improve humanitarian conditions, lifting curfews and easing restrictions on movement of persons and goods, and allowing full, safe, and unfettered access of international and humanitarian personnel.
- AHLC reviews the humanitarian situation and prospects for economic development in the West Bank and Gaza and launches a major donor assistance effort, including to the reform effort.
- GOI and PA continue revenue clearance process and transfer of funds, including arrears, in accordance with agreed, transparent monitoring mechanism.

Civil Society

- Continued donor support, including increased funding through PVOs/NGOs, for people to people programs, private sector development and civil society initiatives.

Settlements

- GOI immediately dismantles settlement outposts erected since March 2001.
- Consistent with the Mitchell Report, GOI freezes all settlement activity (including natural growth of settlements).

PHASE II
Transition—June 2003–December 2003

In the second phase, efforts are focused on the option of creating an independent Palestinian state with provisional borders and attributes of sovereignty, based on the new constitution, as a way station to a permanent status settlement. As has been noted, this goal can be achieved when the Palestinian people have a leadership acting decisively against terror, willing and able to build a practicing democracy based on tolerance and liberty. With such a leadership, reformed civil institutions and security structures, the Palestinians will have the active support of the Quartet and the broader international community in establishing an independent, viable, state.

Progress into Phase II will be based upon the consensus judgment of the Quartet of whether conditions are appropriate to proceed, taking into account performance of both parties. Furthering and sustaining efforts to normalize Palestinian lives and build Palestinian institutions, Phase II starts after Palestinian elections and ends with possible creation of an independent Palestinian state with provisional borders in 2003. Its primary goals are continued comprehensive security performance and effective security cooperation, continued normalization of Palestinian life and institution-building, further building on and sustaining of the goals outlined in Phase I, ratification of a democratic Palestinian constitution, formal establishment of office of prime minister, consolidation of political reform, and the creation of a Palestinian state with provisional borders.

- *International Conference:* Convened by the Quartet, in consultation with the parties, immediately after the successful conclusion of Palestinian elections, to support Palestinian economic recovery and launch a process, leading to establishment of an independent Palestinian state with provisional borders.

- Such a meeting would be inclusive, based on the goal of a comprehensive Middle East peace (including between Israel and Syria, and Israel and Lebanon), and based on the principles described in the preamble to this document.
- Arab states restore pre-intifada links to Israel (trade offices, etc.).
- Revival of multilateral engagement on issues including regional water resources, environment, economic development, refugees, and arms control issues.
- New constitution for democratic, independent Palestinian state is finalized and approved by appropriate Palestinian institutions. Further elections, if required, should follow approval of the new constitution.
- Empowered reform cabinet with office of prime minister formally established, consistent with draft constitution.
- Continued comprehensive security performance, including effective security cooperation on the bases laid out in Phase I.
- Creation of an independent Palestinian state with provisional borders through a process of Israeli-Palestinian engagement, launched by the international conference. As part of this process, implementation of prior agreements, to enhance maximum territorial contiguity, including further action on settlements in conjunction with establishment of a Palestinian state with provisional borders.
- Enhanced international role in monitoring transition, with the active, sustained, and operational support of the Quartet.
- Quartet members promote international recognition of Palestinian state, including possible UN membership.

PHASE III

Permanent Status Agreement and End of the Israeli-Palestinian Conflict—2004–2005

Progress into Phase III, based on consensus judgment of Quartet, and taking into account actions of both parties and Quartet monitoring. Phase III objectives are consolidation of reform and stabilization of Palestinian institutions, sustained, effective Palestinian security performance, and Israeli-Palestinian negotiations aimed at a permanent status agreement in 2005.

- *Second International Conference:* Convened by Quartet, in consultation with the parties, at beginning of 2004 to endorse agreement reached on an independent Palestinian state with provisional borders and formally to launch a process with the active, sustained, and operational support of the Quartet, leading to a final, permanent status resolution in 2005, including on borders, Jerusalem, refugees, settlements; and, to support progress toward a comprehensive Middle East settlement between Israel and Lebanon and Israel and Syria, to be achieved as soon as possible.

- Continued comprehensive, effective progress on the reform agenda laid out by the Task Force in preparation for final status agreement.
- Continued sustained and effective security performance, and sustained, effective security cooperation on the bases laid out in Phase I.
- International efforts to facilitate reform and stabilize Palestinian institutions and the Palestinian economy, in preparation for final status agreement.
- Parties reach final and comprehensive permanent status agreement that ends the Israel-Palestinian conflict in 2005, through a settlement negotiated between the parties based on UNSCR 242, 338, and 1397, that ends the occupation that began in 1967, and includes an agreed, just, fair, and realistic solution to the refugee issue, and a negotiated resolution on the status of Jerusalem that takes into account the political and religious concerns of both sides, and protects the religious interests of Jews, Christians, and Muslims worldwide, and fulfills the vision of two states, Israel and sovereign, independent, democratic and viable Palestine, living side-by-side in peace and security.
- Arab state acceptance of full normal relations with Israel and security for all the states of the region in the context of a comprehensive Arab-Israeli peace.

NOTES

CHAPTER 1. JORDAN'S CHANGING ROLE AND THE EVOLUTION OF THE TWO-STATE SOLUTION CONCEPT

1. The League of Nations mandate that was awarded to Britain combined Transjordan with the Palestine Mandate. However, as the mandate was coming into force on September 1, 1922, the British high commissioner ordered the demarcation between the two areas, and on September 16, 1922, the British were granted a separate administration for Jordan by the Council of the League of Nations.

2. See Yazid Sayigh, *Al-Urdunn wa al-Filastiniyyun, Dirasah fi Wihdat Al-Masir aw Al-Sira' al-Hatmi* (London: Riyad Al-Rayyis, 1987), 12–14.

3. Avi Shlaim, *War and Peace in the Middle East: A Concise History,* rev. and updated ed. (Toronto: Penguin, 1995).

4. For more details of Allon's ideas regarding the final borders of Israel, see Yigal Allon, "Israel: The Case for Defensible Borders," *Foreign Affairs,* October 1976.

5. Allon, "Israel."

6. See King Hussein's interview with Avi Shlaim, "My Secret Meetings with Israelis," *New York Review of Books,* July 15, 1999.

7. Yitzhak Shamir, "Israel's Role in a Changing Middle East," *Foreign Affairs,* Spring 1982, 791.

8. For details on this issue, see William B. Quandt, *Peace Process: Arab Diplomacy and the Arab-Israeli Conflict since 1967* (Washington, DC: Brookings Institution, 1993).

9. Dennis Ross, *The Missing Peace: The Inside Fight for Middle East Peace* (New York: Farrar, Straus, and Giroux, 2004), 46.

10. This is a term used by the Israeli right meaning Greater Israel, comprising all of historic Palestine.

11. In an interview with *Sunday Times,* June 15, 1969, Golda Meir stated, "There were no such thing as Palestinians. When was there an independent Palestinian people with a Palestinian state? It was either southern Syria before the First World War, and then it was a Palestine including Jordan. It was not as though there was a Palestinian people in Palestine considering itself as a Palestinian people and we came and threw them out and took their country away from them. They did not exist."

12. In an interview with the daily Israeli paper *Ma'ariv,* June 26, 1992, as Yitzhak Shamir was leaving office, he was quoted as saying: "I would have carried out autonomy talks for ten years, and meanwhile we would have reached half a million people in Judea and Samaria."

13. *King Hussein's Address to the Nation, July 31, 1988* (Amman: International Press Office, Royal Hashemite Court, 1988).

14. See, e.g., the episode on my meeting with Binyamin Netanyahu, in Chapter 2.

15. For the full text, see *King Hussein's Letter to Prime Minister Abdel Salam Majali, December 4, 1997* (Amman: International Press Court, Royal Hashemite Court, 1997).

CHAPTER 2. FIRST AMBASSADOR TO ISRAEL

1. "Muasher Heads for Tel Aviv Today with Clear Goals," *Jordan Times,* April 6, 1995.

2. "Muasher Presents Credentials," *Jordan Times,* April 11, 1995.

3. "Muasher Visits Orient House, Affirms Stand on Jerusalem," *Jordan Times,* April 26, 1995.

4. *Jordan Times,* April 29, 1995.

5. For a more detailed discussion on settlements and their status in international law, see Chapter 8 on the Israeli separation wall and the International Court of Justice Advisory Opinion on the Legal Consequences of the Construction of a Wall in the Occupied Palestinian Territory, July 9, 2004.

6. Letter from Israeli foreign minister Shimon Peres to Jordanian foreign minister Abdel Karim Kabariti, May 15, 1995. Personal notes.

7. *Note Verbale to the Israeli Foreign Ministry,* Q/12/700, July 4, 1995.

8. "Absentee Property Law, 5710-1950," Article 28, *Laws of the State of Israel: Authorized Translation from the Hebrew,* vol. 4 (Jerusalem: Government Printer, 1948–1987), 68–82.

9. Article 6 of the Knesset law 5755-1995 approving the peace treaty between Jordan and Israel explicitly stipulated that "notwithstanding the provisions of the properties of Absentees Law, 5710-1950, starting the 7th day of Kislev, 5755 (November 10, 1994), property shall not be considered the property of an absentee only on the basis that the person with a right in it was a citizen or subject of Jordan or was present in Jordan after the said date." Article 6 B then states that "the contents of sub-section (A) shall not, in any way, affect the status of a property that became property of an absentee in accordance with the said law prior to the date specified in said sub-section (A)."

10. "Treaty of Peace between the Hashemite Kingdom of Jordan and the State of Israel," available at http://www.kinghussein.gov.jo/peacetreaty.html.

11. *Note Verbale from the Israeli Foreign Ministry,* Jordanian division 64606, July 19, 1995.

12. *Note Verbale to the Israeli Foreign Ministry,* S/15/980, August 31, 1995.

13. *Note Verbale to the Israeli Foreign Ministry,* Q/12/699, July 4, 1995.

14. *Note Verbale from the Israeli Foreign Ministry,* Jordanian division 64609, July 20, 1995.

15. *Note Verbale to the Israeli Foreign Ministry,* MK/1368, November 23, 1995.

16. *Note Verbale from the Israeli Foreign Ministry,* Jordanian division 65053, December 11, 1995.

17. For a detailed account of Israel's treatment of its Arab citizens, see Sabri Jiryis, *The Arabs in Israel* (New York: Monthly Review, 1976).

18. "Jordanian Lionized in Israel," *New York Times,* July 16, 1995.

19. "Ex-Enemies Risk Wrath at Home to Say Goodbye," *New York Times,* November 7, 1995.

CHAPTER 3. THE LAST SIX MONTHS OF KING HUSSEIN'S LIFE

1. Oslo B divided the West Bank into area A, under full control by the Palestinians; area B, under civilian but not military control by the Palestinians; and area C, under full control by Israel.

2. Meeting between King Hussein and Dennis Ross, Washington, DC, June 15, 1998. Personal notes.

3. Christopher Dickey and Joseph Contreras, "The Day After," *Newsweek International,* August 10, 1998, 38–40.

4. Meeting between King Hussein and President Bill Clinton, Wye River Plantation, October 20, 1998. Personal notes.

5. Barton Gellman, "Netanyahu and Arafat Sign Accord," *Washington Post,* October 24, 1998.

6. "Treaty of Peace between the Hashemite Kingdom of Jordan and the State of Israel," Article 8.1 b, available at http://www.kinghussein.gov.jo/peacetreaty.html.

7. Conversation with Ayman Majali, chief of royal protocol, Washington, DC, November 1998. Personal notes.

8. A proconsul, according to *Webster's Eleventh New Collegiate Dictionary,* is "a governor or military commander of an ancient Roman province; an administrator in a modern colony, dependency or occupied area." The term implied that the crown prince was regarding me as the representative of another camp, that is, the king's.

9. *Al-Dustour* (Jordanian Arabic daily newspaper), November 5, 1998.

10. *Al-Dustour,* November 28, 1998.

11. *Al-Dustour,* December 29, 1998.

12. *Al-Dustour,* January 17, 1999.

13. Available at http://www.telaviv.usembassy.gov/publish/president/121498d.html.

14. *Al-Dustour,* January 20, 1999.

15. *Al-Dustour,* January 24, 1999

16. Queen Noor, *Leap of Faith: Memories of an Unexpected Life* (New York: Mira-mar Books, 2003), 427–428.

17. *Al-Dustour,* January 30, 1999.

18. *Al-Dustour,* January 31, 1999.

19. Available at http://www.findarticles.com/p/articles/mi_m2889/is_6_35/ai_54251197.

CHAPTER 4. THE ARAB INITIATIVE

1. The account and content of the king's proposal were given to me by Jack O'-Connoll, the king's lawyer and confidant.

2. Sharon's visit was deliberately provocative; he showed up with a legion of snipers and made deliberations from the plaza about his birthright as a Jew. The Israeli government at first dissuaded him from going but ended up allowing him to do so.

3. Steve Mufson and Marc Kaufman, "Arab Diplomats Meet to Discuss Changing Roles," *Washington Post,* September 17, 2001.

4. Meeting between King Abdullah II and President George W. Bush, Oval Office, Washington, DC, September 28, 2001. Personal notes.

5. The two officials I saw regularly on this point were Bruce Reidel, senior adviser for the president on the Middle East at the National Security Council, and William Burns, assistant secretary of state for Near East Affairs.

6. See, e.g., Bob Woodward, *Plan of Attack* (New York: Simon and Schuster, 2004).

7. Meeting between King Abdullah II and President Bush, Oval Office, Washington, DC, February 1, 2002. Personal notes.

8. Thomas L. Friedman, "Dear Arab League," *New York Times,* February 6, 2002; Thomas L. Friedman, "An Intriguing Signal from the Saudi Crown Prince," New York Times, February 17, 2002.

9. *Jordan Times,* February 21, 2002.

10. Meeting between King Abdullah II and Javier Solana, Aqaba, Jordan, February 28, 2002. Personal notes.

11. Most of the discussions on this issue were held between me and William Burns, then assistant secretary of state for Near East Affairs.

12. *Jordan Times,* March 26, 2002.

13. *Jordan Times,* March 27, 2002.

14. *Jordan Times,* March 27, 2002.

15. *Jordan Times,* March 28, 2002.

CHAPTER 5. THE MIDDLE EAST ROAD MAP

1. After the Palestinian National Authority had been set up in the West Bank and Gaza as a result of the Oslo Accords, Farouq Qaddoumi, the PLO's foreign minister, refused to return to the West Bank and continued to oppose the Oslo

process. Internal politics within the PLO meant that there were now two Palestinian "foreign ministers," one representing the PLO, the other the PNA. Qaddoumi, who differed with Arafat, continued to take personal positions against the peace process and against the official position of both the PLO and the PNA.

2. Israel had demolished many Palestinian camps in the West Bank and Gaza during its military campaign in the weeks preceding the meeting.

3. Arafat had two days earlier admitted he made mistakes and vowed in a speech to the Palestinian Legislative Council to enact sweeping reforms within the Palestinian Authority.

4. Article 11 of UN Resolution 194, passed by the General Assembly on December 11, 1948, states that "the refugees wishing to return to their homes and live at peace with their neighbors should be permitted to do so at the earliest practicable date, and that compensation should be paid for the property of those choosing not to return and for loss of or damage to property which, under principles of international law or in equity, should be made good by the Governments or authorities responsible." See George J. Tomeh, *United Nations Resolutions on Palestine and the Arab-Israeli Conflict*, vol. 1, *1947–1974* (Washington, DC: Institute for Palestinian Studies, 1975), 15–17.

5. On June 18, a suicide bomber belonging to Hamas exploded himself on a bus in Jerusalem, killing nineteen. Israeli tanks entered Jenin that night. On the next day, another suicide bomber, this time from Fatah's Al-Aqsa Brigades, detonated himself at a bus stop also in Jerusalem, killing himself and seven Israelis.

6. Nabil Shaath was working quietly on a new Palestinian constitution and the idea of a provisional state with Prince Saud. The constitution would also call for the establishment of the office of prime minister to circumvent the U.S. refusal to deal with Arafat. Arafat was not keen on this idea also.

7. Meeting with Colin Powell, New York City, July 16, 2002. Personal notes.

8. Meeting at the Oval Office, White House, July 18, 2002. Personal notes.

9. Meeting between King Abdullah II and President George W. Bush at the Oval Office, White House, August 1, 2002. Personal notes.

10. *Jordan Times*, August 14, 2002.

11. "Elements of a Performance-Based Road Map to a Permanent Two-State Solution to the Israeli-Palestinian Conflict," U.S. State Department Draft, 10/15/02.

CHAPTER 6. THE LAUNCHING OF THE ROAD MAP AND THE AQABA SUMMIT

1. Meeting between King Abdullah II and President George W. Bush at the White House, Washington, DC, August 1, 2001. Personal notes.

2. This arrangement ended immediately after the war started.

3. The United States was pushing Syria to close the offices of Hamas and Islamic Jihad, radical Palestinian factions in Damascus, as well as to stop all logistical and political support for the Lebanese party Hezbollah.

4. For a full version of Israel's fourteen conditions, see *Jerusalem Post*, May 26, 2003.

5. Meeting with President Bush at Sharm El-Sheikh, Egypt, June 3, 2003. Personal notes.

6. Elizabeth Kershner, "A Kingdom at Stake," *Jerusalem Report*, June 25, 2003.

7. According to international law, all settlements in the West Bank and Gaza are illegal, not just the ones designated as such by the Israeli government.

8. Meeting between King Abdullah II and President Bush, Camp David, MD, September 18, 2003. Personal notes.

9. For a full text of the document, see the Geneva Initiative official Web site, http://www.geneva-accord.org.

CHAPTER 7. BUSH'S LETTERS TO PRIME MINISTER SHARON AND KING ABDULLAH II

1. Letter from King Abdullah II to George W. Bush, April 8, 2004. Personal notes.

2. For the full text of Ariel Sharon's letter to George W. Bush, see "Letter from Prime Minister Sharon to U.S. President George W. Bush," *Mideast Web*, April 14, 2004, http://www.mideastweb.org/disengagement.htm. Sharon's assertion that the fence was a security rather than a political barrier, repeated by many Israeli officials, proved not to be true. In 2006, the official position of the government of Israel was to implement a unilateral withdrawal from the West Bank and establish permanent borders for the state of Israel largely along the fence lines. Jordan had repeatedly warned that this had always been Israel's intention.

3. For the full text, see "Letter from President Bush to Prime Minister Sharon," available at http://www.whitehouse.gov/news/releases/2004/04/20040414-3.html.

4. Meeting with Colin Powell, State Department, Washington, DC, April 20, 2004. Personal notes.

5. Aluf Benn, "Israel Slams Jordan for Opposing Pullout," *Ha'aretz*, April 21, 2004.

6. For a full text of President Bush's letter to King Abdullah II, see *Jordan Times*, May 7–8, 2004.

7. For a full text of the king's remarks, see "President Bush, Jordanian King Discuss Iraq, Middle East," available at http://www.whitehouse.gov/news/releases/2004/05/20040506-9.html.

8. *Jordan Times*, May 9, 2004.

9. Meeting between King Abdullah II and President George W. Bush, Oval Office, White House, June 15, 2004. Personal notes.

CHAPTER 8. THE ISRAELI SEPARATION WALL

1. See Omar Karmi, "Building Barriers—Israel Is Dancing Alone," *Jordan Times*, December 30, 2003.

2. *Displaced by the Wall: Forced Displacement as a Result of the West Bank Wall and Its Associated Regime* (The Norwegian Refugee Council in conjunction with the Badil Resource Center for Palestinian Residency and Refugee Rights, September 2006).

3. Meeting between King Abdullah II and President George W. Bush, Oval Office, White House, December 4, 2003. Personal notes.

4. As a result of the U.S. veto, the Security Council was unable to act although the issue was on its agenda. This provided the rationale and institutional basis for referring the issue to the General Assembly on the basis of the Uniting for Peace Mechanism, which allows the General Assembly to seize of a matter that is on the Security Council's agenda but is blocked by the council's inability or unwillingness to act because of a member's veto.

5. UN General Assembly Resolution A/RES/ES-10/14, passed December 8, 2003.

6. "Customary international law refers to rules of law derived from the consistent conduct of states acting out of the belief that the law required them to act that way" (Shabtai Rosenne, *Practice and Methods of International Law* [London: Oceana, 1984], 55). The United Nations considers Customary International Law one of the primary sources of international law.

7. "The Big Freeze," *Ha'aretz*, October 9, 2004.

CHAPTER 9. ARAB REFORM

1. See *Arab Human Development Report, 2002: Creating Opportunities for Future Generations* (New York: United Nations Development Programme, 2002).

2. *Arab Human Development Report, 2004: Towards Freedom in the Arab World* (New York: United Nations Development Programme, 2005), 163.

3. See *The State of Democracy in Jordan* (Amman: Center for Strategic Studies, University of Jordan, 2006.)

4. Meeting with Colin Powell, State Department, Washington, DC, March 9, 2004. Personal notes.

5. See, e.g., *The Alexandria Declaration* (Alexandria: Bibliotheca Alexandria, March 2004).

6. Because of problems with the host country, Tunisia, the summit was postponed from its original due date at the end of March 2004.

7. This is a reference to a conference on human rights held in Sanaa by the Yemeni government in January 2004.

8. Comments made at a closed meeting of the G8 leaders with leaders of the Middle East region, Sea Island, GA, June 9, 2004. Personal notes.

9. *Arab Human Development Report, 2004: Towards Freedom in the Arab World* (New York: United Nations Development Programme, 2005), 70.

10. *Arab Human Development Report, 2004*, 53.

INDEX

Page numbers in *italics* indicate maps